The Best American Travel Writing 2012

GUEST EDITORS OF
THE BEST AMERICAN TRAVEL WRITING

2000	BILL BRYSON
2001	PAUL THEROUX
2002	FRANCES MAYES
2003	IAN FRAZIER
2004	PICO IYER
2005	JAMAICA KINCAID
2006	TIM CAHILL
2007	SUSAN ORLEAN
2008	ANTHONY BOURDAIN
2009	SIMON WINCHESTER
2010	BILL BUFORD
2011	SLOANE CROSLEY
2012	WILLIAM T. VOLLMANN

The Best American Travel Writing™ 2012

Edited and with an Introduction
by **William T. Vollmann**

Jason Wilson, Series Editor

A Mariner Original

HOUGHTON MIFFLIN HARCOURT

BOSTON • NEW YORK   2012

www.hmhbooks.com

ISSN 1530-1516
ISBN 978-0-547-80897-0

Printed in the United States of America
DOC 10 9 8 7 6 5 4 3 2 1

Contents

Foreword

WITH EACH PASSING YEAR, we seem to reach another strange milestone in the evolution of travel. I have been seized by this thought each year during the process of putting together another edition of this anthology, and it never ceases to amaze me how much travel has changed since we began publishing *The Best American Travel Writing* in 1999.

This past year it struck me as I was browsing the App Store, downloading English-Spanish editions of popular voice-activated translator apps for my iPhone and iPad. I was doing this at the behest of an editor, who had asked me to test out these apps during a trip to Spain.

Since I was genuinely embarrassed at how badly my Spanish had deteriorated over the years, I was hopeful that the trio of apps I was downloading—Google Translate, SpeechTrans, and Jibbigo—might work better than the reviews suggested. I briefly considered a fourth, iLingual—one in which you take a photo of your mouth and then hold the iPhone or iPod Touch up to your face while the screen animates your lips in the foreign language. Thankfully, for my dignity's sake, I couldn't find iLingual for Spanish, only in French, German, and Arabic.

Eating breakfast at my kitchen table a few days before departure, I gave Jibbigo—the speech-to-speech translator that seemed the most user-friendly on the iPad—a test spin.

"I'm eating French toast," I said slowly, trying to be clear.

"I need in French toast" is what Jibbigo transcribed on its

screen, which then spoke in a sultry female voice: *"Necesito francés en tostada."*

I shushed my kids, who were watching cartoons, and turned down the TV—I'd read that background noise really threw speech-to-speech translators off. Once it was silent, I again pushed the red Record button on the screen. "I am eating French toast," I said, even more slowly and with as much enunciation as I could muster.

"All right and even French toast," Jibbigo transcribed on its screen. *"Está bien incluso y pan tostado francés,"* said Sultry Voice.

"Noooo!" Now my kids began laughing at me and Jibbigo.

One of my sons grabbed the iPad. "Mom, are you cutting pears in the kitchen?" he said through the app to his mother, who was indeed cutting pears in the kitchen. "Are you hiding Harrods in the kitchen?" wrote Jibbigo, which Sultry Voice dutifully said in a bizarre game of mistranslation-down-the-lane.

By then my kids were hysterical. I grabbed the iPad back, pressed the red button, and shouted, "Go get dressed and ready for school!"

"Do you just ready for school?" translated Jibbigo. *"Solo la lista para la escuela?"* said the voice. "Ahhhhhh!"

Needless to say, I was not particularly optimistic about the utility of a speech-to-speech translator during my journeys through the wine regions of Ribera del Duero and Toro. But I was determined to give it a try.

My first chance to use the app—once I'd gotten off the plane and through customs with a mere *"Buenos dias"*—was at the rental car counter. As I approached it, I spoke slowly to Jibbigo. "I have reserved a rental car for Mr. Wilson," I said.

"I have reserved a rental car for Mr. Wilson," transcribed Jibbigo. *"He reservado un coche de alquiler para el Señor Wilson,"* purred the sultry voice.

Okay! I thought. Here we go! Maybe I'd misjudged Jibbigo. Maybe this was all going to work out fine! Reaching the counter, I hit play.

"Yeah, we have that reservation," said the young woman behind the counter. In English. She raised an eyebrow at me. "And no worries, sir. I speak English at a high level."

In fact, in most interactions with tourist-service people—hotel clerks, taxi drivers, cashiers—a speech-to-speech translator was very unnecessary. Basic, polite high school Spanish worked just fine. Jibbigo usually just complicated matters.

In a crowded, noisy café I asked Jibbigo, "May I have a café con leche?" and Jibbigo responded with "May I have a tactical mentioned?" To which Sultry Voice said, *"Puede darme un tactical mencionado?"* Of course, I'd accidentally thrown off Jibbigo by not saying "coffee with milk."

So I simply said, *"Café con leche, por favor,"* to the guy behind the counter—and it all worked out fine.

At one point, driving through a toll plaza, I figured I'd use the translator to ask the toll-taker whether I was going the right way. I pulled out the iPad and said, "Is this the right road for Valladolid?" Jibbigo transcribed, "Is this the right road for liability?" and Sultry Voice said, *"Es este el camino correcto para el obligatorio?"*

The toll-taker looked at me like I was nuts. So instead I did what many Americans do in a foreign country—I pointed wildly ahead and said, loudly, "Valladolid!?"

"Si, si. Claro," the toll-taker said.

Again I knew I'd complicated matters by saying the name of the city rather than just "Is this the correct road?" But honestly, it's not easy to remember Jibbigo's limitations when you're holding up a line of traffic.

This is not to say that all my interactions with translation apps were unsuccessful. In a tapas bar in León, I used Google Translate to help with a nice, informative conversation with the bartender about the Prieto Picudo wines of the region. The bar was so noisy —with Barcelona's league-title-clinching game blaring on the TV —that Jibbigo or SpeechTrans would have been useless.

With Google Translate, I kept surreptitiously tapping my questions and conversation cues into the iPod Touch as the guy poured another customer's drink. It simply looked as if I were perhaps texting friends at another bar. When the barman returned, I had my queries all mapped out in my head.

I did this in a couple of other situations too, and what I realized is that because I already have some competency in Italian, I often knew more Spanish words than I thought. The translation apps helped me fill in the blanks and formulate more coherent sentences. Still, I'm not sure how much they'd help a complete beginner with only *Sesame Street* Spanish.

In the end, there was one situation, a casual dinner-party scenario, in which Jibbigo was relatively useful—and enlightening. I was drinking wine in an ancient wine cellar near Toro, Spain, with a young organic winemaker named Maria. She makes a lovely Toro wine called Volvoreta, which means "butterfly" (and which Jibbigo translated as "Buddha actor").

We sat at a stone table with her father and some family friends, few of whom spoke English. Maria spoke English pretty well and translated, but occasionally we got bogged down by a phrase or a concept.

For instance, they talked for ten minutes about "AYN-stain," and I failed to realize that they meant Albert Einstein until someone typed his name into the translator app on my iPad. At one point we got stuck on the word *musa*. Maria is charming and attractive in a Dionysian earth-goddess sort of way, and someone at the table was suggesting that she was a *musa* to wine writers. Jibbigo clarified that they were suggesting that Maria was a muse.

Maria pointed to a review of her wine in an American wine magazine. After using all the usual descriptors of fruits and aromas and mouthfeel, the critic had referred to her wine as "classy."

"Classy?" she asked. "Tell me what this word means, classy."

Wine is nearly impossible to explain in your native tongue, let alone one you're not proficient in. "Well," I said, fumbling around in my native language, "*classy* is kind of a difficult word to translate. There are several different meanings. You sort of have to know who's using it."

Classy is slightly old-fashioned, and these days can be literal or ironic and mean anything from "elegant" or "stylish" to Ron Burgundy's sign-off in *Anchorman* ("Stay classy, San Diego") to the kind of snarky thing you say to a friend who, say, takes a swig straight from the wine bottle. Wine critics aren't generally known as ironists, but they still are fairly precise in their adjectives—so the choice of *classy* instead of *elegant* or *stylish* meant something.

As I tried to explain the nuance to Maria, one of the friends, slightly impatient, said, "*Elegante.* It means *elegante.*"

"Well, sort of," I said.

"Try your iPad," Maria said.

"Classy," I said into Jibbigo.

"*Elegante,*" said Sultry Voice.

Everyone had a nice laugh at the silly American journalist with the iPad who was trying to complicate everything. Which was a good thing. After all, it was good to be reminded that some ideas, some concepts will never be easily translatable. Sure, people are always inventing new gadgets to make travel easier. And every day it gets easier to reach out and to connect with people of different cultures. But even with the advent of new technologies, it's important to remember that it's still possible to miscommunicate, to get confused, and to become lost. That's the thing about travel—perhaps the essential thing, the thing that teaches us the most—that never changes. And that thing is what this anthology delivers once again this year.

The stories included here are, as always, selected from among hundreds of pieces in hundreds of diverse publications—from mainstream and specialty magazines to newspaper travel sections to literary journals to travel websites. I've done my best to be fair and representative, and in my opinion the best travel stories from 2011 were forwarded to William Vollmann, who made our final selections.

I now begin anew by reading the hundreds of stories published in 2012. I am once again asking editors and writers to submit the best of whatever it is they define as travel writing. These submissions must be nonfiction, published in the United States during the 2012 calendar year. They must not be reprints or excerpts from published books. They must include the author's name, date of publication, and publication name, and must be tear sheets, the complete publication, or a clear photocopy of the piece as it originally appeared. I must receive all submissions by January 1, 2013, in order to ensure full consideration for the next collection.

Further, publications that want to make certain their contributions will be considered for the next edition should make sure to include this anthology on their subscription list. Submissions or subscriptions should be sent to Jason Wilson, Drexel University, 3210 Cherry Street, 2nd floor, Philadelphia, PA 19104.

It was a thrill and an honor to work on this edition with William Vollmann, whose adventurous work I've always admired. I am also grateful to Nicole Angeloro and Jesse Smith for their help on this, our thirteenth edition of *The Best American Travel Writing*.

JASON WILSON

Introduction

"OF THE GLADDEST MOMENTS in human life, methinks, is the departure upon a distant journey into unknown lands." Thus Sir Richard Burton, who knew whereof he spoke. I myself have always been a partisan of that point of view, although Emerson's "travel is a fool's paradise" gratifies me just as much. To set out for someplace far away or strange is to take an active part in that baffling journey of ours through life into death; to stay home and improve one's self-knowledge (perhaps through armchair traveling) is to do the same; both men were right.

My friend Steve Jones, with whom I hop freight trains now and then, eagerly reads this anthology every year. I asked him what he likes best about it, and he said: "I like the variety of the places the writers are going and how odd those places can be, and also the writing style. I like the fact that some pieces are somber and some are just quirky and there are usually a couple of hilarious ones thrown in." During my selection of essays (from sixty-odd finalists, among whom I discovered both the editor of this series and myself; these of course were rejected immediately to avoid any conflict of interest), I tried to consider what might please Steve, in hopes of pleasing you.

Monte Reel's "How to Explore Like a Real Victorian Adventurer," which I have chosen to open this volume, introduces us to the Victorian-era travel guides, which he calls "lovingly compiled tip sheets on the acquired art of paying attention." The epigram from Burton appears in his essay. Emerson also gets his due here, because Reel applies the Victorians to that peculiarly unknown land, the local Sprawlsville. "Instead of being a vacuous purgatory that deserved pity, the mall grew in complexity with each stride. The point that the how-to-explore books collectively hammered home is this: if you sincerely investigate it, every detail hides reason, and any environment is far more sophisticated than our senses appreciate."

Sincere investigation demands an exposition without constraints. When someone asks an author how long his work in progress will run, the best answer is "As long as it takes to say what I need to say, and no longer or shorter." Victorian adventurers, of course, most often traveled on their own capital. What Marx called "the cash nexus" now taints the production of most "professional travelers." Essays in mainstream periodicals are vulnerable to several types of commercial damage. First of all, the editorial department, not the writer, sets the word count, which relates to the subject and the writer's nature only accidentally. Second, the draft received passes through any number of hands, whose cuttings and pastings need not be in concert. It is not only a case of too many cooks spoiling the broth, but also of nobody knowing who has added how much salt. Third, the number of advertisements slated for a given issue goes far in determining how fat it can be. Thus after an essay has been hacked down to meet a given word count, it may be mutilated again, or even expanded. I have occasionally had something excised from an article of mine, only to be asked at the very end, by someone who never saw the original, to add just that, but in a different part of the essay, since the place where it once lived is long gone. These bemusing vicissitudes of the free-lancer's circumstances render the treasures brought home from the voyage—that is, the details, and their causes and meanings—subject to vandalism. Hence "the acquired art of paying attention" is best served outside the marketplace—either by travelers of independent means, such as Richard Burton, or by travelers who control their own means of production, such as the daring train-hopper Aaron Dactyl, a portion of whose self-published magazine appears last in this book. Most of us do sell ourselves, and our work as published by the magazines shows the consequences. My feelings about this are well described by one of Timbuktu's historians: "In my worst dreams, I see a rare text that I haven't read being slowly eaten." He, of course, is referring to bugs, not editors. You will meet him in Peter Gwin's "The Telltale Scribes of Timbuktu," which is perhaps the most traditionally Victorian of this year's travel essays: carefully drawn, rich in anecdotes and observations, complete with romance (of a sad sort) and danger, and set in a locale that we might now call Orthodox Exotic.

To the Victorians, Africa was still the Dark Continent and much of the planet remained unmapped. Nowadays we have gained the semblance of an acquaintance with most of it (excluding the oceans). But insightful travelers perpetually discover the gloriously and ominously unknown darkness of everywhere. When Henry Shukman visits the forbidden country around Chernobyl, he finds an astonishingly rapid alteration into something resembling the Zone in that Tarkovsky movie *Stalker*. Gray wolves and wild boar now roam "a place where the animals are mostly undisturbed, living amid a preindustrial number of humans and a post-apocalyptic amount of radioactive strontium and cesium." Here too are albino birds, red-needled pine trees, and field mice that might be growing resistant to radiation. What if someday the science required to save us from our inevitable new atomic errors comes out of this place? Or what if Chernobyl proves that "moderate" nuclear accidents are worse than we can imagine?

A natural companion to Shukman's essay, Elliott D. Woods's praiseworthy exposition of trash ecology—a topic that is getting ever more attention nowadays—brings us to the outskirts of Cairo, where "a haze produced by the exhalations of some 2,500 black-market recycling workshops carpets a landscape of windowless brick high-rises and unpaved alleys piled high with garbage." The people who live and glean here are called zabaleen. It is unexpected—and heartening—to learn that "in sixty years, the zabaleen have gone from serfs to recycling entrepreneurs." Unfortunately, they lack many rights. As a measure against swine flu, and perhaps "to appease Muslims whipped into a frenzy by the H1N1 scare," the Egyptian government recently killed 300,000 garbage-eating pigs belonging to the zabaleen. All the same, Woods's observations give cause for thought and hope combined. It seems to me that if governments and NGOs were to take note of this essay and encourage appropriate local manifestations of the profit motive to address this problem, then perhaps our future need not involve Soylent Green.

Thomas Swick's account of the group called Addiopizzo, which encourages business establishments not to pay Mafia extortionists, is equally worth reading, because it introduces us to brave people who stand up to evil. That Addiopizzo is necessary in an EU country in this day and age is rather shocking; that it may prove effective would be a still greater surprise. I was very impressed that thirty-five hundred of Palermo's citizens summoned the courage to put themselves on public record that they gave their business to extortion-free bars, restaurants, and the like. At the site where gangsters murdered a man named Paolo Borsellino, a note quotes the victim: "The fight against the Mafia should be a cultural and moral movement that involves everyone, especially the younger generation."

A traveler's experience is necessarily narrow, unique, suggestive at best but never definitive. It is up to us as readers to judge the situations described. What need the Mafia fills today for anyone but its own members remains unknown to us. Very likely Swick could not have interviewed Addiopizzo and the Mafia on the same ticket. His glancing illumination of this subject, like most any one person's, is necessary but not sufficient. In this anthology we are fortunate enough to have two points of view on the situation of Northern Ireland. I have paired Robin Kirk's grim snapshot of Belfast, which is well worth reading for its own close observation and analysis ("what is disturbing about segregation in Northern Ireland is not that there are tradeoffs; it's that the people entrench themselves in segregated communities, and many of their leaders help them do it"), with J. Malcolm Garcia's brave and heartrending investigation into a young man's murder in a small village in this region. In its fidelity to local speech patterns, elimination of the superfluous, and painstaking arrangement of vignettes, Garcia's piece is not only journalism but literature.

While we are on the subject of literary excellence, this seems the place to mention Paul Theroux's lovely vignette of the Maine coast, which draws no less on his historical and literary knowledge than on his accomplished eye, and Michael Gorra's letter from Paris, which rounds out this next plausible pair. The latter ends with the happy Emersonianism of the author and his daughter watching old American movies in the Rue des Écoles, "sitting at home only and precisely because we are also abroad." Both of these offer us the appearance of an organic and intrinsic brevity. Hence they seem undamaged by copy editors' deletions. Both are a pleasure to read in and of themselves.

Another very short piece is Kenan Trebincevic's carefully understated parable of a return to Bosnia, and of an encounter with a neighbor who extorted property from his mother during the war. Anyone who has reflected at all on Yugoslavia's civil war can well imagine the horrors that Trebincevic leaves out. The story he tells is simple, affecting, hideous.

Meanwhile, Bryan Curtis's visit to the Tijuana Sports Hall of Fame seized mordant hold of me: "We miss the gringos, man . . . They all left, like the Mayas did." I never could have imagined that comparison. It is funny, eerie, and true. Curtis alludes to "the bodybuilder Beatriz de Regíl González, who in her bio is compared to a beautiful flower in Tijuana's garden," and I longed to see her portrait, so that I would know how beautiful she was. "Eighty years ago," writes Curtis, "Old Tijuana had a bell tower. It was built to convince Americans they were experiencing European luxury. Now we're standing in a copy of that tower—a Xerox of a dream of Europe . . . Finally, this belltower plays a fake bell." Were I an editorial magnate, I'd invite this writer to spend a year in Tijuana and write down a million crazy details.

Kimberly Meyer's prior residence in Oklahoma eventually led her to the Holy City of the Wichitas, which she describes at greater length and with less cynical bemusement than Curtis does Tijuana. "We do use a donkey and a live baby Jesus," explains an exponent of the passion play. "We've never had to use a doll." What the reader makes of this is up to him. Perhaps the bell tower in Tijuana will come to mind. Or perhaps it will ring significant as an emblem of strict and praiseworthy sincerity. Meyer makes her own point of view gently clear, without telling us what to think.

Dimiter Kenarov's beautifully written essay about Bulgaria's street necrologues (which likewise decorate the street walls and lampposts of Serbia) pays respect to such absurdities as this farewell to the renowned Georgi Dimitrov: "We promise to guard like the pupils of our eyes our maritime border for the successful building of socialism in our beloved Motherland." Here we could almost be in Tijuana's fake bell tower. Kenarov remarks that "the eternal border between the upper world and the underworld, the city and the cemetery, has disappeared in Bulgaria. No one is truly dead without a necrologue, and yet necrologues are meant to keep the dead alive." So it is with Burton and Emerson, Dark Continents and Chernobyl. (As Pink Floyd said: "Matter of fact, it's all dark.")

This ambiguity, or whatever you want to call it, shines out at us in Pico Iyer's account of Varanasi, where Shiva met Vishnu—what could be more emblematic than that? Hence the Ganges with its thirty sewers: "Bathe yourself in its filthy waters . . . and you purify yourself for life." Wandering among sadhus who "want to live in a world of ash," Iyer concludes: "Spirituality in Varanasi lies precisely in the poverty and sickness and death that it weaves into its unending tapestry; a place of holiness, it says, is . . . a place where purity and filth, anarchy and ritual, unquenchable vitality and the constant imminence of death all flow together." Here too he experiences a turning-backward epiphany not unlike that of Gorra in the Parisian repertory theater: Varanasi comes to remind him of his twisting-laned birthplace, Oxford.

Lynn Freed's mini-memoir of the approaching end of apartheid in South Africa is of the highest order, not only for its style but also for its very profound meditation on fear in relation to political change. In his essay, Kenarov references the Bulgarian sociologist Emiliya Karaboeva, who seeks to classify what most recurs in necrologues. She concludes: "The key words are love, pain, and sorrow, but the most important one is love." In Freed's brief vignette the love of what is endangered is implicit: this family, this home which may someday be invaded by killers, this life.

In every anthology of travel writing there should always be a hot-and-miserable piece bookended by a cold-and-miserable one. This year the first is furnished by Luke Dittrich, who shares with us the first installment of his walk along the Mexican-American border. Like many wise journalists, he has provisioned himself with a stroller full of water. Although the voracious mouthparts of copy editors have gnawed random holes in his narrative in obedience to their commercial instincts (I know this area somewhat, and was saddened by the deletion of localities that I know that Dittrich must have passed through), what remains is a pleasing read. His encounters with smiling or poker-faced Border Patrol agents are always an entertainment.

So much for hot. For cold, I give you Mark Jenkins's skiing trek with his brother through Norway's Hardangervidda National Park. Roald Amundsen, who as you probably know led the first successful expedition to the South Pole, tried twice to cross Hardangervidda. Each try almost killed him. Just as Amundsen's own organizational excellence and modest understatement damaged him in comparison to the dead hero Scott, so Jenkins's account (which also shows certain signs of editorial damage) first struck me as less impressive than his accomplishment. But as I thought over that chilly escapade, I grew increasingly glad not to have accompanied the cheerful Jenkins brothers. Although they had the benefit of those newfangled trekking huts, the headwinds and whiteouts described in this story could easily have been fatal. The Jenkins brothers are obviously fine orienteers and in excellent shape. I salute them.

During this same year, Mark Jenkins (are there two of him, or is he just busy?) also managed to spelunk through the beautiful world of Vietnam's Hang Son Doong, which by one measure may be the largest cave in the world. This is travel adventure in Burtonian style, for parts of this place, Jenkins informs us, have not been previously explored. Simple human daring ought to weigh large in an anthology like this. I wish I had been there to see the giant cave pearls—water-formed balls of calcite.

Finally, Aaron Dactyl hops freight trains, without even a donkey, a baby Jesus, or a bell tower among his props. In his way he has gone as far as Richard Burton. I have excerpted a few pages from his Xeroxed magazine *Railroad Semantics*.

WILLIAM T. VOLLMANN

The Best American
Travel Writing 2012

How to Explore Like a Real Victorian Adventurer

FROM *The Believer*

IN ZANZIBAR, LATE in 1856, Richard F. Burton and a caravan of porters prepared to venture into the heart of Africa's interior to search for the source of the Nile River. A ropy knot of scar tissue shined on Burton's cheek—a souvenir from his most recent expedition, upon which he caught a spear to the face during an ambush by Somali tribesmen.

An English diplomat on the island tried to warn Burton against pressing his luck a second time. The diplomat told Burton that a wandering French naval officer recently had been taken prisoner by tribal warriors. The natives had tied the luckless pilgrim to a tree and lopped off his limbs, one by one. The warriors, after dramatically pausing to sharpen their knives, relieved the Frenchman of his misery by slicing off his head. A true story, the diplomat insisted.

Burton wasn't fazed. Severed limbs, rolling heads—even the grisliest of portents couldn't deflate his spirit, not before a journey into uncharted territory. He'd spent his life cultivating a world-worn persona that confronted anything resembling naïveté with open hostility, but a blank space on a map could reduce him to giddiness: "Of the gladdest moments in human life, methinks, is the departure upon a distant journey into unknown lands," he wrote in his journal before that trip inland. "The blood flows with the fast circulation of childhood."

Africa, as it turned out, would wring much of that blood out of him. In the months ahead he would suffer partial blindness, partial paralysis, sizzling fevers. Hallucinations crowded his brain with ghosts. A swollen tongue got in the way of eating. But the bottom line: he would survive to explore again. And years later, flipping through that worn journal from 1856, he would pass retrospective judgment on his pre-expedition enthusiasm: "Somewhat boisterous," he concluded, "but true."

This kind of aimless gusto for all things unexplored defined the golden age of inland travel, which roughly coincided with Queen Victoria's reign (1837–1901) in England. It's no coincidence that these were the same years when steamships and telegraphs began to shrink the globe. Industrialization transformed urban landscapes and fueled the expansion of colonial empires. Railroads standardized the world's clocks, and a new strain of hurried angst —what poet Matthew Arnold labeled "this strange disease of modern life"—began to devour souls by the millions.

Enter a new breed of adventurous explorer, which Burton perfectly exemplified. These men filled the membership rolls of the "geographical societies" that started to pop up in London, New York, Paris, Berlin, and most other capitals of the industrialized world. Geographical expeditions became the antidote to an increasingly ordered, regulated, and unmysterious way of life.

But what purpose would be served if the person who finally entered terra incognita couldn't handle its unpredictable challenges? What was the point of travel if the person who finally laid eyes on the previously unseen didn't really know how to look at it?

It quickly became clear that far-flung voyagers, even those as hearty as Burton, needed focus when confronting the riddles of undiscovered worlds. They needed guiding hands. They needed how-to manuals.

Victorian adventurers rarely took a step into the wild without hauling a small library of how-to-explore books with them. Among the volumes Burton carried into East Africa was a heavily annotated copy of Francis Galton's *The Art of Travel: or, Shifts and Contrivances Available in Wild Countries*. Originally conceived as a handbook for explorers, and sponsored by England's Royal Geographical Society, the book was required reading for any self-respecting Victorian traveler. Before rolling up his sleeves and getting down to the

hard business of exploring, he could turn to page 134 to learn the
best way to do exactly that:

> When you have occasion to tuck up your shirt-sleeves, recollect that
> the way of doing so is, not to begin by turning the cuffs inside-out,
> but outside-in—the sleeves must be rolled up inwards, towards the
> arm, and not the reverse way. In the one case, the sleeves will remain
> tucked up for hours without being touched; in the other, they be-
> come loose every five minutes.

The amiably neurotic Galton left nothing to chance. His index
is studded with gems like "bones as fuel" and "savages, management of." If Burton couldn't find the advice he was looking for
in Galton, he could always consult one of the other books in his
trunk that were written with explorers in mind. The stated aim of
Randolph Barnes Marcy's *The Prairie Traveler: The 1859 Handbook
for Westbound Pioneers,* which Burton himself edited in later editions, read like a manifesto for every handbook of this kind: "With
such a book in his hand," Marcy writes, "[the explorer] will feel
himself a master spirit in the wilderness he traverses, and not the
victim of every *new* combination of circumstances which nature
affords or fate allots, as if to try his skill and prowess."

All of the books advertised practical intentions: if adventurers
are compelled to wander the globe, why not teach them how to
take note of details—be they geographical, anthropological, or
whatever—that might prove useful to science, industry, or empire?

I stumbled upon *The Art of Travel* while researching a book
about African exploration, and continued on to the other titles, all
of which are available for free on the Internet. After reading them,
I can confidently report that the scientific, industrial, and political developments of the intervening century have thoroughly un-
dermined the original intentions of most of their authors. These
titles won't help powerful nations lay claim to new territories and
exploitable populations. As literary genres go, this one is about as
dead as they get.

But it deserves a resurrection.

It's true that the authors are generally eccentric, habitually obsessive, and at times comically misguided. A modern reader will
find plenty of hopelessly dated assumptions to indulge a sense
of cultural superiority. You might chuckle when someone writes

about the best place to buy a pith helmet in London. But that stuff has little to do with these books' contemporary relevance, which goes beyond entertainment value.

While no one was looking, this neglected genre transcended its crudely utilitarian origins to occupy a higher sphere: the books are instruction manuals for the senses, lovingly compiled tip sheets on the acquired art of paying attention.

They're not quick and easy reads. Arcane language and compulsive punctuation force the reader to decelerate. But that is exactly what many of the explorers of the period identified as the most important first step of any successful expedition.

"While traveling in a strange country [I] should always prefer making my observations at a rate not quicker than five or six miles an hour," wrote Richard Owen, the superintendent of the British Museum's natural history departments and a scientific patron for many of the period's most far-reaching expeditions. History has judged him harshly for opposing Darwin's ideas, but when it came to the subject of travel, his philosophy represented the vanguard of his generation's views.

The crux of that philosophy—"Slow down; it's the journey, not the destination," etc.—has ripened into soft travel-guide cliché. Modern writers tend to sound like humorless scolds when they preach about this stuff, but the Victorians avoided the trap of bland sanctimony because they were never content to stop at generalized advice. They always pushed it further. After advising travelers to reduce their speed, they offered hyper-specific instructions about exactly what travelers should observe, and how they should observe it.

The obvious titles illustrating this tendency are Harriet Martineau's *How to Observe: Morals and Manners,* published in 1838, and *What to Observe: The Traveller's Remembrancer,* written by Colonel Julian R. Jackson three years later. Jackson, a secretary at the Royal Geographical Society, explains in his preface that he has "endeavored to excite a desire for useful knowledge by awakening curiosity. The intending traveller, it is hoped, will, from a perusal of the present work see what an immense field of physical and moral research lies open to his investigation . . ."

Everything that meets the eye tells a story, but if viewed skillfully, it also can crack open a Russian-doll wonderland of stories within stories. When looking at a mountain peak, for example, Jackson emphasizes that care must be taken to determine if it's a "saddle-back" or a "hog's back" or a "sugar-loaf"—because the structure might reveal the landscape's geological composition, which in turn can explain its vegetative potential, which can in turn . . . and so on.

Jackson spends thirty pages advising travelers how to look at a river (Is the surface of the water flat, or does it actually appear slightly convex? What sort of debris does it carry?). There is no such thing as an insignificant detail. After reading a few dozen pages of this stuff, his book works like a mind-altering drug. You look up from the page and notice that the world around you is popping into new dimensions. Suddenly the tree outside your window is demanding attention. You start to notice the subtle temperature differences between the air circulating around your head and the soil beneath your feet. If you're not careful, you can get lost on runaway trains of thought.

Jackson recognizes this danger, and he gently reminds his readers to stay on track, to maintain a discipline of focus. When he suggests that travelers should determine if native populations practice beekeeping (among many other things), he cautions against jumping ahead. First, the skillful explorer must fully observe the matter at hand before moving on to related concerns: "The care of bees is seldom an exclusive occupation, and although the honey, and particularly the wax obtained are important objects, we are here to consider merely the care bestowed on the bees themselves."

Martineau's *How to Observe* limits its attention to the proper manner of perceiving humans and their behavior. Like Jackson, she goes to great lengths in listing what travelers should notice —their treatment of criminals, the aspirations of children, beliefs about marriage—and she's a stickler for concrete details. But she also exhibits a respect for the distorting potential of point of view that's downright postmodern.

She urges the voyager to dismantle his assumptions and to always remain vigilant against "the affliction of seeing sin wherever he sees difference." It takes a lot of practice to learn how to see the world clearly, but learning how to gauge the fun-house-mirror refractions of a foreign land is the duty of all who find themselves stumbling into disorienting territory: "A child does not catch a gold fish in water at the first trial, however good his eyes may be,

and however clear the water; knowledge and method are necessary to enable him to take what is actually before his eyes and under his hand. So it is with all who fish in a strange element . . ."

The cameras of this era were cumbersome, delicate, and hellishly
tricky to use in the field. Most explorers didn't even bother. But often they were still expected to provide their sponsoring geographical societies with visual representations of the people and lands
they encountered.

Burton, our tour guide into this lost world, turned to writers
like Jackson and Martineau to broaden the scope of his attentions,
but he delved deeper into his makeshift bookmobile when he
needed to zoom in for a tighter focus. An essential handbook was
The Elements of Drawing in Three Letters to Beginners, by John Ruskin.
Upon publication, in 1857, it immediately found a place in the
luggage of explorers in every corner of the world.

Other travel handbooks, including the Royal Geographical
Society's *Hints to Travellers* (1854), had previously emphasized
the importance of drafting and sketching, but Ruskin provided
detailed, practical know-how. His book simply cannot be cracked
open without intensifying a reader's visual acuity. Without cameras
to record the details for them, explorers needed to develop the
eyes of an artist. *The Elements* aimed to refine their vision:

> The victorious beauty of the rose as compared with other flowers,
> depends wholly on the delicacy and quantity of its colour grada-
> tions, all other flowers being either less rich in gradations, not hav-
> ing so many folds of leaf; or less tender, being patched and veined
> instead of flushed.

Ruskin didn't envision his audience as frustrated painters in-
dulging ambitions to hang a canvas in the Louvre: "My efforts
are directed not to making a carpenter an artist, but to making
him happier as a carpenter." Encouraging such eclecticism seems
strange, not to mention vaguely irresponsible, in our age of hyper-
specialization. But the Victorians were unembarrassed about dipping from one discipline into another.

Consider Burton. He spoke more than twenty languages, wrote
books on subjects ranging from bayonet technique to gold mining, was a spy and a consul, and was generally regarded as the most
accomplished ethno-sexologist of his generation. Before disguis-

ing himself as a dervish to complete a pilgrimage to Mecca, he apprenticed himself to a blacksmith—just in case he came across some available steeds during the journey and needed to make horseshoes. He was an enthusiastic amateur in an era when the word wasn't a slur.

Dedicated travelers didn't limit their aesthetic studies to the visual arts. William Gardiner's *The Music of Nature* (1838) was a treasury of creative listening techniques to be applied in the field. Every sound, as heard by Gardiner, can reveal and instruct.

Using standard musical notation, he transcribed everything from the canter of a horse to the cry of a child. He charted the musical differences between the "yelp of a cur, whose foot has been trod upon" and "the whine of a dog tied up." He encouraged readers to apply a musical ear to every sound they might encounter out in the great wide open, even the speech of the natives. He concluded that the sounds of the Nordic languages are "less pleasing" than those found in milder climates, for example, because "the severity of the regions in which they are spoken keeps the mouth constantly closed, and the act of speaking is principally performed in the throat."

In the ragged chorus of nature, where insects provide the dominant sound track, we find Gardiner at his most enthusiastic. "The lively note of the cricket . . . consists of three notes in rhythm, always forming a triplet in the key of B," he writes.

Remember how Jackson suggested that explorers should notice whether or not a native population keeps bees? With Gardiner, this field of inquiry bursts open with newfound potential. He informs readers that within every hive, certain bees called "fanners" ventilate the premises by the incessant motion of their wings.

"If the ear is placed on the outside of the hive," Gardiner advises, "you may distinguish the mezzo tones that emanate from the host of fanners, who shed a mellow music from their odorous wings, which, on listening, will be found to be in the key of F."

"It is not worth the while to go round the world to count the cats in Zanzibar . . ." That's Henry David Thoreau, gently mocking the fellows of the geographical societies in the pages of *Walden*. When he goes off on this subject, Thoreau sometimes sounds as if he's responding to passages in the handbooks of Galton or Marcy. Other times he sounds as if he's shouting directly into Burton's ear:

What does Africa—what does the West stand for? Is it not our own interior white on the chart? . . . If you would learn to speak all tongues and conform to the customs of all nations, if you would travel farther than all travellers, be naturalized in all climes, and cause the Sphinx to dash her head against a stone, even obey the precept of the old philosopher, and Explore thyself.

Screw Zanzibar, in other words.

But here's something Thoreau neglected to admit in that book: no one was more incurably addicted to expeditionary literature and the how-to-travel books than HDT himself. Not only did he devour the travelogues of Burton and other contemporary explorers, but he energetically consumed the works of almost every author referred to above. Martineau, Owen, Ruskin, Gardiner—references to each of them appear in Thoreau's journals.

Thoreau's love of these books can be reconciled with his stay-at-home instinct, because he recognized the durable potential of the how-to-explore genre even better than its authors did. The lessons of the books could be applied to Zanzibar, but they held up equally well in the bustling hamlet of Concord, Massachusetts —or pretty much anywhere else in a world growing more tired, crowded, and worn with every passing year.

"It is worth the while to see your native village thus . . . as if you were a traveler passing through it," Thoreau wrote in his journal.

There's an idea.

Before I turned sixteen and got a driver's license, I spent a lot of time in the Cross County Mall in Mattoon, Illinois. Within my compressed conception of the universe, the mall was roughly analogous to the Silk Road: a place that marked the eastern edge of the world, where they sold imported goods. I dared go no farther on my bike. Beyond the mall, there was nothing but an interstate and a lot of corn. This was my ultima Thule.

My world has since expanded. My parents still live in Mattoon, and I visit occasionally, but the mall exerts little pull on me. I spent more hours inside the mall during an average day playing video games as a preteen than I've spent there in the past twenty years. It's no longer a destination for me; it's a forlorn piece of architecture that I drive past on the way out of town. One of roughly

50,000 shopping malls crowding roadsides in America, according to the Bureau of the Census. I could ignore it for another twenty years, and it would still feel like the most familiar place in the world.

On a recent morning, I pulled into the mall's parking lot with a Kindle full of downloaded guides: *The Art of Travel, What to Observe, How to Observe, Hints to Travellers, The Elements of Drawing, The Music of Nature,* and *The Prairie Traveler.*

I started by following Jackson's advice to place the area in its broadest context by surveying the surrounding geography, which was ironed flat by a mile-thick glacier that rolled through about 20,000 years ago. Now the landscape imposes rigid Newtonian laws on anything that messes with its uniformity—if you see the mild rise of an interstate overpass (like the one within eyeshot of the parking lot), a small man-made pond of inverse dimension will be found nearby, a couple hundred yards away.

The mall is a 300,000-square-foot retail space anchored by a JCPenney at one end and a Sears at the other. Faithfully observing Owen's speed limit, I walked at a relaxed pace from the entrance of one store to the other. The journey took exactly two minutes, three seconds.

Following Galton's advice, I was sensitive to my first impressions. Evidence of recent economic troubles screamed for immediate attention. Of thirty-eight leasable spaces, sixteen were vacant. But instead of giving off a hollow, abandoned vibe, the mall felt mildly claustrophobic. A dozen separate vendors had set up cafeteria tables in the main concourse, hawking everything from hunting knives to pewter dragons to collectible dolls. You could still find nice stuff in the remaining stores, but these tables represented a lower rung on the retail ladder, and they were clearly taking over.

In place of the landmarks of my youth, like the video-game arcade and the ice cream parlor, I saw a General Nutrition Center and something called "Community Blood Services." Before I made it to Sears, I began to feel as if I were strolling through a world robbed of joy.

But I checked myself. I returned, took a seat on a grated metal bench in the middle of the concourse, and reached into my backpack for my Kindle full of PDFs. Martineau was waiting to remind me to turn my attention outward. She urges her readers to assess the "character of the Pride" of a region—figure out what inspires them to make public proclamations, and you're on the way to cracking their moral code.

A T-shirt table in the middle of the mall attracted my eye. The first shirt I saw featured the letters *GPS,* with smaller letters around them. With exploration on the brain, I naturally gravitated toward it. It read, *If Lost, Use GPS—God's Plan of Salvation.*

I remembered that Jackson, in his chapter about exploring the religion of an unknown locale, advises explorers to look for hints that might answer this question: "What do they hold necessary to be done in this life to receive happiness in the next?" I found some clues on the T-shirt table. *To Get to Heaven, You Need to Get the Hell Knocked Out of You.*

In my pocket notebook, under a few lines of first impressions, I wrote: "Christianity rules here, and it seems to be a combative, hard-won strain." The author of *Hints to Travellers* advises that explorers label all field notations as "good," "very good," "doubtful," etc. I confidently scribbled "v. good" in the margin.

I now think of the first page of that notebook as a necessary warm-up, full of disposable insights. Few who visit could fail to note that whenever this midwestern town doesn't wear its faith on its sleeve, it often wears it emblazoned across its chest. But it was around this time, as I wandered away from the T-shirts, that the tireless focus these books help to instill started to reveal less obvious patterns.

Jackson insists that the ways a society engraves letters, for example, are "cognate and characteristic of the national mind, and are therefore, as such alone, highly worthy of the traveller's attention." I ducked into the Kirlins Hallmark store and found that cursive fonts, particularly those designed to suggest the lightest of pen strokes, could be found on almost all of the sympathy cards. Bold, blocky letters—many inscribed with a caveman sort of imprecision—almost always meant the cards were either meant to be funny or else were for children.

These bare facts led me to really read the signs throughout the mall, and I traced undisguised symbolism everywhere. Thin-bodied letters were used to sell beauty products (you won't find many fat, inky fonts in Bath & Body Works). RadioShack seemed to observe a zero-tolerance policy regarding serifs, which are reserved for products that appeal to classicism and tradition (see the Lands' End clothing section at Sears). Every letter in the mall seemed to exude purpose, as if hand-chiseled by market testers.

Suddenly the mall didn't seem quite as simple as it had just a couple minutes before. Instead of being a vacuous purgatory that deserved pity, the mall grew in complexity with each stride. The point that the how-to-explore books collectively hammered home is this: if you sincerely investigate it, every detail hides reason, and any environment is far more sophisticated than our senses can appreciate. You have no justification for feeling world-weary; even if the modern world bombards you with a million images per second, you have not seen it all. Ruskin writes:

> There was always more in the world than men could see, walked they ever so slowly; they will see it no better for going fast. And they will at last, and soon, too, find out that their grand inventions for conquering (as they think) space and time, do, in reality, conquer nothing; for space and time are, in their own essence, unconquerable, and besides did not want any sort of conquering; they wanted *using*.

For a while, I tried to inventory all of the smells I could detect and trace them to their sources: the dyed fabrics in Maurices clothing store; the brushed suede in Payless Shoes; the jasmine-and-sandalwood of the cosmetics counter in the Elder-Beerman department store. While concentrating hard to identify the characteristic smell of an electronics aisle in Sears (did I really detect the subtle tang of burning circuits?), a three-year-old boy accompanied his mother to inspect the DVD players. The kid wouldn't shut up. "I want this one! I want this one!" Every ten seconds or so, for reasons only he can grasp, he'd shriek like a beluga whale —three high, raspy squawks. My concentration shattered into a hundred pieces. I lost the scent.

But I remembered that I was carrying an electronic voice recorder—a device that I believe the author of *The Music of Nature,* had he lived into our century, would carry on his person at all times. I fished it out of my pocket and covertly began recording the boy's voice.

For the next half hour or so, I digitally captured the discrete units of sound that collectively composed the mall's soundscape. The hum of the refrigerator at Mom's Legendary Foods. The splash of the decorative water fountain in the geographic center of the concourse. The squeaky wheel of one of the race-car-shaped strollers available near the main entrance. The rapid-fire percussion of a cash register.

Some things, surely, deserve to be ignored, for sanity's sake. At times, I worried I might have been too loose with my attentions at the mall. Emerson had warned against this sort of thing, believing that indiscriminate observation could turn a person into a mere child—"the fool of his senses, commanded by every sight and sound, without any power to compare and rank his sensations, abandoned to a whistle or a painted chip, to a lead dragoon or a gingerbread-dog, individualizing everything, generalizing nothing, delighted with every new thing . . ."

It's true that the techniques outlined in these books can be abused, and they should be applied sparingly, medicinally. But I was discovering unexplored territories within the commonplace, and it felt as if I was beginning to correct an imbalance that had taken hold years before, when I'd pedal out to the mall to pump tokens into Galaga and Tempest, losing hours staring into a digital display. Video games train players how to react quickly to abrupt changes in the visual field, something that researchers now call "target vision." Young gamers—the ones who don't have to go to arcades but can play at home, token-free, for hours—are really good at it. But that skill, if overdeveloped, can erode a person's "field vision," which is the ability to register what's going on before and after those abrupt changes happen. Field vision requires proactive, not reactive, awareness. Without it, the bigger picture is lost.

The Victorians valued that way of looking at the world, considering it a critical skill when wandering into strange and bewildering territories. It still is. Behind a trash can near Sears, a single-serving carton of milk lay partially spilled. After reading Galton, the image was infused with intrigue: he tells us that milk, when applied to paper and subjected to a low flame, works as invisible ink, useful to explorers in hostile territories. The carefully designed GNC storefront display, with its labels advertising protein supplements and antioxidants, read like a sociological essay. The ragged chorus of the mall's concourse, captured on my digital recorder, then analyzed using music-studio software, revealed itself as music in the key of B-flat major, and the screech of a toddler, instead of being something that annoys and distracts, rang out in a perfectly pitched D.

PETER GWIN

The Telltale Scribes of Timbuktu

FROM *National Geographic*

The Salt Merchant

In the ancient caravan city of Timbuktu, many nights before I
encountered the bibliophile or the marabout, or comforted the
Green Beret's girlfriend, I was summoned to a rooftop to meet
the salt merchant. I had heard that he had information about a
Frenchman who was being held by terrorists somewhere deep in
the folds of Mali's northern desert. The merchant's trucks regularly crossed this desolate landscape, bringing supplies to the
mines near the Algerian border and hauling the heavy slabs of salt
back to Timbuktu. So it seemed possible that he knew something
about the kidnappings that had all but dried up the tourist business in the legendary city.

I arrived at a house in an Arab neighborhood after the final
call to prayer. A barefoot boy led the way through the dark courtyard and up a stone staircase to the roof terrace, where the salt
merchant was seated on a cushion. He was a rotund figure but
was dwarfed by a giant of a man sitting next to him, who, when he
unfolded his massive frame to greet me, stood nearly seven feet
tall. His head was wrapped in a linen turban that covered all but
his eyes, and his enormous warm hand enveloped mine.

We patiently exchanged pleasantries that for centuries have
preceded conversations in Timbuktu. Peace be upon you. And
also upon you. Your family is well? Your animals are fat? Your
body is strong? Praise be to Allah. But after this prelude, the

salt merchant remained silent. The giant produced a sheaf of parchment, and in a rich baritone slightly muffled by the turban over his mouth, he explained that it was a fragment of a Koran, which centuries ago arrived in the city via caravan from Medina. "Books," he said, raising a massive index finger for emphasis, "were once more desired than gold or slaves in Timbuktu." He clicked a flashlight on and balanced a mangled pair of glasses on his nose. Gingerly turning the pages with his colossal fingers, he began to read in Arabic, with the salt merchant translating: "Do men think they will be left alone on saying, 'We believe,' and that they will not be tested? We did test those before them, and Allah will certainly know those who are true from those who are false."

I wondered what this had to do with the Frenchman. "Notice how fine the script is," the giant said, indicating the delicate swirls of faded red and black ink on the yellowing page. He paused. "I will give it to you for a good price." At this point I fell into the excuses that I regularly used with the men and boys hawking silver jewelry near the mosque. I thanked him for showing me the book and told him that it was far too beautiful to leave Timbuktu. The giant nodded politely, gathered the parchment, and found his way down the stone stairs.

The salt merchant lit a cigarette. He had a habit of holding the smoke in his mouth until he spoke so that little puffs would tumble out along with his words. He explained that the giant did not really want to sell the manuscript, which had been passed down through his mother's ancestors, but that his family needed the money. "He works for the guides, but there are no tourists," he said. "The problems in the desert are making all of us suffer." Finally he mentioned the plight of the Frenchman. "I have heard the One-Eye has set a deadline."

During my time in Timbuktu, several locals denied that the city was unsafe and beseeched me to "tell the Europeans and Americans to come." But for much of the past decade the U.S. State Department and the foreign services of other Western governments have advised their citizens to avoid Timbuktu as well as the rest of northern Mali. The threats originate from a disparate collection of terrorist cells, rebel groups, and smuggling gangs that have exploited Mali's vast northern desert, a lawless wilderness three times the size of France and dominated by endless sand and rock, merciless heat and wind.

Most infamous among the groups is the one led by Mokhtar Belmokhtar, an Algerian leader of al Qaeda in the Islamic Maghreb (AQIM). Reputed to have lost an eye fighting the Russians in Afghanistan, he is known throughout the desert by his nom de guerre, Belaouer, Algerian-French slang for the One-Eye. Since 2003 his men have kidnapped forty-seven Westerners. Until 2009, AQIM had reached deals to release all of its hostages, but when the United Kingdom refused to meet the group's demands for Edwin Dyer, a British tourist, he was executed—locals say beheaded. His body was never found. In the weeks before my arrival, Belaouer and his cohorts had acquired a new inventory of hostages: three Spanish aid workers, an Italian couple, and the Frenchman.

"Belaouer is very clever," the salt merchant emphasized. He described how AQIM gained protection from the desert's Arab-speaking clans through Belaouer's marriage to the daughter of a powerful chief. One popular rumor describes him giving fuel and spare tires to a hapless Mali army patrol stranded in the desert. Such accounts have won him sympathizers among Timbuktu's minority Arab community, which in turn has angered the city's dominant ethnic groups, the Tuareg and Songhai.

Up on the roof the temperature had dropped. The salt merchant pulled a blanket around his shoulders and drew deeply on his cigarette. To the north, the city's lights gave way to the utter blackness of the open desert. He told me that the price AQIM had set for the Frenchman's life was freedom for four of its comrades arrested by Malian authorities last year. The deadline to meet these demands was four weeks away.

I asked him why the Mali army did not mount an offensive against the terrorists. He pointed the red ember of his cigarette toward a cluster of houses a few streets over and described how Belaouer's men had assassinated an army colonel in front of his young family in that neighborhood a few months earlier. "Everyone in Timbuktu heard the shots," he said quietly. He mimicked the sound, *bang, bang, bang.* Then he waved the cigarette over the constellation of electric lights that revealed the shape of the city. "The One-Eye has eyes everywhere." And then, almost as an afterthought, he added, "I'm sure he knows you are here."

The Bibliophile

Sand blown in from the desert has nearly swallowed the paved road that runs through the heart of Timbuktu to Abdel Kader Haidara's home, reducing the asphalt to a wavy black serpent. Goats browse among trash strewn along the roadside in front of ramshackle mud-brick buildings. It isn't the prettiest city, an opinion that has been repeated by foreigners who have arrived with grand visions ever since 1828, when Réné Caillié became the first European to visit Timbuktu and return alive. Yet it is a watchful city: with every passing vehicle, children halt soccer games, women pause from stoking adobe ovens, and men in the market interrupt their conversations to note who is riding by. "It is important to know who is in the city," my driver said. Tourists and salt traders mean business opportunities; strangers could mean trouble.

I found Haidara, one of Timbuktu's preeminent historians, in the blinding midmorning glare of his family's stone courtyard, not far from the Sankore Mosque. He wanted to show me what he said was the first documentary evidence of democracy being practiced in Africa, a letter from an emissary to the sheikh of Masina. The temperature was quickly approaching 100 degrees, and he sweated through his loose cotton robe as he moved dozens of dusty leather trunks, each containing a trove of manuscripts. He unbuckled the strap of a trunk, pried it open, and began carefully sorting the cracked leather volumes. I caught a pungent whiff of tanned skins and mildew. "Not in here," he muttered.

Haidara is a man obsessed with the written word. Books, he said, are ingrained in his soul, and books, he is convinced, will save Timbuktu. Words form the sinew and muscle that hold societies upright, he argued. Consider the Koran, the Bible, the American Constitution, but also letters from fathers to sons, last wills, blessings, curses. Thousands upon thousands of words infused with the full spectrum of emotions fill in the nooks and corners of human life. "Some of those words," he said triumphantly, "can only be found here in Timbuktu."

It is a practiced soliloquy but a logical point of view for a man whose family controls Timbuktu's largest private library, with some 22,000 manuscripts dating back to the eleventh century and volumes of every description, some lavishly illuminated in gold and decorated with colorful marginalia. There are diaries filled with subterfuges and plots, as well as correspondence between sovereigns and their satraps, and myriad pages filled with Islamic theology, legal treatises, scientific notations, astrological readings, medicinal cures, Arabic grammar, poetry, proverbs, and magic spells. Among them are also the little scraps of paper that track the mundanities of commerce: receipts for goods, a trader's census of his camel herd, inventories of caravans. Most are written in Arabic, but some are in Haidara's native Songhai. Others are written in Tamashek, the Tuareg language. He can spend hours sitting among the piles, dipping into one tome after another, each a miniature telescope allowing him to peer backward in time.

The mosaic of Timbuktu that emerges from his and the city's other manuscripts depicts an entrepôt made immensely wealthy by its position at the intersection of two critical trade arteries—the Saharan caravan routes and the Niger River. Merchants brought cloth, spices, and salt from places as far afield as Granada, Cairo, and Mecca to trade for gold, ivory, and slaves from the African interior. As its wealth grew, the city erected grand mosques, attracting scholars, who in turn formed academies and imported books from throughout the Islamic world. As a result, fragments of the Arabian Nights, Moorish love poetry, and Koranic commentaries from Mecca mingled with narratives of court intrigues and military adventures of mighty African kingdoms.

As new books arrived, armies of scribes copied elaborate facsimiles for the private libraries of local teachers and their wealthy patrons. "You see?" said Haidara, twirling his hand with a flourish. "Books gave birth to new books."

Timbuktu's downfall came when one of its conquerors valued knowledge as much as its own residents did. The city never had much of an army of its own. After the Tuareg founded it as a seasonal camp about A.D. 1100, the city passed through the hands of various rulers—the Malians, the Songhai, the Fulani of Masina. Timbuktu's merchants generally bought off their new masters, who were mostly interested in the rich taxes collected from trade. But when the Moroccan army arrived in 1591, its soldiers looted the libraries and rounded up the most accomplished scholars, sending them back to the Moroccan sultan. This event spurred the great dispersal of the Timbuktu libraries. The remaining collections were scattered among the families who owned them. Some were sealed inside the mud-brick walls of homes; some were buried in the desert; many were lost or destroyed in transit.

It was Haidara's insatiable love for books that first led him to follow his ancestors into a career as an Islamic scholar and later propelled him into the vanguard of Timbuktu's effort to save the city's manuscripts. Thanks to donations from governments and private institutions around the world, three new state-of-the-art libraries have been constructed to collect, restore, and digitize Timbuktu's manuscripts. Haidara heads one of these new facilities, backed by the Ford Foundation, which houses much of his family's vast collection. News of the manuscript revival prompted the Aga Khan, an important Shiite Muslim leader, to restore one of the city's historic mosques and Libyan leader Muammar Qaddafi to begin building an extravagant walled resort in anticipation of future academic congresses.

I asked Haidara if the problems in the desert are impeding Timbuktu's renaissance. "Criminals, or whoever else it may be, are the least of my worries," he said, pointing to pages riddled with tiny oblong holes. "Termites are my biggest enemies." Scholars estimate many thousands of manuscripts lie buried in the desert or forgotten in hiding places, slowly succumbing to heat, rot, and bugs. The question of what might be lost haunts Haidara. "In my worst dreams," he said, "I see a rare text that I haven't read being slowly eaten."

The Marabout

After the salt merchant's talk about the One-Eye, a local man suggested I consult a certain marabout, a type of Muslim holy man. For a price, he could provide me with a gris-gris, a small leather pouch containing a verse from the Koran imbued by the marabout with a protective spell. "He is the only one who can truly protect you from Belaouer," the man had confided.

Arriving at the marabout's house, I entered a small anteroom where a thin, bedraggled man was crouching on the dirt floor. He reached out and firmly held one of my hands in both of his. A few of his fingernails had grown long and curved off the tips of his fingers like talons. "Peace upon you," the man cried out. But after I returned his greeting, he didn't let go of my hand. Instead he sat on the ground, rocking slightly back and forth, firmly holding on, and smiling up at me. Then I noticed a chain fastened around his ankle. It snaked across the floor to an iron ring embedded in the stone wall.

The marabout, a balding man in his late forties who wore reading glasses on a string around his neck, appeared. He politely explained that the chained man was undergoing a process that would free him from spirits that clouded his mind. "It is a thirty-day treatment," he said. He reached out and gently stroked the crouching man's hair. "He is already much better than he was when he arrived."

The marabout led the way to his sanctum, and my translator and I followed him across a courtyard, passing a woman and three children who sat transfixed in front of a battered television blaring a Pakistani game show. We ducked through a bright green curtain into a tiny airless room piled with books and smelling of incense and human sweat. The marabout motioned us to sit on a carpet. Gathering his robes, he knelt across from us and produced a matchstick, which he promptly snapped into three pieces. He held them up so that I could see that they were indeed broken and then rolled up the pieces in the hem of his robe. With a practiced flourish worthy of any sleight-of-hand expert, he unfurled the garment and revealed the matchstick, now unbroken. His powers, he said, had healed it. My translator excitedly tapped my knee. "You see," he said, "he is a very powerful marabout." As if on cue, applause erupted from the game show in the courtyard.

The marabout retrieved a palm-size book bound with intricately tooled leather. The withered pages had fallen out of the spine, and he gently turned the brittle leaves one by one until he found a chart filled with strange symbols. He explained that the book contained spells for everything from cures for blindness to charms guaranteed to spark romance. He looked up from the book. "Do you need a wife?" I said that I already had one. "Do you need another?"

I asked if I could examine the book, but he refused to let me touch it. Over several years his uncle had tutored him in the book's contents, gradually opening its secrets. It contained powers that, like forces of nature, had to be respected. He explained that his ancestors had brought the book with them when they fled Andalusia in the fifteenth century after the Spanish defeated the Moors.

They had settled in Mauritania, and he had only recently moved from there with his family. "I heard the people of Timbuktu were not satisfied with the marabouts here," he said. I asked who his best customers were. "Women," he answered, grinning, "who want children."

He produced a small calculator, punched in some numbers, and quoted a price of more than a thousand dollars for the gris-gris. "With it you can walk across the entire desert and no one will harm you," he promised.

The Green Beret's Girlfriend

The young woman appeared among the jacaranda trees of the garden café wearing tight jeans and a pink T-shirt. She smiled nervously, and I understood how the Green Beret had fallen for her. Aisha (not her real name) was twenty-three years old, petite, with a slender figure. She worked as a waitress. Her jet-black skin was unblemished except for delicate ritual scars near her temples, which drew attention to her large, catlike eyes.

We met across from the Flame of Peace, a monument built from some three thousand guns burned and encased in concrete. It commemorates the 1996 accord that ended the rebellion waged by Tuareg and Arabs against the government, the last time outright war visited Timbuktu.

Aisha pulled five tightly folded pieces of paper from her purse and laid them on the table next to a photograph of a Caucasian man with a toothy smile. He appeared to be in his thirties and was wearing a royal-blue Arab-style robe and an indigo turban. "That is David," she said, lightly brushing a bit of sand from the photo.

They had met in December 2006, when the U.S. had sent a Special Forces team to train Malian soldiers to fight AQIM. David had seen her walking down the street and remarked to his local interpreter how beautiful she was. The interpreter arranged an introduction, and soon the rugged American soldier and the Malian beauty were meeting for picnics on the sand dunes ringing the city and driving to the Niger River to watch the hippos gather in the shallows. Tears welled in Aisha's eyes as she recounted these dates. She paused to wipe her face. "He only spoke a little French," she said, laughing at the memory of their awkward communication.

Aisha's parents also came from starkly different cultures. Her mother's ancestors were Songhai, among the intellectuals who helped create Timbuktu's scholarly tradition. Her father, a Fulani, descended from the fierce jihadis who seized power in the early 1800s and imposed Sharia in Timbuktu. In Aisha's mind, her relationship with David continued a long tradition of mingling cultures. Many people pass through Timbuktu, she said. "Who is to say who Allah brings together?"

Two weeks after the couple met, David asked her to come to the United States. He wanted her to bring her two-year-old son from a previous relationship and start a life together. When her family heard the news, her uncle told David that since Aisha was Muslim, he would have to convert if he wanted to marry her. To his surprise, David agreed.

Three nights before Christmas, David left the Special Forces compound after curfew and met one of Aisha's brothers, who drove him through the dark, twisting streets to the home of an imam. Through an interpreter the imam instructed the American to kneel facing Mecca and recite the *shahadah* three times: "There is no God but Allah, and Muhammad is his prophet." He gave the soldier a Koran and instructed him to pray five times a day and to seek Allah's path for his life.

When David returned to the compound, his superiors were waiting for him. They confined him to quarters for violating security rules. Over the next week, he was not allowed to mix with the other Green Berets nor permitted to see Aisha, but he was able to smuggle out three letters. One begins: "My dearest [Aisha], Peace be upon you. I love you. I am a Muslim. I am very happy that I have been shown the road to Allah, and I wouldn't have done it without meeting you. I think Allah brought me here to you . . ." He continues: "I am not to leave the American house. But this does not matter. The Americans cannot keep me from Allah, nor stop my love for you. *Allahu Akbar.* I will return to the States on Friday."

Aisha never saw him again. He sent two e-mails from the United States. In the last message she received from him, he told her that the army was sending him to Iraq and that he was afraid of what might happen. She continued to e-mail him, but after a month or so her notes began bouncing back.

As she spoke, Aisha noticed tears had fallen onto the letters.

She smoothed them into the paper and then carefully folded up the documents. She said she would continue to wait for David to send for her. "He lives in North Carolina," she said, and the way she pronounced *North Carolina* in French made me think she imagined it to be a distant and exotic land.

I tried to lighten her mood, teasing that she had better be careful or Abdel Kader Haidara would hear of her letters. After all, they are Timbuktu manuscripts, and he will want them for his library. She wiped her eyes once more. "If I can have David, he can have the letters."

Uncertain Endings

A month after I left Timbuktu, Mali officials, under pressure from the French government, freed four AQIM suspects in exchange for the Frenchman. The Italian couple was released, as were the Spanish aid workers after their government reportedly paid a large ransom. Since then AQIM has kidnapped six other French citizens. One was executed. At press time five remained in captivity somewhere in the desert. The marabout and his family disappeared from their home. Rumor spread that he had been recruited by the One-Eye to be his personal marabout.

I e-mailed David, who was serving in Iraq and is no longer in the Special Forces. He wrote back a few days later. "That time was extremely difficult for me, and it still haunts me." He added, "I haven't forgotten the people I met there, quite the contrary, I think of them often."

I called Aisha and told her that he was still alive. That was months ago. I haven't heard any more from David, but Aisha still calls, asking if there is any news. Sometimes her voice is drowned out by the rumble of the salt trucks; sometimes I hear children playing or the call to prayer. At times Aisha cries on the phone, but I have no answers for the girl from Timbuktu.

HENRY SHUKMAN

Chernobyl, My Primeval, Teeming, Irradiated Eden

FROM *Outside*

THE WILD BOAR is standing 30 or 40 yards away, at the bottom
of a grassy bank, staring right at me. Even from this distance I
can see its outrageously long snout, its giant pointed ears, and the
spiny bristles along its back. It looks part porcupine, a number
of shades of ocher and gray. And it's far bigger than I expected,
maybe chest-high to a man. The boar is like some minor forest
god straight from the wilderness, gazing wild-eyed at the strange
spectacle of a human being. For a moment it seems to consider
charging me, then thinks better of it. When it trots away, it moves
powerfully, smoothly, on spindly, graceful legs twice as long as a
pig's, and vanishes into the trees.

I climb back into our VW van, tingling all over. The sighting
bodes well. I've come to what is being dubbed Europe's largest
wildlife refuge in early July, when I knew spotting animals wouldn't
be so easy. (Winter, with its scarcity of food and lack of foliage,
makes them more visible.) And within a couple of hours I've
ticked a wild boar off the list. Maybe luck is on our side.

But luck isn't our only obstacle to wildlife spotting here. This is
northern Ukraine's Chernobyl Exclusion Zone, a huge area, some
60 miles across in places, that's been off-limits to human habita-
tion since 1986. Even now, nineteen years after the collapse of
the USSR, nothing happens in this former Soviet republic without sheets of paper typed and stamped in quintuplicate. It took
months of e-mails and phone calls to get permission to spend a

few days here. Yes, we're only a couple of foreign vagabonds—
photographer Rory Carnegie is an old travel buddy of mine from
England—but we have cameras and a telephoto lens, and my note-
pad has lines in it: obviously we're spies. The Soviet Union may
have died, but the Soviet mind-set has not.

At the Chernobyl Center, a kind of makeshift reception building in the heart of the old town, I had to hand over a solid 9
inches of local bills—hryvnia, pronounced approximately like the
sound of a cardsharp riffling a deck—sign a stack of agreements,
compliances, and receipts, and then get checked on an *Austin Powers*-style Geiger counter made out of chrome. Finally, under the
protection of a guide, a driver, and an interpreter, we were free
to set off into the zone—as long as we did exactly what our guide
said.

A handful of dilapidated roads cross the zone, half overgrown
with weeds and grasses, and the whole area is littered with pockets
of intense radiation, but nature doesn't seem to mind. All nature
seems to care about is that the people, along with their domestic
animals, are for the most part gone. The zone is reverting to one
big, untamed forest, and it all sounds like a fantastic success story
for nature: remove the humans and the wilderness bounces right
back. Lured by tales of mammals unknown in Europe since the
Dark Ages, we're setting out on an atomic safari.

It was soon after 1 A.M. on the night of April 26, 1986, that one of
the world's nightmare scenarios unfolded. Reactor 4 in the huge
Chernobyl power station blew up. The causes are still the subject
of debate, but it was some combination of a design flaw involving the control rods that regulate reactor power levels, a poorly
trained engineering crew, a test that required a power-down of the
reactor, and a dogged old-style Soviet boss who refused to believe
anything major could be wrong. At any rate, it was spectacular.
Eight-hundred-pound cubes of lead were tossed around like pop-
corn. The 1,000-ton sealing cap was blown clear off the reactor.
A stream of raspberry-colored light shone up into the night sky
—ionized air, so beautiful that inhabitants of the nearby city of
Pripyat came out to stare. When it was all over, estimates former
deputy chief engineer Grigori Medvedev, the radioactive release
was ten times that of Hiroshima.

Chernobyl had been a mostly peaceful settlement for one thousand years and a predominantly Jewish town for the past three centuries, famous for its dynasty of Hasidic sages. Since the Russian Revolution, the Jews have thinned a lot, but even today there are two shrines to the Hasidim where once a year devotees come to light candles and pray. It's incredible what survives a disaster. As Emily Dickinson said, "How much can come and much can go, and yet abide the world."

In 1970, 9 miles from the town, the Soviet Union started building what they hoped would become Europe's largest nuclear power station. (Only four of the planned eight reactors had been completed when disaster struck.) To go with it, they erected a brand-new concrete city, Pripyat, whose 50,000 inhabitants greatly outnumbered the 12,000 living in Chernobyl. The nuclear industry fell under the military complex, and the traditional Soviet culture of secrecy was all over it. Radiation is bad enough, but compound it with Soviet pride and paranoia and you have a potent mix of Kafka and Ray Bradbury.

The first the rest of the world knew of the Chernobyl disaster was when workers at a Swedish power station more than 1,000 miles away reported for work two days later, checked themselves with a Geiger counter, and found they were highly radioactive. By the following day, April 29, radioactive clouds had been carried by prevailing winds right across Western Europe and into Scandinavia, and the *New York Times* ran a front-page story about the catastrophe. The Soviet newspaper *Pravda* devoted a full eight lines to the "accident" that day—on its third page. It wasn't till May 15, three weeks later, that General Secretary Mikhail Gorbachev finally announced what had happened.

Thirty people died on the night of the explosion or soon after. Two days later, a convoy of 1,100 buses shipped out all the inhabitants of Pripyat, turning it into a ghost city overnight. The vast might of the Soviet Union went into overdrive with a massive cleanup operation involving 600,000 workers. A layer of topsoil was removed for miles around the site. (The government has not said where it went, but many believe it was dumped in the nearby Dnieper River, where silt would have buried it.) Hundreds of thousands of trees were planted, to bind the ground and reduce the spread of radioactive dust.

But the cleanup turned out to be even more lethal than the explosion itself. Soldiers were offered two years off their service in exchange for just two minutes shoveling nuclear waste. Thousands of people won medals for bravery and were declared Heroes of the Soviet Union but at the same time picked up cancer and thyroid problems that would dog them for the rest of their lives. Thousands of evacuated locals and cleanup workers are said to have died in the ensuing years from radiation doses, and it's reckoned that some 2.7 million people alive today in Ukraine, Belarus, and Russia have been directly affected by it.

In the following weeks, bureaucrats in Moscow designated an 1,100-square-mile Exclusion Zone—roughly the size of Yosemite —reasoning that the farther from Chernobyl people were, the better. This is mostly true: almost all of the crew working at the reactor when it blew died within a few weeks, as did several of the firemen who arrived on the scene minutes later, but the backup laborers who got there later mostly survived, albeit with dire health problems.

In all, two towns and an estimated ninety-one villages were emptied. But radiation doesn't travel consistently or evenly. If radioactive dust is picked up by a cloud, it will fall where the rain falls. There are still parts of Wales where the sheep farmers can't sell their meat, and last summer thousands of wild boars hunted in Germany were declared dangerously radioactive.

Today, around five thousand people work in the Exclusion Zone, which over the years has grown to an area of 1,660 square miles. For one thing, you can't just switch off a nuclear power plant. Even decommissioned, it requires maintenance, as does the new nuclear-waste storage facility on-site. The workers come in for two-week shifts and receive three times normal pay. Any sign of disease at the annual medical, however, and they lose their jobs.

There are also some three hundred people living in the zone: villagers who've been coming home to their old farming lands since not long after the disaster and teams of radioecologists from around the world who've come to study the effects of radioactive fallout on plants and animals. They've effectively turned the zone into a giant radiation lab, a place where the animals are mostly undisturbed, living amid a preindustrial number of humans and a post-apocalyptic amount of radioactive strontium and cesium. On the outside the fauna seems to be thriving: there have been huge resurgences in the numbers of large mammals, including gray wolves, brown bears, elk, roe deer, and wild boar present in quantities not recorded for more than a century. The question scientists are trying to answer is what's happening on the inside: in their bones, and in their very DNA.

Once you enter the zone, the quiet is a shock. It would be eerie were it not so lovely. The abandoned backstreets of Chernobyl are so overgrown, you can hardly see it's a town. They've turned into dark-green tunnels buzzing with bees, filled with an orchestral score of birdsong, the lanes so narrow that the van pushes aside weeds on both sides as it creeps down them, passing house after house enshrined in forest. Red admirals, peacock butterflies, and some velvety brown lepidoptera are fluttering all over the vegetation. It looks like something out of an old Russian fairy tale.

Ukraine officially opened Chernobyl up to tourism in January 2011, but small groups have been able to visit the zone for the past few years. There are small tour operators based in Kiev that take visitors on day trips. You don't need Geiger counters or special suits; you just have to stay with the tour, pass through several checkpoints, and get tested for radiation on your way out. The tours will shuttle you around some of the main sites—the deserted city of Pripyat, a small park filled with old Soviet army vehicles used in the cleanup, various concrete memorials to the fire crews who lost their lives after the blast. Visitors are strictly confined to areas the authorities have scanned and declared safe.

Staying longer than a day is more complicated. The Chernobyl Center has a guesthouse where nonofficial visitors like us can stay and be fed delicious if overpriced Ukrainian stews and escalopes. At sundown each evening there's a curfew. Walk to the nearby shop where the local workers buy their beer and bread and you could get yourself arrested.

Chaperoning Rory and me at the center and on our daily excursions is our guide, Sergey. He lives in a town near Kiev, but for the past ten years he's been spending two weeks out of every four in the zone, showing visiting scientists and the odd tourist around. Sergey is a tough, taciturn guy who looks like an old sergeant major, with a silver mustache and a head of cropped white hair. Our plan is to explore the forest, the old town of Chernobyl, the nearby rivers, the empty city of Pripyat, and some villages where a few peasants are still living. One of the papers we had to sign when we entered was an agreement that if we stepped anywhere Sergey hadn't told us to, we wouldn't hold the authorities responsible for any health issues.

So far, the only visible sign of radiation has been a digital read-out on the mostly deserted post office building in Chernobyl. Instead of telling the time and temperature, it shows the micro-roentgen levels in different sectors of the zone, which fluctuate according to changes in background radiation and the weather.

The most contaminated of the villages were bulldozed and bur-ied soon after the explosion, with only a few mounds and ridges left to show they were ever there. The meadows are mostly gone, replaced by forest. Russia is a land of forests, but the true forest, the primeval untouched forest that human eyes may never even have seen, is called *pushcha*—which roughly translates as "dense forest." This is what has been reestablishing itself at Chernobyl, regenerating at an unprecedented rate.

At the edge of Chernobyl, we stop by the half-mile-wide Pripyat River. It's unbelievably peaceful. A black dog, which knows Sergey, slumps down in the grass beside us. A handful of long, stoved-in rowboats moored at the shore take me back to the punts of my Oxford childhood. They're stamped with the initials of the local KGB and must have been moldering here since Soviet times. Frogs plop into the water, boatmen skedaddle across the surface, dragonflies hover—it's like a weight has been lifted from the world. A sparrow-hawk turns in lazy circles; a pair of ducks race by, low down, necks stretched, and make it to a willow on the far bank with a clatter of relief.

We pass two brick sheds with padlocks on their doors: the shrines of zaddiks, Jewish wise men.

"Why locked?" I ask Sergey.

Not missing a beat, he says, "Many people don't like Jews." (Something else that survived the apocalypse.)

We meander along the sleepy brown river. The main sounds are the different shades of hissing of wind in the trees: high nearby, deeper and steadier farther away. Occasionally the wind picks up, flicks a ripple along the surface. This must be what life was like one thousand years ago, when the entire human population of the globe was roughly 250 million. There's space for everyone, time for everything.

On our way down off the bridge, we spot a slender roe deer 200 yards up the road. It stands still a moment, head cocked, then like a sylph it slips into the trees, so swiftly I don't even see it go. A little farther on, we spot an elk between two bushes. He looks at us, head lifted, then strolls out of sight.

The van drops us off at a dark footpath that winds up through the woods, past a chain of collapsed wooden houses. Inside, their floors are littered with clothes, bottles, stuffing from mattresses. Pieces of gutted insulation lie strewn like corpses under the trees. It's not so much a town with trees in it as a forest with an old town falling to pieces within it.

Sergey tells us about the herds of boar he has seen, fifty strong, rampaging through the forest. And about a starving wolf pack that surrounded a scientist friend of his in a wood one winter day. He had to shoot every last one to get away.

It's not just the forest that's come back but all its creatures. It's the land of Baba Yaga, the old witch of Russian folktales. Is this the world before humanity? Or after? Is there a difference?

Traveling in Ukraine can be quite a party. The Ukrainians prefer not to engage in talk on its own. It's better with a bucket of vodka and a carton of cigarettes.

It's three in the afternoon of our second day when seven of us settle at a makeshift table beneath a spreading mulberry tree in the luscious garden of Ivan Nikolayevich's home. Officially, no one is supposed to live here, but within a few months of the disaster, several hundred farmers, families like this one, returned to their ancestral homes and have been quietly living here ever since, tolerated by the government and apparently free of any unusual health problems.

We're in the tiny village of Upachich, deep in the zone. There's Ivan himself, dressed in a sleeveless shirt with only one button and a pair of trousers that have seen so much yard work he could be a man from any of the past few centuries. When we met him half an hour ago, he had just finished gathering up his small field of hay with a pitchfork, building the kind of hayrick Monet and Van Gogh loved to paint. There's Ivan Ivanovich, his son, who was helping him, with designer stubble and a wristwatch that place him somewhere in the past few decades. The two of them are still dripping and red-faced from their labors. And there's young Ivan's mother, Dasha, wearing a timeless Russian babushka headscarf and a subtle, sublime smile.

It feels like we haven't walked into a home so much as a story by Gogol. Corncobs are drying on a line. Indoors, there's a big stove with a built-in shelf on top for sleeping on in winter, buckets of potatoes standing on the floor, scraps for the hens, a basin with its own cistern you fill up from the well.

Ivan the son is busy wiping down the table, spreading out sheets of newspaper for all the foodstuffs: eggs from chickens pecking under our feet, tomatoes from the garden, bread, a bowl of tiny forest raspberries, a whole dried river fish, crystallized and orange from its time smoking in a homemade stove. It's all local and it all looks great, but most tempting of all are the mulberries hanging above my head. They resemble elongated blackberries, and there's something about the way they're growing among the elegant oval leaves of the tree that makes them irresistible. I'm dying to reach up and grab one, but they frighten me. We're only 10 miles from the power station.

Whatever you do, friends advised before we came, don't eat anything that grows there.

The older Ivan comes out of the house carrying a glass jar full of clear fluid in his trembling hand.

"Vodka," someone declares appreciatively.

That'll be safe, I think to myself: shop-bought.

"No, no. Samogon," Sergey explains, eyeing the jar with a gleeful twinkle. "Better than vodka."

Samogon?

"Homemade."

My heart sinks. The local moonshine. But before I can ask if it's really safe to drink, we're clinking glasses, wetting our fingers, and I cautiously take a sip.

"You're not exactly drinking as you should," Sergey notes, suggesting that I chug.

"Clean—it must be clean!" declares one of the Ivans.

Sergey is already slamming down his empty glass. What can I do but oblige?

Conversation begins to flow. Sergey starts expatiating on the advantages of village life. "When you want make business, make networking, you live in the city. But here, there is natural food, for example this samogon, it is so good for you."

I'm far from sure, but the dad gets up and shows me round the garden. He wants me to see where the tomatoes grow, and the grapes and vegetables, and where he finds the root he uses in his special medicinal vodka. Swaying, puffing, he pulls up a little plant, then lumbers off to the pond to rinse it: a lump of ginseng.

A couple of samogon shots later, my fears have abated and I'm tucking in like the rest. The fish is so smoky my eyes water, and soon my hands are stained blood-red from all the mulberries I've eaten. A bird starts singing. Flakes of sunshine shift over us. The hay is in, there's a pig fattening for Easter, and the oats are almost ready for the scythe. If this isn't rustic life at its timeless, bibulous best, what is?

Most everyone in Chernobyl displays a predictable bravado about living with radiation. In the relative cool of the evening, the workers on their two-week shifts gather outside the guesthouse to sit on tree stumps and chew the fat, drink beer, smoke cigarettes. With a line of dark chestnut trees nearby and the pale night sky overhead, amid the silence and stillness of the deep forest, it's a lovely scene, even with the insistent black mosquitoes that bob around our faces.

"Radiation is good for you," one of them tells me. "Every year I get younger," says another. And another: "I work here so when I come home glowing my wife will think I'm a god."

A particularly hearty-looking man who works as a janitor asks me, "How old do you think I am?"

"Sixty," he answers himself. A preposterous answer: he looks not a day past thirty.

The best decontamination? "A bottle of vodka."

But radiation is scary. It's particularly scary because it's mostly undetectable to the senses. If you feel sleepy and have a chemical taste in your mouth, it might be because of radiation. If you're able to see it, in the form of purple ionized air—as they did that night in April—or, worse, feel it in the form of instant-tanning heat, it's probably too late for you.

Still, it's a fact of life. We all live under constant radioactive bombardment: there's solar radiation, terrestrial radiation, there's even radiation in our food, since all living things contain radioactive potassium-40 and our food consists mostly of once-living things. There are different units of measurement—like dps, or disintegration per second, and curies, grays, sieverts, rads, rems, roentgens, and so on. The average terrestrial dose is 3 microrems per hour—but in some parts of the world this goes as high as 100 microrems, with no perceptible ill effects. (In fact, there's some evidence that cancer rates are lower in these areas; perhaps mild stress to the immune system makes it work better.)

A dangerous dose is hard to pin down. Worldwide, for most people, those daily microrems add up to about 360 millirems per year. Scientists agree that humans can safely handle 1,000 a year. Astronauts on the International Space Station receive 18,000 millirems of cosmic radiation over six months—but it's once in a lifetime, so it's seen as an acceptable, voluntary risk. But edge that up to 30,000 millirems and you're looking at what caused increased cancer rates among the blast survivors of Hiroshima and Nagasaki. And yet animals can handle even more than this: large mammals and birds are generally safe with 36,000 per year, small ones with even higher doses, and reptiles with higher still. The more complex the animal, the more sensitive it is.

Nuclear power involves various radioactive substances that differ from the hydrogen isotopes in a modern thermonuclear weapon. There are the fissile materials (which make the reaction happen) like plutonium and uranium, and the fission products (which result from it) like radioactive iodine, cesium-137, and strontium-90. It's these last two, along with some plutonium, that mostly contaminate Chernobyl today. Some emit alpha or beta particles, some gamma rays. Alpha particles have a short range: in air, 1 to 2 inches; in skin, one to two thousandths of an inch. So if they're coming from outside you, they can't penetrate your skin. But if inside—if you've eaten something contaminated, for example—they're nasty. Their short range means they're more likely to deposit their energy within a small area—small enough to attack both strands of a DNA molecule, possibly causing cancer. Beta particles, meanwhile, can travel about 20 feet through air and a quarter of an inch through skin; they can't reach internal organs from outside the body. Gamma rays are essentially X-rays. They can be more or less penetrating, depending on strength.

The half-lives of radioactive materials vary too. Cesium's and strontium's are around thirty years, plutonium's is eighty-eight years, but with uranium-238—the base product used to create plutonium—it's more than 4 billion years. A long half-life means the substance remains radioactive much longer but gives off its radiation more slowly. The half-life of radioactive iodine is only one week, which means it gives off a lot of radiation quickly—another reason the Soviet authorities were so irresponsible in not announcing the Chernobyl disaster sooner: a lot of lethal, iodine-contaminated food got eaten those first few days after the explosion.

All through our trip, Sergey has been telling us how healthy he is, in spite of ten years in the zone. Only at the end will he reveal that he can't run anymore because of pains in his legs. Too much "strontsy," he says. But he's fine, he adds, because the strontsy is only in his muscles, not the bones. Not yet, anyway.

One of the workers tells me he doesn't drink, not even beer. "I do sports, so I cannot drink," he says, lighting up another cigarette.

"But what about the radiation?" I ask him.

He shrugs. "Life itself is dangerous, my friend."

The world beyond the apocalypse may not be so great for humans, but for the other denizens of the planet it looks like a bonanza. Today there are around 5,000 adult wild boars in the Chernobyl Zone. In 1995 there were many more, but they suffered an epidemic and have now stabilized. There are 25 to 30 wolf packs, a total of maybe 180 adults. Many more lynx live here than before, along with foxes, barsuks (a Ukrainian badger), hundreds of red deer, and thousands of roe deer and elk. Out of the disaster comes a paradise of wildlife. The Garden of Eden is regenerating.

But it's not so straightforward.

For seventeen years, biologist Igor Chizhevsky has been studying how animals metabolize cesium and strontium. He works with the Chernobyl Radio-Ecological Center and is a friendly, serious, broad-faced man. He has made Chernobyl his career. When he comes to talk with us in the guesthouse, he sits stolidly in an armchair, barely moving at all for an hour, while telling us in a doleful Slavic voice about how things are really going down here for the animals.

When humans abandoned the zone, he says, it wasn't just them and their domestic animals—including 135,000 cattle—that left. The "synanthropic" species that live around humans—pigeons, swallows, rats, and the like—also left the territory in large numbers, leaving it free for a wild ecosystem to reestablish itself.

"Structure of entire fauna system change," Igor says.

House mice, which thrived on grains no longer grown here, have been replaced by forest and field mice. Likewise with the bird species. But it's the larger mammals we're interested in.

On the surface, Igor says, the wildlife seems to be thriving, but under the fur and hide, the DNA of most species has become unstable. They've eaten a lot of food contaminated with cesium and strontium. Even though the animals look fine, there are differences at the chromosomal level in every generation, as yet mostly invisible. But some have started to show: there are bird populations with freakishly high levels of albinism, with 20 percent higher levels of asymmetry in their feathers, and higher cancer rates. There are strains of mice with resistance to radioactivity—meaning they've developed heritable systems to repair damaged cells. Covered in radioactive particles after the disaster, one large pine forest turned from green to red: seedlings from this Red Forest placed in their own plantation have grown up with various genetic abnormalities. They have unusually long needles, and some grow not as trees but as bushes. The same has happened with some birch trees, which have grown in the shape of large, bushy feathers, without a recognizable trunk at all.

"Genomes, er, unpredictable," says Igor. "Genome not exactly same from generation to generation. They change."

This is not good for a species. Genomes are supposed to stay the same. That's what holds a species together. No one knows what these changes could result in.

"Soon or late," Igor says, "new species will evolve."

In other words, new animals could actually be in the making here. The area has become a laboratory of microevolution—"very rapid evolution," says Igor—but no one knows what will emerge or when.

One Stanford scientist I spoke to later had a terse summary: if there are genetic changes, and if these pass down to the next generation, and if they survive natural selection, then it's reasonable to talk of evolution. There are two theories about why this may happen. In classic Darwinism, random genetic changes that help an organism survive in its environment are naturally selected through generations, because the individuals with those characteristics do better. But "mutagenesis," an alternate theory, posits that organisms deliberately adapt to their surroundings. The process is not accidental. For example, in Chernobyl, if mice are developing radiation resistance by passing down cell-repair systems, is that because some individuals just happened to develop this attribute and to fare better, or is it because the species deliberately developed this capacity in response to the environment?

Sergey takes us to a real-life laboratory nearby: just an old house, but inside it's been gutted, and the walls are lined with shelves of cages, each one full of scurrying white mice. A rank stench hits us as soon as we walk in.

The white-coated lab technician—yet another Ivan—notices my grimace and smiles. "Yes," he says. "And we just cleaned the place this morning."

He explains that they're studying the effect on the mice of the radioactive spectrum here in the Chernobyl Zone. They took probes from the Red Forest and recreated the conditions here at the lab, then started giving the mice food laced with cesium and strontium.

Why here? I ask.

"This is already a contaminated area. So we don't risk spreading radiation elsewhere." In other words, the zone has become a kind of refuge for radiation research.

He and his team are studying the mice to understand their resistance to radioactivity. They've found sensitivity to ionization, which results in certain tumors, and some of this passes down through the genes. But they're also finding heritable radiation resistance—which could perhaps be beneficial to humans someday.

In spite of being a clearheaded scientist, Ivan gives us a surprise when asked if he's okay being photographed. He starts laughing nervously. "I'm afraid of American shamans and what they may do to me," he confesses. Apparently some old-time beliefs are still being inherited around here too, even in a science lab. The Ukrainians are complex people: part Soviet, part soulful Slav, part subsistence farmer. Even this lab has its own vegetable patch out front.

On our last morning I wake up early, and as I lie in my bed at the dorm I hear, quite distinctly, a wolf howling. It holds its note a long time before reaching for a higher one, then a still higher one. It sounds like a healthy howl. But no biologist has yet been able to study these wolves in sufficient numbers to have a clear idea of their genetic health. They know what their bellies are full of, but the meat has its own genetic instability. These wolves may have a vast untracked forest to roam, but what is happening deep in their DNA no one knows. Will there be new species in a few generations? There may already be, out in the forest, and we wouldn't even know.

Later that morning, on our way to the ghost city of Pripyat, we see a fox darting across the road—nothing more than a black silhouette, curiously low to the ground. Or perhaps it was a small wolf, says Sergey. Then a big bird, which turns out to be an eagle, is suddenly ahead of us, grappling with a sapling it has attempted to land on, bending it down low, then letting the young tree spring back up again as it rides away on giant brown wings.

Sergey tells us that Pripyat used to be the most beautiful, spacious city he ever saw. More roses grew there than anywhere else he ever knew. There were never any shortages, and you could get fine clothes, Czech-made shoes. It was a model of what communism was supposed to have been.

It's weirdly distressing to be here. As a human, it's like staring down the barrel of our likely fate. We may wipe ourselves out with a nuclear holocaust, or with carbon and methane, or some other way we can't yet conceive of. Or nature may do it for us. When it happens, trees may or may not mind. Cyanobacteria poisoned their own atmosphere two and a half billion years ago by releasing vast quantities of a gas that was poisonous to them—oxygen—and in the process created an atmosphere suited to higher forms of land life. Who knows what creatures may adapt to a high-carbon, high-methane atmosphere if we keep going the way we are? They may include us, or not.

From Pripyat we drive on to the old power station itself. It's a large area of vast concrete buildings. One of them is the stricken Reactor 4, some 200 feet tall, with a giant chimney still rising out of it. For almost twenty-five years it's stood encased in a "sarcophagus" of cement, but the seal is far from perfect, and it leaks dangerously. We park 200 yards away to look at it but stay only a few minutes. A new steel sarcophagus is slowly being built; when finished, it will be the world's largest movable structure.

There are canals threading through the giant buildings, which provided water for the old coolant system, and in one of them the catfish have grown to prodigious sizes. We stop on a metal bridge and gaze down into the brown water. Suddenly the monsters rise to the surface, some of them a good 10 feet long, black, whiskered, curling around as they hunt for the bread people feed them.

They're not big because of radiation, Sergey insists. It's just that they haven't been fished for a quarter of a century.

The whole area is like this: fecund, scary. Later Sergey takes us to an army barracks where some soldier friends of his keep a few wild pets. From the dark doorway of one of the sheds issues a terrific subterranean grunt, and a moment later, as if in a hurry, out trots another wild boar. It comes straight at the fence, presses against it with the weird, wet sucker of its long, long nose, then raises its bristly head and eyeballs me as if I'm something from another planet.

In a pen next door there's another forest sprite—the barsuk, a very close relative of our badger. When it comes out of its kennel, it runs up a woodpile, turns at the top, and proceeds to stare right into me with deeply strange eyes. Something in me seems to recognize something in it, and I feel a pang of longing. Is it for the deep forest, the *pushcha*? For the trees, the smell of autumn leaves, of mushrooms and mold? For the freedom to live our own way, far from society?

Crouching and staring, the barsuk doesn't move a muscle. It could be a stuffed animal, with eyes of glass. Or perhaps a new species, staring at the world with new eyes.

ELLIOTT D. WOODS

Garbage City

FROM *VQR*

PERCHED ATOP THE Moqattam Cliffs, where Pharaonic slaves cut limestone for the pyramids, the Monastery of Saint Simon and its accompanying cathedral boast a commanding view of Cairo. On a smog-free day, if you peek around the cliffs to the south, you can see clear to the Great Pyramids of Giza. Looking west, you have a fine view of more recent history; you can almost throw a rock at the Citadel of Salah Ed-Din or into the endless expanse of tombs that make up el-Arafa—the City of the Dead. On the western horizon, the Cairo Tower stands apart from the deceptively modern skyline of downtown. Right below your feet, largely invisible to the outside world, you'll find Izbet Az-Zabaleen. The Garbage City, as it's known in English, is a hive of entrepreneurial recyclers called *zabaleen*, literally "garbage people," nestled at the edge of Manshiet Nasser, a teeming slum on Cairo's eastern outskirts. A haze produced by the exhalations of some 2,500 black-market recycling workshops carpets a landscape of windowless brick high-rises and unpaved alleys piled high with garbage, the raw material of zabaleen industry. Rooftops serve as storage for stockpiles of plastic bottles, but also for herds of sheep and pigeon coops.

Women cluster in the trash-lined dirt streets, sorting organic waste from recyclables. They hunt for aluminum, tin, steel, and sixteen types of plastic—from the kind used to make Ziploc Baggies to the crash-resistant stuff of car fenders. Bands of barefoot children play amid the waste. To the uninitiated, the scene appears downright infernal—like the fiery orc workshops of *The Lord of the Rings*. But looks are deceiving; the zabaleen swear they're living better than ever.

In sixty years, the zabaleen have gone from serfs to recycling entrepreneurs. Palaces have risen from the trash, bricks purchased bottle by bottle. There are real-life garbage kings in the village with informal businesses worth millions of dollars, but most of the 60,000 zabaleen in the Garbage City live modest lives defined by hard labor and strong family obligations. They and others like them throughout the city collect an estimated 4,500 tons of garbage from Cairo and Giza each day, and they claim to turn 80 percent of everything they collect into postwaste, salable materials. By comparison, Switzerland—which claims to have the best-organized recycling program in the world—recycles just over 50 percent of its waste.

Almost all zabaleen are Coptic Christians whose families migrated to Cairo from Upper Egypt (the country's agricultural south, called "upper" because it's upstream from Cairo) in the 1940s, when government land reforms brought down a centuries-old feudal system and forced tens of thousands of peasant farmers into the cash economy. Like their Muslim compatriots, Coptic zabaleen remain deeply religious. Family homes are plastered with icons and biblical quotations, and the monastery above the Garbage City is the zabaleen's private paradise. Hundreds of people stream up the hill in the afternoons to visit the gardens and breathe the comparatively clean air. For thousands of zabaleen women who rarely leave the Garbage City, Saint Simon is the only sanctuary from a life lived among the refuse of 16 million.

Moussa Zikri and I are admiring the view from Saint Simon one afternoon when his phone rings. His face goes gray as he listens to the voice on the other end. When he hangs up, he asks politely if we can leave.

"What's wrong?" I ask.

"There is a fire at my dad's work," he says. "I have to go there now."

We begin walking briskly downhill.

"Do you want to run?" I ask.

"Yes," he says, and he takes off.

I sprint too, past girls on their way up to the monastery, who giggle as we run by, past men hunched under ridiculously large sacks of garbage. We pick our way around donkey carts, squished rats, and puddles filled with sludge. Moussa flags down a car at the bottom of the hill. I walk the remaining distance, orienting myself toward a growing plume of black smoke. When I arrive, I find Moussa panting before a flaming heap of plastic bottles.

"My materials!" he shrieks.

Moussa's father works as a guard at a parking lot where garbage collectors keep their trucks when they're not working. Moussa, twenty-three, is the youngest of three brothers. He recently got into the bottle recycling business with the help of a $2,000 microloan, and he stockpiles his bottles in the parking lot, where his dad can keep an eye on them. Somehow a fire sprang up this afternoon, and it's consuming weeks of work right before his eyes.

Moussa's little sister brings pails filled from a hose, and his brothers sling the water over the flames. The fire hisses and pops, mocking their efforts. Finally firemen arrive and unleash a blast of high-pressure water from their fire engine. In minutes Moussa's mountain of bottles has been reduced to a steaming slag heap.

Moussa and Samaan, his older brother and partner in the bottle recycling business, rush up the street to buy a bundle of giant woven sacks made from recycled grain bags to gather the surviving bottles. They salvage enough to load a Datsun pickup to three times my height, but Moussa remains inconsolable.

"Today is a big misfortune for me," he says. "I probably lost eight hundred kilos today." Moussa travels all over Cairo to buy bottles from garbage collectors spread throughout the city. He hoards bottles with his own capital, then turns a small profit by shredding them into chips and reselling them to an exporter.

Moussa estimates the fire damages at about thirty dollars—a seventh of his monthly income. He's sure the firemen would have arrived sooner if the address were somewhere other than the Garbage City. Manshiet Nasser is an "informal" development, in the language of Egypt's Ministry of Planning; Moussa and his family are technically squatters, and they and the other zabaleen receive little in the way of government services.

I follow Moussa upstairs to his living room after he and Samaan finish unloading the unburned stock into their basement. The door frames and walls are coated in black grime. A ceiling fan casts a choppy shadow over the room. Samaan's one-year-old son,

Abanoub, stumbles around behind his mother, screaming bloody murder. He was circumcised the day before and has developed an infection. Abanoub's mother paces around frantically, clutching the phone and begging Samaan to call the doctor.

Moussa's two-year-old nephew waddles into the room with a Styrofoam plate of potato chips. He trips and spills the chips on the floor at Moussa's feet.

Moussa bends over to pick up a chip from the floor. He crunches it in his mouth, and a fleeting grin appears beneath his glazed eyes.

"I'm going crazy," he says.

Today's zabaleen were preceded by a group of garbage workers called the *wahaya,* or "oasis people," who emigrated to Cairo from Saharan waterholes in the early twentieth century. The wahaya made money by gathering waste paper and selling it to public bathhouses in downtown Cairo, where it was used to heat bath water. The government eventually prohibited the use of wastepaper fuel in public baths, and the wahaya had to find a new business model.

In came the first waves of Coptic farmers from Upper Egypt. They struck a deal with the wahaya: they would collect the garbage and use it to raise pigs, and the wahaya would keep the rights to garbage collection routes and monthly collection fees charged to residents. The wahaya would provide each Copt family with a pigsty and two pigs to get them started, and the Copts could buy out their pigsties over time.

In the 1940s, the first zabaleen neighborhoods sprouted in Torah and Imbaba, two greater Cairo areas that were once on the outskirts of the city but have since been enveloped in the city's endless sprawl. The Giza Governorate forced the zabaleen out of Imbaba in the seventies and many families relocated to the arid and inhospitable desert below the Moqattam Cliffs.

The wahaya no longer collect garbage, but they guard their roles as middlemen between the trash and the profits. They still control the garbage collection routes and take a three-fifths cut of all collection fees. The tradeoff between zabaleen and wahaya remains essentially the same: zabaleen families keep all the garbage they want; only now, instead of feeding it to pigs, they mine it for recyclable materials.

Sherif, the collector who worked my building with his brother and nephew in May and June 2010, paid the wahaya with rights to my neighborhood about sixty cents out of the dollar he collected monthly from each of the 250 apartments on his route. Sherif's three-man team thus earned around $100 per month from collecting six hours a day, six days a week. The bulk of their monthly income came from selling plastic bottles to shredders like Moussa.

In 1983 the Cairo and Giza Cleansing and Beautification Authorities (CCBA, GCBA) divvied up collection routes between the biggest wahaya families and gave them legal recognition, but the zabaleen missed out on the deal. Their livelihood remains technically illegal, and they often pay petty bribes to street cops to avoid fines for using donkey carts in the city and driving trucks overloaded with garbage. Rather than draw more attention to their community by agitating for a more equitable system, the zabaleen try to fly below the radar.

In June 2009 the zabaleen took the biggest hit to their livelihood in history: in a panic over the spread of H1N1, swine flu, which had yet to reach Egypt, the government slaughtered 300,000 pigs belonging to zabaleen families. The pig cull struck the zabaleen as a personal assault. Many Copts believe they are the de facto scapegoats whenever Egypt runs into problems, and they suspect the government of killing the pigs to appease Muslims whipped into a frenzy by the H1N1 scare.

Pig farming had been the core of the zabaleen's business since they began their relationship with the wahaya in the 1940s. The zabaleen were so well known for their pigs that many Cairenes referred to their neighborhoods as *zarayyib*—pigsties. The pigs were a vital organ in the system; they sorted organic garbage from the recyclable materials with their mouths, allowing the zabaleen to profit from the garbage in three ways: by selling pork to fellow Christians at market, by selling truckloads of manure to rural farmers as fertilizer, and by selling recyclable materials to workshops in the Garbage City. Families took fattened pigs to market every six months, and a dozen hogs could generate as much as $1,500 of supplemental income. "The use of pigs was very clever," explained Nicole Assad, who has volunteered in the Garbage City for nearly thirty years with the Association for the Protection of the Environment (APE). "The pig is the only animal we know that can consume such quantities of organic garbage—thirty-two kilos a day." When the pigs vanished, it was as if the zabaleen machine suddenly had to run without an engine.

A forty-three-year-old mother of six named Naema—who, like many women in the Garbage City, spends her days sorting the garbage her husband brings home at night—told me that the worst consequence of the pig slaughter is that they can no longer handle as much trash. "We used to have two hundred pigs, and now the pigsty is overflowing with trash. We can't keep up." Absent hundreds of voracious mouths, the sorting process takes much longer—and produces fewer recyclables. "We want the pigs back," another woman told me. "It was a perfect system: they ate the garbage, and we ate them."

As they adapt to a hog-free world, the zabaleen have to contend with another roadblock: the arrival of multinational waste management consortiums. In 2003, in an attempt to modernize the capital, the Egyptian government invited corporations to bid on multimillion-dollar contracts for the collection and disposal of Cairo's garbage. When green-suited waste workers hit the streets with their compaction trucks and dumpsters, the zabaleen feared their days were numbered.

But Cairo itself seemed to come to their defense. Much of the city—from the ancient Fatimid arcades to the modern slums— rose around narrow alleys meant for foot traffic and donkey carts, not for cars or trash trucks. Even in modern Zamalek, where I stayed, most streets allow for the passage of only a single car between rows of cars parked two-deep along the sidewalks. On the wider axes, paralytic traffic makes a grueling slog out of the shortest journeys. Before long the multinationals were up to their ears in trash, utterly overwhelmed by Cairo's garbage.

Logistics were not the multinationals' only problem. They were also unable to convince Cairenes—accustomed to leaving their trash at their apartment doors for the *zabal*—to carry their trash bags down to dumpsters each day. In many locations where residents brought trash out to curbside bins, corporate garbage trucks failed to pick it up frequently enough, and the dumpsters overflowed. Dumpsters became feeding troughs for cats, dogs, rats, and weasels. The populace grew indignant.

Cairenes were also infuriated by the government's decision to charge them for trash collection directly on their utility bills. Suddenly they were paying twice—one payment to the multinationals, and another payment at the door for the people who actually collected the trash: the zabaleen.

To learn how multinationals were coping with their dilemma, I make an appointment with Ahmed Nabil, general manager of International Environmental Services (IES), in his glass-and-steel office next to the American embassy. IES won a $6.5 million annual contract to collect waste from Giza, but after six years on the ground the company still pays huge sums in fines for repeatedly failing to empty dumpsters on time. The fines have hobbled IES and prevented them from expanding their fleet or offering more jobs to the city's legions of unemployed. (Nabil would not disclose a figure, but Luigi Pirandello—the Italian manager of another multinational firm called AMA Egypt—told me his company pays 7 percent of its revenue in fines.)

After bemoaning myriad forms of GCBA harassment and waxing nostalgic about his sojourn in Houston as a young engineer, Nabil—wiry, with a thin silver mustache and a raspy smoker's voice—turns to the zabaleen. He sips his double espresso and tamps out his fifth cigarette, folding the filter neatly over the ember and pressing down with his thumb. "Of course the zabaleen are part of the plan," he says. "From the social point of view, we have a responsibility to keep them working, and from the point of view of experience, they can do what no one else can. The question now is how should they be integrated?"

When the multinationals first arrived, they attempted to hire zabaleen as collectors at about $60 a month, the going rate at the time for manual labor in Cairo. The zabaleen never showed much interest, partly because working for them would be seen as betrayal of the community—like a scab breaking a strike line—but more because the zabaleen recoil at the idea of simple wage labor.

"The zabaleen are business people in their own right," explained Bertie Shaker, a researcher with CID Consulting, a Copt-owned firm that has advised the government and the multinationals. "They don't want to be beholden to corporate interests, or to turn over the methods and expertise they've spent generations developing in exchange for a wage."

Executives like Nabil have a strong financial interest in co-opting the zabaleen: illegal dumping by zabaleen is the main source of multinationals' fines. The problem spun out of control after the May 2009 pig cull. For the zabaleen, dumping was partially an instrument of revenge. Mountains of trash shot skyward from vacant lots across the capital, and multinationals took months to get the situation under control.

Nabil hopes to discourage illegal dumping by bringing the assets of his company and the zabaleen in line. By contract, IES must recycle 20 percent of all garbage collected, a mark the company has never met. Nabil thinks the zabaleen could help his company reach the bar, and he plans to scratch their backs in return. He has advocated the construction of a transfer facility the zabaleen could use instead of an illegal dump site to sort recyclables from organic waste. The zabaleen could cart off all the recyclables they could manage, and IES could truck the organic waste left behind to composting facilities, where it could be turned into environmentally safe fertilizer for donation to rural farmers and counted toward IES's recycling percentage.

"If they dump garbage on the street, we incur more expenses to collect it, but if there was a place where they could come and sort in a hygienic plant, they could double or even triple their efficiency," Nabil says. "To waste their experience is wrong. To use their experience is a win-win situation."

It's just after eight on a May morning, and Moussa and Samaan are preparing for a long day at the shredder with *taamiya* sandwiches and tea at a hole-in-the-wall coffee shop down the street from their house. Today the machine under Moussa's house will eat 1,700 pounds of plastic soda bottles. Baba Shenouda, the Coptic pope, drones from a fuzzy TV mounted in a corner. Moussa puffs on a gurgling waterpipe and hums along to the liturgy. One of the Zikris' friends, a guy named Beshoul, takes it upon himself to introduce me to everyone in the shop. This is so and so, he works with PET plastic, he says, and this is so and so, he works with cardboard. Every zabaleen recycler has a specialty—they are master guildsmen of trash.

Back at the house, Moussa and Samaan hoist open the corrugated iron door to their garage. Sunlight sends rats scurrying into the shadows. We scramble over filthy bags of bottles stacked to the ceiling to get to the back of the garage, where the shredder is plugged into a high-voltage socket. Wedged into a corner, we're completely walled in by a fortress of 8-foot-tall bags stuffed with bottles. All that plastic does little to dampen the agonizing whine of the circular grinder Samaan uses to sharpen the shredder blades. I put on my sunglasses to protect my eyes from the bursting sparks, but Samaan just squints scornfully and keeps grinding.

The men work with astonishing speed. Their shredder consumes each giant bag of bottles in about five minutes, and little by little the magic machine chews its way out of the hole. Like Rumpelstiltskin spinning a heap of straw into gold, these men are turning worthless bottles into cash. After a while the machine gets hot and begins to put off bitter fumes, a mix of diesel exhaust and vaporized plastic. There's no ventilation except for the open garage door. Moussa tries to hide his running eyes from the smoke rising from the mouth of the machine. Veins bulge from his thin arms as he plunges bottles into the blades with a giant Aquafina jug. Samaan fills the hopper and shovels the growing pile of chips. He hangs empty bags by a nail driven through an icon of the Virgin Mary.

At some point Samaan passes me cotton balls to stuff in my ears, but the damage is done. For the rest of the day I feel like I'm underwater. We take a break at noon and head to the coffee shop for a smoke. We wade through a 2-foot layer of 7-Up and Sprite bottles to get out of the garage—it feels and sounds exactly like wading through the balls at a McDonald's PlayPlace. We stop to say hello to Moussa's mother and father, who are squatting in a garage across the street, sorting plastic shopping bags into color-segregated bins. A donkey is tethered to a post next to where they're sitting, and chickens are pecking at the dusty floor.

Three giggling boys pile around the table where Moussa and I are sitting at the coffee shop. Their names are Samaan, Abanoub, and Gergis—names as common to Copts as Mohammed, Ahmed, and Mustapha are to Muslims. Moussa arm-wrestles with the boys, who clearly admire him. He's a hotshot among the younger generation of zabaleen, with his microloan and his progress in the Recycling School, a nonprofit established to reach out to zabaleen kids left behind by the formal education system.

Samaan sits alone in a corner of the coffee shop, scowling. His relationship with Moussa is frayed, but I haven't found out why. We pay and go back to Moussa's house, where his sister-in-law has prepared a lunch of chicken and stewed tomatoes. We pick hunks of meat off the chicken with pieces of flatbread. Moussa and Samaan don't speak a word to each other, but Moussa's sister-in-law is more relaxed today, now that Abanoub's infection has passed. She sits with us and laughs at my Palestinian-accented Arabic. Samaan, suddenly in a foul temper, sucks the joy from the room. He snarls at the kids whenever they stray too close.

After lunch Moussa takes me to visit his English tutor, a thirty-two-year-old bachelor named Rizeq Youssef. We find him at a table on the street in front of his grandmother's house at the edge of the Garbage City, where the zabaleen's realm butts up against the vast Muslim slums. We wait for Riz, as Moussa calls him, to wrap up a business deal on his mobile. Riz runs a bustling PET-chip exporting business—PET is the variety of plastic used to make soda bottles—and the café next to his grandmother's place is the closest thing he has to an office.

As we wait, Riz's workers unload grain sacks full of unwashed green plastic chips from a truck. Each sack weighs about 80 pounds, and there must be thirty of them. Riz has just purchased the chips from a shredder, and now his workers will wash the chips in a series of vats to remove debris and remnants of labels. Then they'll dry the chips in the sun and repackage them for shipment to China.

Riz is tall with graying hair, a mustache, and a pocked, chubby face. He got into the PET business about ten years ago, and he's got his operation down to a science. He exports one ton of chips to China for a total cost of about $515, including labor and shipping expenses. He exports 40 to 60 tons of PET each month to Chinese importers, who resell the chips to textile manufacturers at a 20 percent markup. Riz splits the profit with the importers. The real value enters when Chinese manufacturers turn the chips into polyester, which eventually makes its way to American shopping malls in the form of tracksuits and sneakers.

Riz's business only works on an economy of scale. He buys chips from dozens of shredders, including Moussa, and deals in huge volumes. He employs seven men and runs his washing workshop six days a week. "I'm happy if I make fifty dollars per ton," he says. At $50 a ton and 60 tons a month, Riz earns about $36,000 a year.

Hardly a king's ransom, but he has ambitions. He's saving to buy a machine that will help him increase his output to 15 tons daily, putting him into serious cash.

Riz considers himself extremely lucky. His father was a science teacher at a government school who went out on a garbage collection route on the weekends, and his mother worked as a garbage sorter. His parents scrimped to send him to the private Gabbal Moqattam School, founded in 1981 by a Belgian nun named Sister Emanuelle. There were no schools at all in the Garbage City prior to the opening of Gabbal Moqattam, and Riz was one of the first enrolled students. Today he is one of the school's most celebrated graduates.

Riz went on to get a university teaching degree and become a teacher, "but I was always working both jobs," he said, and "my business was suffering. I like teaching, but I think my mind is more suited to business." Still, Riz can't shake a sense of community obligation, so he spends his free time outside his grandmother's house writing down English vocabulary for neighborhood kids and coaching them through their homework. As we talk, Moussa plucks words out of our conversation and scrawls them out in shaky English letters in his notebook. Riz pauses occasionally to correct him.

Moussa listens with wonderment as Riz rattles off calculations: so many tons of chips from the shredders equals so much profit from China. If Moussa keeps working and studying, he could develop a business like Riz's someday. As we walk back from Riz's in the dwindling sunlight of early evening, however, Moussa grows sullen. I quickly understand why. When we arrive at his street, Samaan comes flying out of the coffee shop in a rage.

"Where were you!" he screams. "I've been calling you all afternoon!"

Moussa had taken off after lunch to visit Riz and left Samaan alone to contend with the sea of green bottles.

"My battery died! Besides, I told you I had a lesson today," Moussa growls. Samaan throws up his hands and storms off. Moussa and I keep walking toward the highway, where I'll catch a taxi home.

"Sometimes when I'm alone," he says, "I write my whole life down. I ask myself, what can I do with my life? Can I live outside?

Maybe I can leave Egypt. I am tired of this life. I am tired of carrying my whole family."

He mumbles something.

"What did you say?" I ask.

"Ar-rab yesouah aarib min i-khaifeen."

The Lord Jesus is close to the afraid.

Ezzat Naem has come a long way since his childhood years, when he spent his days sorting garbage with his parents. Now he's director of the Spirit of Youth Association, which oversees the Recycling School for Boys. "Children's education is the first thing to go during economic hardships," Ezzat told me. A successful girls' school program founded by the Association for the Protection of the Environment in the 1980s, centered on crafts projects and literacy, paved the way for the Recycling School, which now has a hundred and fifty boys enrolled.

Moussa is the equivalent of an eighth-grader at the Recycling School, which focuses on literacy and arithmetic while striving to harness students' entrepreneurial zeal. There is no telling how sophisticated young zabaleen could become with strong foundations in mathematics and market analysis. Like most boys of his generation, Moussa never received any formal education before starting at the Recycling School at age sixteen. Government schools in Manshiet Nasser average sixty students per classroom, and the overcrowding deprives students of individual attention. Parents pay for after-school private lessons in order for their kids to pass yearly exams. But lessons cost nearly $200 per year, and zabaleen kids are also sorely missed during the workday, when they care for siblings and help process garbage.

In order to convince parents to send their kids to school, teachers had to show that students could still contribute to family income. Students at the APE girls' school received a dollar per day for the weaving work they did between lessons, and upon graduation they received a loom in their home and free rug-making material. The school would then buy the girls' woven products and sell them to wealthy Egyptians. The girls' school is now in its thirtieth year, and the Recycling School hopes to emulate its success.

About half of the boys enrolled at the Recycling School earn money by gathering, weighing, and destroying shampoo and conditioner bottles. Procter & Gamble funds the school as part of its Corporate Social Responsibility (CSR) regimen, but also because it was losing hundreds of thousands of dollars each year to counterfeiters, who used to buy stockpiles of bottles, refill them, then sell them on the street. Since the Recycling School opened in 2004, its boys have destroyed 250,000 bottles.

I visited Moussa at school one day and found him sitting at a low table with two students about his age and two little boys who were about twelve. The walls were painted in exuberant purples and pinks and the ceilings were strung with shampoo bottle craftwork. The room had the feel of a kindergarten, and a fair number of the boys in the room looked about kindergarten age. They were the lucky ones, to have such an early jump on education.

Moussa was taking down dictation in Arabic from a young female teacher. At another table, little boys worked math problems with an abacus. Moussa didn't seem worried that his classmates were less than half his age. He lives and breathes the Recycling School. He is studying hard for an exam that will allow him to matriculate to high school, and he would probably live at the school if they'd let him.

"Moussa can make it if he believes in himself," said Ezzat Naem, another one of Moussa's heroes. It was Ezzat and the staff of the Recycling School who helped arrange Moussa's microloan. "He snatches at opportunities. He's hungry for chances and willing to work hard. If he is ambitious enough, he can do anything."

Mariam Abdel Malik must have been expecting me to arrive at the Ministry of Planning with an entire television crew. She had a dozen plates of cookies set out on the giant conference table, and I think she was disappointed when she realized I had come alone. I had come to the Ministry of Planning to glean their plans for the future of the Garbage Village and the rest of Manshiet Nasser, and Mariam was going to be my guide.

There is a lot of anxiety in the Garbage City about the possibility of a forthcoming eviction, and a lot of historical evidence to suggest it might happen.

Ezzat Naem singled out real estate developers—not multinational waste management firms—as the greatest threat to the zabaleen community. He fears the government will force the zabaleen from Garbage City just like they were forced out of Imbaba forty years ago. They survived the previous eviction, but it's different now. Back then zabaleen lived in shacks and owned only the clothes on their backs and their pigs. Now they live in a city they're proud of, that they've built with their own hands and the sweat and ingenuity of generations. "The house is the primary investment and the primary site of business," Ezzat told me. "You can't do this work from an apartment. It just doesn't work. Families need their garages to store materials and to keep their machines."

I keep Ezzat's anxiety in mind as Mariam, a middle-class Egyptian who happens to be Christian, leads me through a PowerPoint on the Greater Cairo 2050 Master Plan. "Seventy-five percent of the population of Cairo lives within a twenty-kilometer diameter," she tells me. "The population density is extreme, and the purpose of the plan is to decentralize Cairo to reduce population density."

Illustrations flit across the screen of a place that looks like Orlando, not the traffic-choked, polluted mess outside the ministry's doors. Leafy trees line wide boulevards devoid of people and cars, and aerial sketches show swaths of jungle canopy over much of the city's slums. The few cars there are conspicuously observe the limits of their lanes—the surest sign that these images are from a fantasy Egypt.

When Mariam comes to a slide of a giraffe bending down to lick an ice cream cone held out by a blond woman in a sports car in the middle of the desert, a ministry employee named Nahed deadpans, "Now this is the future."

"Yes, this is too much," Mariam laughs.

I ask Mariam to return to a slide diagramming Cairo's residential areas according to three status labels: planned, unsafe, and unplanned. Part of the Master Plan, as Mariam explained, is to relocate everyone living in unsafe and unplanned areas to new satellite cities in the desert. The government will demolish the slums —including large portions of the historic City of the Dead, where an estimated 25,000 squatters have turned tombs into homes— and attempt to bring back the expansive green spaces that existed in Cairo's Nile watershed just twenty years ago.

"We will build new apartments in unpopulated areas for the people in unsafe areas who are to be relocated," she says. Unsafe areas include areas under power lines, areas where access streets are not wide enough to permit emergency vehicles, flood-prone areas, and areas under cliffs. Those conditions describe almost all of Cairo's most crowded downtown neighborhoods, as well as large areas of Giza, including the slums that abut the Great Pyramids.

The entire Moqattam area is unsafe in at least two of those categories—it's on the cliffs, and its tiny alleys would be all but impossible for an ambulance driver to navigate. I was on hand two years ago when a rockslide in the Duweiqa neighborhood next to the Garbage City killed over a hundred people. In this instance, the rockslide happened at a place that was easy for ambulances and fire trucks to access, but it didn't matter. It took days for the Egyptian rescue services to finally admit that they had no idea how to break apart the giant boulders to unearth those buried beneath. The most tragic aspect of the disaster was that the government had finished construction several years before on hundreds of new apartments for families living under and above the Duweiqa cliffs, but had never distributed them. Rumors surfaced after the rockslide that the bureaucrat in charge of placing at-risk families in the new apartments sold them to his friends instead.

As Mariam tells me about the relocation plans and shows me mockups of the Disneyesque Future World the government will build for Cairo's poor, I think of the giant boulders on top of crushed Duweiqa homes and the lines of riot police. Not in another forty or a hundred years could I imagine a relocation project on the scale Mariam is describing. If the government won't invest in proper schools and hospitals for the poor, why would it hand them the keys to a new city?

I inquire directly about the ministry's plans for Manshiet Nasser. "Unsafe areas will be *khalas*," Mariam says, wiping off an imaginary slate. "They will have a choice between an apartment or money."

"So there will be no people living here in 2050?" I ask, pointing to the Garbage City on the map.

"No."

If you hang around the Garbage City long enough, you start to think that things aren't so bad. You give up trying to keep your shoes clean and you stop worrying about where you sit or the fact that no matter how many times you clean your fingernails, they're always lined with black. After a while you don't think about it when you shake someone's hand who has just had their arm elbow-deep in trash. You leave your Purell at home.

And if you listen to the older zabaleen, you start to think the younger generation has it pretty good. A stout, perpetually smiling mother of five who went by the name Um Michael told me, "When I was a kid there were no schools. There were not even any houses! We used to live in wood and tin one-level shacks right next to the pigs. We even used to go to the bathroom in the pigsty." Um Michael was born in 1968 in Imbaba. She said life has gotten much easier for women in particular. "Twenty years ago we couldn't even leave the house!" she said.

The zabaleen are Christians, but they're still rural Egyptians and cling to the same conservative social practices as their Muslim counterparts; until this century, female circumcision was widespread in the Garbage City (it has nearly been eliminated thanks to NGO activism), and widespread adherence to traditional Egyptian codes regarding the protection of feminine virtue—observed by Muslims and Christians—prevented women from working outside the home in any capacity.

After puberty, women's lives were restricted almost exclusively to domestic work and child-rearing. "There was no education at all for girls," Um Michael said. Now forty-two, she is taking literacy classes at Saint Simon and has attained an eighth-grade reading level. She is immensely proud. In a living room scrawled with biblical graffiti, she fed me watermelon and pungent aged cheese that masked the smell of the streets outside. "I'm sorry the house is so dirty," she said. "It's not usually like this, but I've been studying so hard I haven't had time to clean."

Marianne Marzouk, Um Michael's oldest daughter, lives a life that Um Michael never could've imagined as a young woman. Marianne has a university degree, speaks English, and recently got a loan to start her own business. It'll just be a small clothing shop underneath her house, but her decision to quit her pharmacy job and strike out on her own shows that entrepreneurial spirit is not limited to zabaleen men alone. It's also notable that Marianne, at twenty-two, is not already married with children; young men and women from the zabaleen community are waiting longer to marry and having fewer kids, allowing them to pursue their work and educational interests with greater freedom.

Many younger zabaleen have visited relatives in their ancestral farming villages, and they are happy to leave the clean air and green vistas behind to return to the Garbage City. "I went with my father once to Assiut," Moussa told me. "There was nothing to do, and I asked my father if I could come home early. I hated it!" Naema came north to be married as a teenager and has never looked back. "In the village the men work all day under the burning sun for two dollars. They don't own the land and there is no opportunity," she explained. "Here the men can work as much or as little as they please. The amount of money they make depends on how hard they work."

In so many ways, a brighter future has already arrived for the zabaleen. They have achieved most of the improvements in their community through their own cooperative labor and ingenuity. All they ask now is for the freedom to continue improving their community at their own pace without government interference in the form of aggressive regulations or, in the worst case, forced relocation.

I was surprised to learn that Ezzat supports Ahmed Nabil's idea for transfer facilities where zabaleen can turn over organic waste to the multinationals and sort their recyclables outside the Garbage City. "If we can convince the government that we are the experts with garbage and recycling, and they help us upgrade our systems and our technology, then our living conditions will improve immensely," he said. Rizeq Youssef said he is already planning to move his washing operation out of the Garbage Village once the government makes industrial land available. "There are many people looking to buy land," Rizeq said. "I'm trying to invest in land too, because I need space to make my business bigger."

Dr. Atwa Hussein, a soft-spoken Ministry of Environment employee with olive-green eyes and a neat desk, does not conform to my idea of a scheming bureaucrat. In his office near Cairo's old city, he told me that the government has plans to construct two sorting facilities in the desert surrounding Cairo exactly like the one Ahmed Nabil described. "The biggest problem from the Ministry of Environment's point of view is informal dumping and the accumulation of garbage," he said. Informal dumps are more than eyesores—they catch on fire and pose a serious threat to adjacent areas, and they also exude methane and pollute the water table.

Informal dumps are also factories for disease, especially when located close to overpopulated megacities like Cairo.

Dr. Hussein admitted that the government rushed into reckless contracts with the multinationals in 2003, and that new contracts should account for the zabaleen, who Dr. Hussein sees as Cairo's most important waste management asset. His office is reworking waste management contracts to shift to a service-by-ton model—a shift they believe will lead to a cleaner Cairo and a more productive relationship between the government, the multinationals, and the zabaleen. "Service by route and pickup times does not incentivize the companies," he explained. "A service-by-ton model will mean that companies will get paid to work as much as they can." As for the zabaleen, "In the new contracts we will make it possible for the zabaleen to work officially as subcontractors for the multinationals. They will get paid a rate per ton of garbage they take to the sorting facility multiplied by the kilometers driven from the pickup point to the facility."

Zabaleen collectors with whom I spoke said multinationals already allow them to dump organic waste in their trucks at night, and some even said the multinationals pay the wahaya to organize transfers. Where many parties see a hopelessly complex set of competing interests, Dr. Hussein sees an opportunity to expand and improve a system that's already working. "In a perfect system," he said, "zabaleen will be formally licensed as the owners of their recycling businesses. In such a system, they could make even more money." Of course the government will benefit too. Dr. Hussein hopes the eradication of illegal dumping and the transition to environmental landfills will reduce future cleanup costs related to soil and water contamination.

Unlike the Ministry of Planning's PowerPoint, Dr. Hussein's plans are rational and plausible—especially because most of the cooperation he describes is already happening. The cooperation between multinationals and zabaleen just needs to be formalized to achieve maximum efficiency and to promise that the zabaleen get a fair cut.

While I was in Cairo, the Spirit of Youth Association was working with a Gates Foundation grant to explore possibilities for the zabaleen to integrate with the formal waste management sector. The organization surveyed eight hundred garbage collectors to ask if they wanted to be licensed, and the overwhelming response was yes. For all the zabaleen have been able to build out of trash, they've never been able to achieve real security. Formalization would legally sanction their operations and protect them from exploitation.

On the downside, formalizing the zabaleen and moving recycling workshops out of the Garbage City might erode the sturdy village culture that has allowed the community to thrive. In the Garbage City, the family is the best guarantee of security one can hope for; people still pay into collective pots to help friends get married or to handle medical emergencies, marriages are still arranged the old-fashioned way, and children take care of their parents as they grow old. An incredibly complex web of business relationships exists in the Garbage City, but family relationships are the anchors of existence. The zabaleen have always been more like farmers who barter and trade at the village market than factory workers and owners whose relationships and decisions are based entirely on financial transactions. But large export businesses like Rizeq Youssef's are all the evidence one needs to conclude that things are changing fast. The village is getting bigger, and so are the ambitions of its entrepreneurial youth.

If any of the Garbage City elders fear a new era in which the younger zabaleen base their decisions on money instead of family, Riz will allay their concerns. While he invests in growing his business, he also invests in his family; Riz pays tuition for all of his younger siblings, takes care of his grandmother, and even set his father up with a small shop in the neighborhood. He pays his workers more than they would earn with a multinational—more, in fact, than Riz made as a government teacher. Riz has never forgotten where he came from.

At about midnight one evening toward the end of my trip, I ride up to the Garbage City to meet a garbage collector who agreed to take me on his route. The taxi driver laughs when I ask him to take me to Manshiet Nasser.

"You're kidding, aren't you?" he asks.

When I get to the coffee shop where I arranged to meet the collector, he's nowhere to be found. He probably got worried that I would attract too much attention from the police—the most common reason every collector but him refused to take me along. As luck would have it, I find Riz at an Internet café across the street. He joins me for a cup of anise-flavored *yansoon*.

I tell him that Moussa and Samaan have been fighting constantly and that Moussa threatened to give up recycling altogether and try to find work as a tour guide. I tell him how Moussa said, "I am tired of carrying my whole family."

"It's not true," Riz says. "It's just that he has changed and now he looks at them as simple. He just doesn't see how much they do for him." Riz takes a sip of his *yansoon* and leans in across the table.

"Believe me," he says, "nobody does anything alone in this place."

THOMAS SWICK

My Days with the Anti-Mafia

FROM *The Missouri Review*

SHE SAT READING in the garden of Monreale Cathedral, dwarfed by an ancient, leathery ficus. Except for the book, she fit the popular image of the young Siciliana: black hair, black dress, black shoes. She looked as if she'd come from Mass. I took a seat at the other end of the bench, from where I could make out the title of her book: *The Portrait of a Lady.* "That's a good book," I said.

"Scusi?" she asked, startled by my intrusion.

"Henry James is a wonderful writer."

She smiled without looking at me. "I'm trying to improve my English," she explained.

Her name was Rosalina. She had recently returned from Milan to look after her ailing mother in Palermo. "A lot of young people leave Sicily," she said. Her brother lived in Milan. "We are not good citizens," she said bluntly. "Do you know what I mean?"

I mentioned the litter, which, after only two days, had made an impression.

"Yes. We live in a kind of paradise. We have the sun and the sea. We think everything will take care of itself."

I told her I had come to write about the anti-Mafia organization Addiopizzo.

"I think a lot of people don't understand the importance of this organization," she said.

"Perhaps the new generation will."

She looked unconvinced. "People were more active in the '80s," she said.

My bed-and-breakfast sat at the end of a quiet street not far from the port. I had arrived on a cruise ship Friday evening and stayed onboard for the weekend excursions, the last of which was to Monreale. There was no sign outside the building, just the name SoleLuna among the names of tenants on the list by the door. I took the elevator to the third floor and rang the bell on the right. The door opened to reveal a woman in big round glasses with a tousle of salt-and-pepper hair. "I am Patrizia," she said, pretty much exhausting her English, if not her warm welcome. Then she showed me to my room, where two single beds sat a little forlornly under a high ceiling.

Going out to explore, I found Palermo in a deep sleep. It was midafternoon on a Sunday in mid-August. Streets narrowed and darkened, at one point opening up to a sunlit intersection of stupendous decay. Abandoned buildings, sick with graffiti and boarded-up windows, seemed in competition to see which one could hold up the longest. I had read that some bombed-out neighborhoods in the city had never been restored after World War II, that Sicily was perennially ignored by Rome. But stumbling upon a decades-old dereliction—after two days of churches and palaces—was deeply alarming. This looked like Havana, not a major city of the European Union.

I crossed Via Vittorio Emanuele and plunged into another maze. A clutter of balconies blackened the airspace until I emerged into a small square filled with café umbrellas. An aproned waiter stepped from a door above which were the words *Antica Focacceria S. Francesco.* I knew the place from photographs, though they had always shown armed guards near the entrance, placed there because the owner had not only refused to pay protection money; he had gone to court and identified his extortionist. I imagined their absence was due to the drowsiness of August.

Via Merlo led to Piazza Marina, where the shuttered windows of old palazzos overlooked the dusty Giardino Garibaldi, its fence a rusting riot of nautical themes. It struck me as possibly the psychological heart of the city, the place where people would gather —if there were people. As I was admiring one of the ficuses in the garden, I came upon a plaque:

IN QUESTO LUOGO IL 12 MARZO 1909 ALLE ORE 20:45
PER PRODITORIA MANO MAFIOSA TACQUE LA VITA DI
Joe Petrosino
Lieutenant della Polizia di New York

LA CITTÀ RICORDA ED ONORA IL SACRIFICIO DELL'
INVESTIGATORE ITALO-AMERICANO

(IN THIS PLACE ON MARCH 12, 1909, AT 8:45 P.M.
THE HAND OF THE MAFIA SILENCED THE LIFE OF
Joe Petrosino
New York Police Lieutenant
THE CITY RECORDS AND HONORS THE SACRIFICE OF THIS
ITALIAN-AMERICAN INVESTIGATOR)

Not far away, an inscription on a wall, in Italian and German, identified the house as a place where Johann Wolfgang von Goethe had stayed while on his visit to Palermo in 1787. It noted that his subsequent book, *Italian Journey*, had called Sicily "the key" to understanding Italy.

A little to the east, Piazza Kalsa showed some life. Two boys rode one bicycle back and forth, and a father pulled down his son's pants so the boy could urinate into the bushes. Smoke from grills wafted over from surrounding streets. Next to the Church of Santa Teresa, a large hand-painted cart held a statue of the Virgin. The floor of the cart was covered on two sides with artificial roses, while the center sparkled with shards of broken glass. It seemed an odd decorative touch, but perhaps it doubled as a glittery warning to would-be thieves.

I ate my first breakfast at SoleLuna in the company of two young women from Genoa. They had come to the B&B on the recommendation of a friend. They hadn't realized that it was a member of Addiopizzo, the organization that supports businesses which refuse to pay protection money (*pizzo*) to the Mafia. They were accidental ethical tourists.

Patrizia joined us, and I asked Francesca to inquire about her membership in Addiopizzo. She said she had never been asked to pay the *pizzo;* she had joined the organization out of a sense of solidarity. (The full name of her lodging is SoleLuna della Solidarietá Bed & Breakfast.) I wondered if she was afraid. "No, no, no," she said dismissively, waving her hands and shaking her mop of salt-and-pepper hair. "No problem."

Addiopizzo was launched in 2004, when a few recent university graduates were considering opening a bar in Palermo. Of course it would entail, as someone pointed out to them, paying protection money. At the time the Mafia extorted an estimated $200 million annually from Palermo businesses, with rates that ranged from about $300 for a bar to as much as $1,500 for a large hotel. Instead of starting their new business, the young men went out late at night and blitzed the city with stickers that read: "An entire people that pays the *pizzo* is a people without dignity."

It was a courageous act. In 1991 Libero Grassi, the owner of a textile firm, had sent an open letter to the *Giornale di Sicilia* that began: "Dear Extortionist." Nine months after it was published, he was killed. Other people who had stood up to the Mafia had had their factories torched, their stores ransacked, their pets killed. The retaliation of the so-called Honored Society is a well-documented phenomenon.

Support for Addiopizzo grew, so that today it has over 460 members—ranging from the Accademia Siciliana Shiatsu to the Zsa Zsa Monamour *discoteca*—that refuse to pay protection money. Considering all the businesses in Palermo, this is still a modest number, however, and skeptics say that many people who claim they don't pay the *pizzo* actually do. There is a store on Via Vittorio Emanuele that sells only products made by *pizzo*-free enterprises. Comitato Addiopizzo has a comprehensive website, giving information in most EU languages (including Finnish and Lithuanian), and it even has a travel arm, which offers anti-Mafia tours. I was signed up for one on Tuesday.

That first day, however, I needed to go shopping, as I hadn't seen my suitcase since check-in in Miami. I walked the length of Via Roma, stopping in every men's store I passed. As disheartening as the merchandise—shirts defaced with logos, zippers, bogus coats of arms, meaningless scraps of English—was the reception from the shop assistants. It wasn't a surprise, though: in *The Honoured Society: The Sicilian Mafia Observed,* the British travel writer Norman Lewis wrote: "By comparison with the Italy of Rome—above all of Naples—Sicily is morose and withdrawn." Lewis developed a great affection for the place but noted in a later book, *In Sicily,* that he rarely heard the sound of laughter there.

The shop assistants along Via Roma and Via Maqueda lived up to the stereotype. Granted, it was a stifling week in August, when anyone still working had a right to be irritable and pining for the beach. But at most of the places I went in Palermo—cafés, newsstands, gelaterias—I was met with an impassive stare that seemed the fixed facial expression of a people who had long ago learned to be suspicious of strangers.

In every store, I wondered if the owner paid the *pizzo*.

The bus traveled north along Via della Libertá and dropped me on a wide boulevard lined with large apartment houses. Heading toward the entrance of one of them, I saw a handsome young man dressed in a T-shirt and shorts. He introduced himself as Edoardo, the man I'd been corresponding with by e-mail. The T-shirt, I now noticéd, displayed an anti*pizzo* message.

I followed Edoardo up to his office on the second floor. He told me the previous tenant had been a mafioso. In one corner hung a large cutout of a tree with head shots of men—Libero Grassi, Giovanni Falcone, Paolo Borsellino (the two anti-Mafia magistrates assassinated in 1992)—pasted on its branches. Above them arched the words, in Italian, "You are not alone anymore."

Edoardo gave me a booklet that listed Addiopizzo businesses and a large city map with their locations, including that of his office, clearly marked. Then, taking a seat, he told me his story.

In 2004 he had been working at a small publishing company with one of the originators of the sticker campaign. He asked if he could join them. They would go out once a week, often as late as 2 A.M.; some wore hoods to hide their identities. "We were scared," Edoardo admitted. "We were not sure what we could risk."

After spreading their message through stickers and the Internet (methods ancient and modern), they started to recruit businesses. It was hard to ask shopkeepers to join a *pizzo*-free organization, so they began with businesses that had never paid the *pizzo* or whose family members had been Mafia victims. After two years Addiopizzo had a hundred members.

They also recruited consumers. Edoardo got up to show me another wall hanging, a framed page from the *Giornale di Sicilia*. It contained a list of names of "normal citizens," 3,500 of them, who were committed to shopping at *pizzo*-free establishments and, even more impressively, who allowed the fact to be reported in the newspaper. It was a striking testament to the courage of the common Sicilian. And it seemed to refute what Rosalina had said.

Edoardo stressed that Addiopizzo is not running a boycotting campaign. "We don't want to accuse those who pay the *pizzo*," he said. "Most of them are victims. And they are scared."

People who have refused to pay have paid the price. Having armed guards outside your restaurant, for instance, is not exactly a boon to business. One man with a paint and hardware store saw his warehouse destroyed by fire. "In the last years," Edoardo said, "the Mafia prefers not to kill people. But destroying this man's business was like killing him."

But, he added, it didn't work. Addiopizzo gave him assistance, as did a lot of those "normal citizens," who collected money for his employees. Usually employees flee a company that's been attacked by the Mafia.

The government provided the man with another warehouse, and the boss who had ordered the fire and the henchman who had set it were both arrested. It was a critical moment, Edoardo said. It demonstrated that the city had changed, and that people were ready to stand up to the Mafia.

Our chat was interrupted by the arrival of the tour group. They entered the room and took seats in a circle; then Edoardo gave them an extensive briefing. He spoke more fluently in Italian than in the English he'd been using in our own conversation, but with the same quiet intensity. When he finished, he asked everyone to say something about themselves. There were two middle-aged women from Rome, a couple from Milan traveling with their teen-aged son, a twenty-something couple from Verona, three young women from Veneto, and a vintner, Beatrice, from central Italy, who sat next to me and occasionally translated. Even when a bottle of wine was opened and some cookies passed around, the assembly had more the air of a mission than that of a holiday.

We were too numerous to all fit in the van, so I joined the women from Veneto in their rental car. We drove down residential streets and parked in front of a ten-story apartment house. A small olive tree stood in front, its branches dripping with caps, ribbons, an Italian flag. Here, Edoardo explained, Paolo Borsellino had been killed by a car bomb, along with his bodyguards. He had just come from paying a visit to his mother, who lived in the building.

Eighteen years later, stuffed animals and scrawled messages still sanctified the site. *Not all Sicilians are Mafia and not all Mafia are Sicilian,* read one note. Another said, *The fight against the Mafia should be a cultural and moral movement that involves everyone, especially the young generation. —Paolo Borsellino.*

Back in our vehicles, we headed out of the city and up Mount

Pellegrino, site of the Santa Rosalia Sanctuary. ("The Mafia are very Catholic," Beatrice had explained to me, in a voice heavy with exasperation at the irony.) The patron saint of Palermo, Rosalia is revered for having saved the city from the plague in 1624.

A yellow convent backed into a cliff at the top of a series of unfolding steps. "In 2005," Edoardo said as we climbed upward, "Addiopizzo put a sign on the sanctuary that said, 'Santa Rosalia —free us from the *pizzo*.' She once freed us from the plague," he explained. "Now the plague is the Mafia."

Inside the chapel, everyday crowds jostled their way past sacred objects. The spectacle of commotion mixed with reverence, common to any pilgrimage site, was here amplified by the fact that it was contained in a cave 1,400 feet high. The devout and the curious made their way through the dank cavity to a statue of Rosalia, backlit in blue. As I was leaving, I noticed, high on a wall in the vestibule, a plaque commemorating the visit of Goethe, who had "contemplated the primitive simplicity of the sanctuary" and the devotion of the people. Not much had changed in the ensuing two centuries.

It was important for Addiopizzo to relate to the Church, Edoardo said when we got outside, because it still had a great deal of influence on people. In the past the Church had been indifferent to or even accepting of the Mafia, but that was changing. After the murder of Giovanni Falcone, Pope John Paul II spoke out against the Mafia. (A rare papal condemnation of the organization that came, perhaps not coincidentally, from the first non-Italian pope since the sixteenth century.) In 1993 the Mafia killed a priest, Father Giuseppe "Pino" Puglisi, who worked in a poor neighborhood of Palermo. Edoardo told us Puglisi "tried to organize free-time activities for kids" who would otherwise have gone to the Mafia.

Back in the car, Agnese apologized for her English, which was infinitely better than my Italian. "Problem in Italy," she said. "People only speak Italian."

"Yes," I said. "Outside of Italy, Italian's not really spoken much."

"Only Formula One," she said. "And opera."

We came down from the mountain and were soon driving along a street sprinkled with beachgoers and lined with villas. This was Mondello, Palermo's resort town. We found the rest of the group on the seaside promenade, in front of an impressive Art Nouveau bathhouse.

As we strolled, I asked Maria where she lived in Rome. "Near St. Peter's," she said, adding that she had been baptized in the basilica. "My father worked at the Vatican. He wasn't a priest," she said, smiling. "He was an architect."

Among the many decals on the door of the Renato Bar was one identifying the place as *pizzo*-free. "At first they didn't want to put it," Edoardo said. "But after they did, they saw that more people came."

We pulled a few of the outdoor tables together, and they soon filled with bowls of gelato, plates of brioche, and tulip glasses of granita, the delicious flavored ice that is a specialty of Sicily. The young man from Verona insisted I take some of his brioche and dip it into my almond granita; I did, blissfully putting sweet on sweet. I learned that the group was spending the entire week on an Addiopizzo tour, staying at a *pizzo*-free hotel on the beach. Very few hotels are members of Addiopizzo. When I asked Edoardo why, he said it could be because they've been paying the *pizzo* longer than most businesses—in the past, smaller business had been left alone.

The next day I picked up my new trousers, which had needed to be shortened, put on my new shirt, its blue stripes partially disguising the logo, and walked out of the SoleLuna feeling like a Palermitano, a sensation that only increased when I bought a bouquet. But I still wanted my suitcase back.

Beatrice (another Beatrice, not the vintner) lived in a modern building on a quiet street a few blocks west of the designer shops on Via della Libertá. She was a writer, a friend of a friend. Her apartment was on the top floor, and when she opened the door, her daughter's new puppy headed enthusiastically for my white pants.

Her daughter was studying anthropology in Turin, her son philosophy in Berlin: the far-flung children of Sicilian intelligentsia. The university in Palermo, the son said, had some good professors, but "the worst administration in Italy."

A friend by the name of Maruzza arrived, and we moved to the table. "I hope you like pasta," Beatrice said, passing me a bowl of fusilli cooked with eggplant and tomatoes. This was followed by cold plates: meatballs, pecorino cheese, slices of potato, more egg-plant and tomatoes. The daughter opened a bottle of wine, then placed it on the table, where it sat untouched. Was it the guest's duty to pour in Sicily? Nothing I'd read had indicated that.

Maruzza did most of the talking, telling us all about her hand-bags, made by women in the worst slum in Palermo, a place with the unlikely name of Zen 2. There was also a Zen 1, I was told, the name an acronym for "northern extension zone."

"It is the Bronx of Palermo," someone said.

"The police won't go there," someone else added. "Everyone there is Mafia."

I said I'd like to see it.

Beatrice got up and unwrapped a box that Maruzza had brought. It contained not pastries but exquisite miniature ice cream cones, each tiny individual scoop encased in a dark chocolate shell.

When we'd eaten them all, Beatrice showed me the apartment: the wraparound balcony, with a distant view of the sea; her office off the living room, the walls lined with books. Despite these com-forts, she spent quite a bit of time on the mainland. "It is hard to live here," she said, forgoing an explanation, as she had the wine.

Maruzza picked me up near the SoleLuna the following after-noon. We drove out of the center, passing through Parco della Favorita, which Norman Lewis had described affectionately as a prowling ground for prostitutes, who—back then, at least—were called *lucciole* (fireflies). Now all we saw was litter.

Eventually we entered a bright, spacious compound of housing that looked like a failed cubist experiment. Long, straight streets were lined with small-windowed apartments. At lunch the day be-fore, Maruzza had downplayed the danger, and now she drove through the compound with seeming nonchalance. Residents passed us on the street—there were more people loitering than driving cars—but few paid us any attention, though I looked at them. After all the talk about the Mafia, I wanted to see a mafioso. I felt a bit like V. S. Naipaul, traveling through the South on a mis-sion to find a redneck.

The compound was harsh but not ghastly, and drenched in sun-shine. In his novel *The Leopard,* Giuseppe di Lampedusa wrote that not even the "vibrant Sicilian light" could disperse Palermo's per-vasive sense of death. But here it helped diminish an atmosphere of menace.

We parked by the church and entered the annex. The priest had offered a work space to Maruzza and her group, who were currently on summer hiatus. Father Miguel was not in, so we took a walk along the "piazza." That word carries such connotations of stateliness for a foreigner that it sounded odd when applied to a vacant, garbage-strewn lot whose only inhabitants were two mangy dogs.

Maruzza pointed to the building running along its edge. "Many of the women I work with live there," she said. She had started the project two years earlier, teaching the women to make luxury handbags. Though of different designs, they each carried the large label LABZEN2, like a declaration of faith or a sign of radical chic.

Maruzza said most of the bag makers were married to mafiosi, who didn't appreciate their wives working, going out of the house, acquiring a feeling of empowerment. "They don't like me," she said with blithe resignation.

Zen 2 was also a center of the drug trade. Kids were recruited as couriers, and residents of Palermo made the trip out to do their "shopping." It was the old, sad story of hopelessness and crime, here combated by a pragmatist with a penchant for bags.

On the drive back to Palermo, Maruzza said she'd get me a meeting with the owner of Antica Focacceria San Francesco. Then we made a stop for gelato.

Thursday morning, Edoardo came by the SoleLuna to continue our talk which had been interrupted by the tour group. The group was spending the day with a coworker; in fact, I was meeting them for lunch. We sat in the living room, the French doors of the balcony open to the heat. I told Edoardo that I'd been to Zen 2. He said the Mafia doesn't like that the schools are there and added that the teachers have to fight against the culture of the parents. About the piazza, he remarked, "It doesn't look like Italy. It looks like a Middle East place." He mentioned a plan—a dream?—to build a garden park there. If you wanted to be effective in the fight against the Mafia, you had to create something that could be used in the poorest neighborhoods. If they understood that they had a garden there because of the anti-Mafia, that could be helpful, he said.

He told me more about the growth of Addiopizzo. While it began by recruiting members, now it waited for business owners to come to it. One man, a publican in the nearby town of Caccamo, wrote to Addiopizzo, quite distraught. He had gone to the police with the name of his extortionist, and in the process lost most of his customers. Edoardo, along with some colleagues, drove out to his pub to have a beer—a gesture he called "an act of ethical consumerism." And they continued going, every Saturday night, taking friends with them to fill the place. They started organizing parties there. This made an impression on the youth of Caccamo —normally for nightlife, people from Caccamo go to Palermo.

Still, Edoardo confessed disappointment at the pace of Addiopizzo's growth. "In 2008 a lot of shopkeepers testified against the Mafia in trials," he said. "We expected more would say no to protection money, but it didn't happen. When you think 460—it is really a minority. I was thinking from one year to another maybe a thousand. That is not happening."

But there was cause for hope. Fifteen years ago, he said, if you thought about not paying protection money, you thought about Libero Grassi. Now you might think about the 460 who don't pay.

I asked Edoardo about the Mafia souvenirs—black T-shirts with pictures of Marlon Brando, caps with *Kiss My Hand* in Italian— that one sees in Palermo's tourist shops. "They are twisting the image of the Mafia," he said. "They are focusing on picturesque aspects. If Americans come with this notion, they have no idea what the Mafia is. Making money with these *Godfather* shirts is to me a crime."

In Corleone, a town some 40 miles south of Palermo, they sell Don Corleone liqueur and organize Mafia tours. "It's very fake," Edoardo said. "The most serious thing is they don't say a word about what the Mafia was—and still is. And they don't talk about the anti-Mafia movement." Addiopizzo takes tourists to Corleone, but instead of the bar, they show them the anti-Mafia museum, which was opened by the mayor in 2000.

I asked Edoardo if his parents worried about him. "Yes," he said. "They are proud, but at the same time worried. They say, 'You should be prudent.'

"I would be worried if Addiopizzo lost the support of the people. That's a situation when the Mafia could attack because we'd be isolated. Libero Grassi was completely isolated. The Sicilian Industrialists' Association criticized him, saying he should not make so much noise. Now the Industrialists' Association supports Addiopizzo and expels members who pay the *pizzo*.

"Right now it's unlikely that the Mafia will attack us. Addiopizzo is under the spotlight. The backfire would hurt them. But the strategy can change very quickly," he added.

Edoardo headed off to another appointment, and I made my way to Via Vittorio Emanuele, where I was meeting the group for one last time at the store that sold only *pizzo*-free products. It was easy to find; a large yellow-and-green sign over the door read: PUNTO PIZZO FREE with the word L'EMPORIO underneath it. Unlike the small decal on the door of the Renato Bar, this signage stuck out like a boast or even a taunt.

Inside, a petite young woman with a bright, round face sat behind the cash register. She had an openness I'd seldom seen in Palermo shop assistants, and I pictured the most hardened mafioso wandering in and immediately melting. It would be like trying to extort money from your kid sister.

Valeria, the woman at the register, said it was her husband, Fabio, who had gotten the idea for a store that specialized in products from *pizzo*-free enterprises. Business was good, she said; when the store opened, over two years earlier, it had received widespread coverage that had brought in locals as well as tourists from abroad. "When people ask if we are afraid, we say we are so exposed all over the world, so we feel protected."

In addition to the shop, Valeria and her husband had started an agency that organizes *pizzo*-free events. "We had a *pizzo*-free wedding—flowers, photographer, singer, hotel." While sharing in her obvious joy at their accomplishment, I was struck by how much of a Sicilian's life is connected to the Mafia, unless one works at making it otherwise.

On the wall hung a quote from Giovanni Falcone, which Valeria translated: *"Man passes, but ideas remain . . . Everyone has to continue to do his part, big or small, everyone has to make his contribution to improve the living conditions of Palermo."*

The group arrived, with reddened shoulders and sun-kissed hair, the result of a morning swim in the sea. They roamed around the store, examining the cheeses and pastas, the teas and chocolates, the soaps and lotions, the jars of pesto and pine nuts, the bottles of wine and olive oil. There were shelves of *coppole,* the caps traditionally worn by Sicilians before the Mafia appropriated them as its symbol, and shelves of books. There were even two computers providing *pizzo*-free Internet access.

Eventually we made our way down a side street to Antica Focacceria San Francesco. As on Sunday, no armed guards stood in front. There were twelve of us; we took the stairs to the second floor and commandeered three tables under large black-and-white photographs. The place was packed, and I hadn't yet met the owner, but out of the chaos emerged, in fairly short order, drinks for everyone, followed by croquettes of mashed chickpeas, followed by numerous pastas and a few of the famous cow-spleen sandwiches. Spleen, I discovered on trying my neighbor's, tastes pretty much as you'd expect spleen to taste. We concluded our final meeting with a dozen large cannoli.

In the evening I took the bus out to Falcone-Borsellino Airport and picked up my suitcase, which had, remarkably, been brought back from oblivion. Returning to the city, I deposited it in my room and then headed out for a celebratory meal. A small crowd stood outside a pizzeria on Piazza Castelnuovo, including a trio speaking accented English. I asked them if the place was good, and the shorter of the two men told me it had the best pizza in Palermo —and that was coming from a Neapolitan. He introduced me to his friends, a young couple from Paris, and invited me to join them.

After we were seated, I asked him what he was doing in Palermo.

"I am a carabinieri captain," he said.

He had wanted an assignment in Milan; he got Palermo instead. He said he knew Zen 2. Though I'd been told the police didn't go near the place, he said he had been there fairly recently, with a large unit. "This is a terrible period for Italy," he said. "People are stupid—they watch TV and they believe what they hear. They don't read books. It takes too much time."

I brought up the Mafia. He said that after the killings of Falcone and Borsellino, the Mafia realized it couldn't beat the state, so it decided to infiltrate it. "The sergeants are in Palermo," he said, "the generals are in Rome."

"You mean the politicians?" his Parisian friend asked.

"Yes," he said coldly.

Father Miguel made a rare trip into town to meet me for lunch, though he ordered only juice. With apologies, he explained that he'd been testifying in court the day of my visit. Then he looked around the outdoor terrace of the Bar Aluia, just off the upscale Via della Libertá, and said with a smile, "This is not Palermo."

He appeared to be in his late thirties, a handsome man of easy-going warmth in a white, short-sleeved shirt with a Roman collar. He was Argentinean, but his parents were Italian, and he had studied biblical languages in Rome. He had been teaching in the capital when, in 2008, he was assigned to San Filippo Neri parish in Zen 2. "I am a priest," he said, "but also a missionary."

Of the six thousand families in Zen 2, half did not have work — *legal* work, he clarified. Children didn't study; boys stopped going to school after the fifth grade.

"There are people forty and fifty years old who don't know the cathedral. Boys who don't know the sea. And it is two kilometers away. You can't talk of culture. You can't talk of foreign countries. The newspaper doesn't exist."

The place was shut off from the rest of the world. "Inside the Zen quarter, you feel there is no Italy. Palermo doesn't invest in our neighborhood to get people to become citizens," he lamented. Politicians periodically showed an interest, though: some paid as much as 50 euros for a vote.

That payoff paled in comparison to the 500 euros a kid could make selling cocaine for a night, though Father Miguel said that a carabinieri station was going to open soon and that would deter Palermitanos from coming out to buy drugs.

"There are many good people, good families," he insisted, estimating that of the 30,000 people who live in the two Zens, possibly a thousand were connected to the Mafia. The Zens also had one of the youngest populations in Italy: six hundred children in catechism classes.

I asked him about the difficulty of his work. "You can forget that you are a priest," he said. "You can think that you are a social worker. We must do social work, but as priests."

He and his two fellow priests always dressed in clerical garb. "People respect priests," he said. "They like priests." He noted that people like Maruzza, as well as NGOs, do good work in the neighborhood, but they always leave at the end of the day. "We are the only ones that live there, and that's a big difference. But that's why people feel that we love them. Because we are like them." Yet that hadn't prevented a resident from trying to kill him. Father Miguel mentioned the fact casually, dispassionately, saying the would-be assassin was a man (not a mafioso) who was trying to do something that would bring him attention. I assumed this was why he'd been testifying in court. I asked if he knew the people involved.

"Yes," he said. "I live with them. We are a family." He laughed. "A special family."

There was one more person I wanted to see in Palermo, and on one of my last days in the city I made my way down now-familiar streets to Antica Focacceria San Francesco. On the way I stopped at L'Emporio to say hello to Valeria and to buy my only Sicilian souvenir: a white T-shirt imprinted with a drawing of a tombstone inscribed 'U Pizzu and backed by a crowd of cheering children.

Inside the restaurant I asked at the register for Vincenzo Conticello. My pronunciation and my tortoiseshell glasses must have marked me as harmless, because after only a slight hesitation the man pointed outside to two men sitting at a table under an umbrella, just in front of the Focacceria café.

Sipping mineral water at a nearby table, I waited for Vincenzo to finish his meeting. When, after twenty minutes, he joined me, I asked about the history of the place. He told me the Focacceria had opened in 1834 and been in his family for five generations. When he and his brother took over in the '80s, they expanded the menu, adding pastas and fish, and put tables in the piazza. "Before, this was used for parking," he said, "and rubbish. There was rubbish everywhere."

I mentioned that the last picture I'd seen of the restaurant showed armed guards standing in front.

"They're still here," he said quickly, "now in plainclothes. Look behind you."

I turned and saw two fit young men sitting at a table and conversing quietly. I'd noticed them earlier and hadn't given them a second thought. "I have four bodyguards with me twenty-four hours a day," Vincenzo said. "Three more work in the piazza. I don't come here very often," he added. "It's not safe."

It had started in 2005, when he found a letter in his car demanding that he pay 50,000 euros and indicating that the price of refusal would be his life and the lives of his family. Then one day a mafioso visited the Focacceria. As soon as he was gone, Vincenzo called the carabinieri. An investigation followed, and five men were arrested; Vincenzo attended the trial and identified his extortionist. That man and the four others were sentenced to a total of fifty-five years in prison.

"Palermo is a very complicated town to work in," Vincenzo said, showing a gift for understatement. His cat had been killed, and his business had suffered.

Remembering the crowd at lunch the other day, I expressed surprise about the effect on his business.

"Many people in Palermo that like the Mafia don't come to Focacceria," he explained. "Especially politicians. And owners of shops that pay the *pizzo*." He said a lot of his business comes from foreign tourists and students who attend the university and the international school.

He had had big plans for expansion—not only in Italy but in Europe and the U.S.—but the events of 2005 had sapped his energy, which was only starting to return.

I asked about children. He had a daughter, but she was no longer living in Sicily, and he didn't identify her new home. "To see my daughter is very complicated," he said wearily. "I must make four or five reservations in different towns."

The waiter approached, and Vincenzo translated the day's pasta specials. I ordered the spaghetti with tomatoes, swordfish, and mint. When he was gone, I asked Vincenzo about vacation.

"I prefer to take my vacation outside Italy," he said. "Because in Italy it would be with carabinieri."

He estimated that 20 to 25 percent of Sicilians are connected to the Mafia and that another 25 percent have "a mafioso mentality." And it would take generations for the situation to improve. "Mentality is very difficult to change. The teachers in the schools work well," he said, echoing Edoardo, "but the families don't do the same at home."

We sat quietly for a while; then Vincenzo leaned forward and said, sotto voce, "This man is a killer."

The words registered, but barely. I looked up as a hulking man in a white T-shirt and red suspenders lumbered past our table. Before he had even reached the street, Vincenzo motioned to the guard who had been standing watchfully by the café entrance. They exchanged words, the only one of which I understood was a sharp *Attenzione*. Then Vincenzo got on his cell phone to another guard, one of the two who had been sitting behind me and who now stood in front of the Focacceria, into which the man had just walked.

I had seen my mafioso—unfortunately, while dining with one of the Mob's most wanted.

Vincenzo continued talking on his cell phone, alerting his men. He was visibly riled, which made me even more nervous. In a matter of seconds the Mafia had moved, for me, from a distant notion, an endless topic of discussion, to a graspable reality, a galvanic presence in red suspenders. Suddenly the idea of gunfire strafing a café—a familiar trope of gangster movies—seemed not at all far-fetched.

Our pastas arrived. They added, I couldn't help but think, another potential cinematic cliché.

The food put a dent in our already disrupted conversation. We ate while lost in our own private thoughts, though our fates, for the moment at least, were inexplicably tied.

"He killed four people," Vincenzo said finally, adding also that the man had recently been released from prison after fifteen years. "He is a terrible mafioso."

I mentioned that I'd seen him enter the Focacceria.

"Yes," Vincenzo said, a bit more calmly. "He looks here. He looks in there. He studies."

Finished with his pasta, Vincenzo explained that he had another appointment. He apologized, and insisted that I stay for dessert. I thanked him for his time and then watched him climb into the backseat of a squad car, followed by his bodyguards. I hoped some of their colleagues were sticking around.

The waiter appeared shortly, bearing the dessert tray like a frothy distraction. I chose the gelo di melone, another specialty of Sicily. It was delicious, but difficult to enjoy.

ROBIN KIRK

City of Walls

FROM *The American Scholar*

THE NUMBER 1 CITY BUS up the Antrim Road is a leap into Belfast's troubled past and still-turbulent present. Like all bus routes in Northern Ireland's capital city, the Number 1 starts downtown amid glass-and-steel high-rises, trendy shops, and cafés. Locals, international business travelers, and tourists mingle on streets newly adorned with two-story-high curved copper ribs intended to evoke the city's maritime heritage, including the building of the *Titanic*, launched here on May 31, 1911.

Once outside these ten blocks, however, the Number 1 crosses what might as well be an astral divide. Belfast is one of the most segregated cities in the world, an occasionally Molotov-cocktail-bombed landscape of "interfaces" and "peace walls" that have grown higher, longer, and more numerous in the thirteen years since the Good Friday Agreement. The 1998 settlement formally ended the three decades of violence called the Troubles.

In Belfast, an interface is where Protestant and Catholic communities battle and, in the best of times, grimly turn their backs on one another. According to the Belfast Interface Project, there are at least ten in the one-mile stretch between the place where the Number 1 starts and the city's lone synagogue north of downtown. If you go the same distance east and west, the number of interfaces easily triples.

At first interfaces are hard to spot. Uniformed schoolchildren get on and off the bus as they do in any metropolis. Mothers with strollers equipped with plastic shields (for the frequent rain showers) wrestle the carriers to the bays behind the driver and then wrestle them off.

But interfaces quickly become obvious, even to visitors. Snapping in the salty breeze, red-white-and-blue flags mark a Protestant Unionist neighborhood loyal to the British queen, her Union Jack, and the United Kingdom. Across the interface, Catholics and Nationalists who yearn for a united Ireland do errands under the gaze of glowering, ski-masked gunmen depicted in a mural topped by the Irish tricolors. Many Protestants embrace Rangers, a Glasgow-based soccer team. The most visible fans are copiously tattooed men who congregate and smoke in front of a pub as they show off their muscles in light-blue Rangers shirts. In contrast, musclemen in front of Catholic pubs, loyal to the Glasgow team that has a Catholic fan base, wear Celtic-knot tattoos and shamrock-green Celtic shirts.

Belfast boosters want visitors to focus on the *Titanic* and the paddywhackery of the pub crawl. Yet there is brisk business in so-called dark tourism, where guides explain the murals celebrating people like Bobby Sands, a member of the Irish Republican Army (IRA) and hunger striker elected to Parliament on April 9, 1981. He died of starvation twenty-five days later, in prison. In Protestant areas, memorials to Britain's horrific losses at the 1916 Battle of the Somme are common because Protestant volunteers from Ulster took some of the heaviest casualties. Throughout Belfast, images of gunmen conjured from thick paint point their automatic rifles at passersby. Although these threatening figures represent the past, there is no mistaking the fresh touchups that keep them vivid.

Despite a dedicated and creative peace effort, including millions of pounds spent for inquiries and security—not to mention a dozen years of hard, post-Troubles political work—minds and hearts remain staunchly divided here. The negotiations at the peace table were exhausting; to create peace on the ground is harder and comes at a staggering cost. The only thing more expensive, it sometimes seems, would be letting the violence that marked the Troubles continue.

Ninety percent of Belfast's public housing is segregated on religious grounds. Since 1998 it has become more segregated, not less, and some communities without walls are petitioning for new walls to be built. The Berlin Wall came down after twenty-eight years; Belfast's walls have not only stood for thirty-five but proliferated. When the Good Friday accords were signed, an estimated twenty walls stood; thirteen years later there are more than eighty.

Ninety percent of all school-age children attend segregated schools—Catholics in private, tuition-free, Church-run institutions and Protestants in public schools. City planners often dole out resources in pairs: sports centers, clinics, parks, fire stations. If the city doesn't duplicate services, the results can be dire. A friend of mine who lives on the Unionist Shankill Road once drove an ailing family member on a forty-five-minute detour to get to the Royal Victoria Hospital, since the traffic gates on the West Belfast peace wall, open during the day, shut at midnight. The hospital is on the Falls Road, firmly Nationalist. "Thank God she survived, but that's the reality of daily life here," he told me.

The payout for parallel services, at a time when Westminster is slashing spending, is immense. According to government figures, state spending per head in Northern Ireland is even higher than in England's economically depressed northeast. "At an estimated cost of £1 billion [$1.6 billion] per year, division affects everything from health to education to public transport, to access to services and—at times—two of everything literally a few streets apart," wrote Deputy Chief Constable Judith Gillespie in a recent post on the Police Service of Northern Ireland's blog. "This situation is not and should not be seen as normal."

Most officials aren't so frank. Instead of *division,* a term often used is *shared space.* Policymakers embrace shared space as the goal of the peace process, funneling more millions into nongovernmental and grassroots organizations that do cross-community work. Under the city's often gloomy skies, shared space is no abstraction. Where can locals go and be sure they won't be threatened or attacked for their perceived identity? Or where in public can a football fan wearing a Rangers or Celtic shirt go and be sure he won't be beaten up?

"Everyone talks about shared spaces, but that is a short-term solution," says Dominic Bryan, a Queens University anthropologist who has studied the conflict. Every year since 2006, Bryan and a team of researchers have traveled the province counting public displays of flags in the weeks preceding July 12, the Protestant celebration of the 1690 victory of King William III over the Catholic King James at the River Boyne. Led by the Orange Lodges, Protes-

tant flute bands flanked by mostly middle-aged men in bowler hats
march along interface routes as an expression of identity as well
as, it must be said, to batter Catholics with "kick-the-pope" lyrics:

> Hullo, Hullo,
> You'll know us by our noise.
> We're up to our knees in Fenian blood.
> Surrender or you'll die.

The flags mark territory, according to Bryan, as well as identity
and sectarian fervor. In five years of counting, the number and
type of flags have remained stubbornly fixed. "So far," he says,
"*shared* has different meanings, including as long as you get yours,
I'll get mine. Everyone is treated equally, but separately."

The communities — Catholic-Nationalist-Republican and Prot-
estant-Unionist-Loyalist — remain in their respective corners like
punch-drunk boxers. Northern Ireland has no truly shared space,
no place where anyone can come at any time. One interpretation
of shared space is what happens when Protestants and Catholics
quietly trade off the small chunk that is central Belfast, ceding it
one day to the Protestants for a military march and the next to the
Catholics for a St. Patrick's Day parade.

On a rainy Sunday this May, I walked with Shankill residents as
Unionists from around the city converged on city hall to protest
the decision not to hold a homecoming parade for the British Army's Royal Irish Regiment after a six-month tour in Afghanistan.
The 2008 homecoming parade had prompted a massive police
operation devoted to keeping Unionist supporters and Nationalist protesters separated, so the appetite for a repeat near-riot was
slight. As Unionists waved the regiment's black-and-green flag,
nary a Nationalist was to be found.

Longtime observers interpret this as a kind of progress, because at least opponents aren't maiming or killing one another.
The Nationalists get the St. Patrick's Day parade, which wasn't celebrated until 1998, the year the Good Friday accord was signed.
The Unionists get July 12, and so on. Public safety, one reason
to limit shared space, is no mean goal in a province still grieving
for the 3,500 killed and many more maimed in thirty years of the
Troubles.

What is disturbing about segregation in Northern Ireland is not that there are tradeoffs; it's that the people entrench themselves in segregated communities, and many of their leaders help them do it. For Americans, one analogy is to imagine what the South might look like had federal courts not forced integration in the face of violence. Certainly the civil rights movement alone would have made some gains. But it's also likely that states would have adapted in different ways, with some investing in segregation as a way of stemming violence. "Separate but equal" would be thought a virtue, not the disgrace we now understand it to be.

The most famous interface has a peace wall that separates the lower Springfield Road, part of the Catholic Falls, from the Protestant Shankill. The wall was never meant to be permanent. In 1969 it was a stretch of barbed wire hastily rolled out by British troops after clashes between Unionist and Nationalist communities left tiny Bombay Street a smoking ruin. Then came temporary dividers, then concrete topped by metal sheeting and more barbed wire. Today a memorial marks the rebuilt Bombay Street, where new row houses back onto a wall that is more than 40 feet high and is under twenty-four-hour TV police surveillance. Still, projectiles make it over. Residents encase their back porches in metal cages for protection.

Daniel Jacks is a pink-cheeked Republican who works with a cross-community peace project. When there is trouble, he says, kids born after the IRA's formal ceasefire in 1994 usually create it. "They don't really remember what it was like during the Troubles, but they think it was cool." "Recreational riots" are frequent, he says. They happen when young people agree over Facebook or Bebo to start a melee.

A 2009 study by the Belfast-based Institute for Conflict Research found that kids still identify themselves along sectarian lines. It's a question not of religious doctrine but of belonging—your people versus mine. When it comes time to confront, these young people are as handy with the slurs as their grandparents might have been, hurling such epithets as *Huns* (referring to the German origin of the British royal family) and *Prods* or *Fenians* (supporters of a united Ireland) and *Taigs* (from the Irish name *Tahdg*) along with bricks, bottles, and Molotov cocktails.

Most locals lament sectarianism and the walls. But they don't

want the walls removed. "Hugodecat," posting on the popular political blog Slugger O'Toole, put popularly held feelings into this
May 31 post:

> I live on a peace line, and like many of my neighbouring home own-
> ers, we are quite happy to see it stay. It means that when trouble does
> brew we can sleep soundly and not worry about bricks through our
> windows and arson attacks. But I do understand that in many ways
> the walls are divisive, allowing the sectarian louts to perpetuate the
> myth that the human beings on the other side are somehow a dif-
> ferent species.

In June the province watched aghast as the worst rioting since
the Troubles put East Belfast under a pall of greasy gasoline smoke
for several nights. As the long summer day dimmed, youths with
their faces masked under balaclavas pelted Catholic homes in
Short Strand, just steps away from the city's busy Central Station.
Police riot vehicles went up in flames.

Many put the responsibility for the virulence of sectarianism
squarely at the feet of Westminster, Stormont (the provincial parliament), and the province's leading political parties. Protestants
align increasingly behind the Democratic Union Party, and Catholics back IRA-linked Sinn Féin. A media-friendly cordiality goes
on display when blood has been spilled. For instance, after the
dissident Republicans known as the Real IRA murdered a Catholic police officer in April, "Shinner" Deputy Prime Minister Mar-
tin McGuinness, a one-time chief of staff of the Provisional IRA,
urged people to provide the police with information. "These are
people who are pledged to destroy the peace and destroy a peace
process that many of us have invested much of our adult lives in
trying to bring about," he said during a press conference.

Yet there is also a stubborn unwillingness to accept that some
of the past's gruesome acts poison the present. The 1984 killing
of Mary Travers is emblematic. She was a twenty-three-year-old
primary-school teacher born and raised in Belfast. Her father,
Tom, was a magistrate. That may not seem a dangerous profes-
sion, yet the Travers family was Catholic. To the IRA, any Catholics
working for the state, especially the justice system, were traitors. A
murder team shot the Travers family as they left church, injuring
Tom and killing Mary. IRA militant Mary McArdle was quickly arrested, convicted, and sentenced to life. In May 2011 controversy

erupted after McArdle—released under the terms of the Good Friday Agreement—was hired as a top adviser to Sinn Féin Culture Minister Carál Ní Chuilín. Mary Travers's sister, Ann, gave a heart-wrenching interview to news channel UTV. "I just feel physically sick, disgusted," she said. "I think about Mary every day. Then I hear one of the people involved in her murder is given a well-paid job at Stormont and it all comes crashing back."

On the one hand, Sinn Féin insists that McArdle did prison time and worked on the party's peace-building projects. Yet that is a coldblooded response to a family—and a people—still in agony. None of the actual shooters were ever identified or charged (McArdle was part of the getaway team). For her part, McArdle called the killing "a tragic mistake" and expressed regret but never apologized. A *Belfast Telegraph* editorial said the statement fell "far short of what is required . . . The clear inference is that had Mr. Travers died and Mary been spared then the murderous mission would have been deemed a success."

Combatants are understandably the first to justify their actions, the first to close the door on the past, and the first to accuse victims who want to revisit the past of wasting everyone's time. Yet victims have given up more than anyone for peace and have so far received the least in exchange. In this case, the Travers family hasn't even received elemental justice.

One of McArdle's staunchest defenders is Gerry Kelly, a Shinner assemblyman who represents North Belfast. In 1973, Kelly planted four bombs in London, killing one person and injuring hundreds. On the other side of the interface, former Loyalist gunmen continue to "speak for" Unionist communities that at best see the gunmen as necessary evils—and at worst thugs who also traffic drugs, run prostitutes, and carry out criminal vendettas cloaked in patriotism. To be sure, barring anyone with a paramilitary past from working is foolish. At the same time, allowing assassins to go free is abhorrent.

There is some good news along the River Lagan. Despite the summer's riots, violence is sharply down. The British troops that once patrolled are long gone. Most former gunmen and bomb makers have retired; many do good and necessary work in their communities or abroad as peacemakers. Although the Real IRA continues to launch attacks, no one doubts that the peace process is robust.

The unfortunate truth is that increased segregation may just well be the price of peace. Americans can hardly be surprised, since many of us have lived in communities segregated by race since before the Civil War. When one delegation from Israel visited Belfast recently, a friend told me that the earnest visitors grilled their Irish hosts for the secret-sauce recipe that brought peace to this corner of the Emerald Isle. Only partly in jest, my friend merrily replied, "Build a wall. It worked for us."

J. MALCOLM GARCIA

Now Ye Know Who the Bosses Are Here Now

FROM *McSweeney's*

THIS YOUNG MAN sitting beside me, eyes tearing, balls of his feet bouncing ceaselessly off the pavement, tells me that he knew Paul Quinn for seven, eight years. Friends, so they were. Through school and driving tractors together and running bales in the summer.

He played soccer the night Paul died. Paul watched the game until halftime, left for something to eat, came back to pick his friend up. This young man, his feet still tapping the ground, eyes saucers of pain, tells me it doesn't go away, that sound. The sound of batons and metal pipes striking Paul and Paul screaming and then not screaming.

(The police say they have intelligence that my life is under threat.
I understand.
Don't use my name.
I'll use a letter. C.
Aye.
Take me back to that night.)

It's October 20, 2007. About 5:30 P.M. A good evening. Good enough, like. Not hot, not cold. C and Paul don't have plans after the game. Just spinning about, like. Shooting the craic. Driving the back roads of their Northern Ireland village, Cullyhanna. They decide to stop at Paul's house and get on his computer and mess about. Bored with that, they drive around Cullyhanna again.

Then Anthony, a friend, rings Paul. Anthony says some bulls is coming to his father's fucking farm this evening. He needs help cleaning a pen.

C and Paul mess about for another five minutes. Then decide, Fuck this, we have to help Anthony. His farm is near Castleblayney, just over the border in the Irish Republic, the "Free State." On the way, Paul has second thoughts. Take me home, he tells C. He can't be bothered. Fucking cows. C can't be bothered either. But it won't take long, C says. How long can it take?

(I thought it was funny that Anthony called Paul.

Why?

He would have called me, usually. I was closer to him. I thought to myself, He couldn't get through on my phone so that's why he called Paul.)

At the farm C and Paul park outside a shed where Anthony is to meet them. Still light out. Around ten to six, so it was. No one in sight. They stop, look around, pondering like.

A yellow lorry stands down a ways. Bright yellow. C walks toward it. He's almost reached it when a man wearing a black mask, black jacket, black jeans, and black boots jumps out at him, shouting *You fucking scumbag bastards!*

C turns around, yells at Paul.

Go! Run, run, run!

Three more masked men come at C from his left. More are running out from behind hay bales. Another three, from other directions.

(At first I thought it was a joke, like.

A prank?

Yeah, quite a joke, Anthony, yeah, good on ye.)

C shoves one of them away, but there are too many to fight off. Other men are on top of Paul. They drag C and Paul into the shed, hitting them with iron bars. Shouting, You bastards!

Three or four men stay on top of C until someone comes over and drags him into a pen. He sees Anthony tied up next to another one of their mates, Connor. On their knees, faces against the wall. Someone kneels on C again. Shouting, Shut it, shut it, shut it!

C can hear them bashing Paul about. He hears the *whoomp, whoomp* against his friend's body, hears Paul screaming, Stop, stop, fuck, fuck, stop, stop!

Then he stops screaming.

(*Just stopped, like. All of a sudden.*)

But they keep hitting him. Two minutes more, at least. Then they stop. The air still. The men breathing hard through their masks.

(*Did they say anything?*

Now ye know who the bosses are here now. Shouting, like. Now ye know!)

I am staying in a bed-and-breakfast in Crossmaglen, a small town fifteen minutes' drive from Cullyhanna.

In 1969, at the start of the Troubles, the police barracks here was attacked by the IRA. In 1971, British Army soldiers killed a Crossmaglen man who they wrongly thought was armed. The killing drove many young Catholics to join the fight. The community became much more insular and suspicious of outsiders. A characteristic it retains to this day.

With my long beard and ponytail, I stand out. People ask one another, Who's the hairy man walking about Crossmaglen and Cullyhanna?

The name sticks.

Hey, Harry, a man shouts to me one day, what about ye?

You enjoying your stay, are you, Harry? another man says.

What about Obama, Harry? Cheeky bastard, wha? declares a third.

But when I bring up the subject of the Paul Quinn killing, the good humor disappears and we quickly find something else to discuss.

However, if, at the end of the day, I meet someone alone in a pub or on the road or leaning on a fence post and considering the hazy distance across the field before them, when the evening hour has slowed and hesitates between light and dark and what lurks beneath the surface rises more easily, then I find people willing to talk about Paul.

Paul was a cheeky lad, so he was, Harry.

Good with his dukes. Wouldn't back down, don't you know. Not one to be pushed about, our Paul Quinn. He took a lot but didn't like someone with no authority telling him what to do. That was his downfall, aye.

Cullyhanna is naught but a church, a pub, and a convenience store. Everyone knew Paul. Everyone knows everybody. There's so-and-so's son. People look at their neighbor now and wonder, Was ye part of them that done him? People look at themselves and think, What could I have done to stop it?

Them boys who done Paul, they lured Anthony and that other boyo, Connor, to that shed by promising them some work. They broke Connor's ankle, so they done. Anthony cracked, then, made the call.

What would any of us have done had we been him?

Everyone keeps an eye on our Father Cullen. They tell the Quinn family, Father Cullen's talking to so-and-so. Maybe they done it. Maybe they're asking forgiveness. Father Cullen says our humanity has sunk to a new level.

What they done to him you wouldn't do to a dog. Beating him like that. Pipes and bats with nails in them. Breaking every bone in his body below the neck, so they done. The word got around. Young man battered to death. Just twenty-one. The savagery of it.

Sinn Féin says no Republicans were involved. Ludicrous. They know that if another crowd did that to a Catholic boyo, the IRA would have stepped in and dealt with them, ceasefire or no ceasefire. But the IRA hasn't stepped in. No Sinn Féin counselor came to the Quinn house to pay their respects to a Catholic family that lost a son to murderers. Very strange. Normally they arrive quick like, if for no other reason than to get their picture taken for the newspapers.

Maybe they didn't mean to kill him. Maybe they meant to leave him in a wheelchair to look out a window for the rest of his wee life. A message to other young people born after the Troubles. Look at Paul Quinn and remember: respect the IRA. Whatever they planned, they beat our Paul to death, so they done.

There were good men in the IRA when the struggle was going on. It's the bad men that remain. They want to keep control. Like dogs killing sheep. Bolder and bolder. If they hadn't a killed Paul, they'd a killed others.

Kids today, the Troubles are forgotten history. It's something they read in a book. They don't remember it. Some asshole says he used to be somebody in the IRA, who the fuck are they, wha? Kids used to think, When we grow up we'll be one of the boys. But the new generation says, No we won't. Fuck the IRA.

It's created a void, so it has.

Paul was born in 1986 and raised on a farm in Cullyhanna, in County Armagh. By the 1990s the South Armagh Brigade of the IRA had grown to about forty members. Thomas "Slab" Murphy, an alleged member of the IRA's Army Council, has been the organization's Armagh commander since the 1970s, according to British security personnel.

The South Armagh Brigade has not confined itself to paramilitary activities. Irish and British authorities accuse it of smuggling millions of dollars' worth of gasoline and diesel north across the Irish border every year. As much as 50 percent of the vehicle fuel used in Northern Ireland has been estimated to have been obtained in this way. Gas is cheaper in Ireland proper.

Paul's parents, Stephen and Breege, were never involved with the IRA, they tell me. They would stop and listen to news reports about a pub bombing or attacks on the RUC and then get on with their day. Paul never called Breege mum. Just Breege. That was his way. He'd call and ask about dinner and pretend to be somebody else. Make up an accent, like. Every night before going to bed, he would shout *Au revoir.*

French for goodbye, you know, Breege explains.

He had a jolly way. He would always buy a chocolate and a drink and put change in the charity box in town. He'd help old folks carry their bags, so he would.

When Breege stood by the sink he'd come behind her and lift her up. He was just full of life and was all the time smiling. Even when she gave out a scolding, he'd smile.

He loved to hear drinking stories about his father. He would come home and tell Stephen what he'd heard and watch his face turn red. He enjoyed listening to old men talk to other old men. All those stories and the laughter. It never was serious talk.

He liked having his potatoes peeled for him.

Mommy's boyo, Breege says.

Paul worked on farms. He also drove lorries for smugglers. Sometimes he came home and the house filled with the smell of diesel.

Smuggling was always a way of life, Stephen says. When I was a wee thing, my father smuggled, and his father, and his father before him. Where there's a border, there's smuggling. Only way to make a living. Is it criminal? Then you'd have to call everyone a criminal. Everyone.

Stephen was fixing a wall with some other fellows the day Paul died. Looking at it more than fixing it, truth be told, Stephen says. Paul came home in a car belonging to a friend and stayed long enough to make a bacon sandwich. After he ate, he said he was going to pick someone up. Siphoned some diesel from a petrol tank near the driveway, maybe a gallon, and then drove off. Stephen watched him go and never saw him alive again.

Breege saw Paul for the last time the night before. She came home from an evening with friends and he was in the kitchen eating cereal. She said goodnight and went to bed.

Au revoir, Paul said.

Jim McAllister meets me at McNamee's Bakery, a few blocks away from my bed-and-breakfast.

Jim helped start the Quinn Support Group, a loosely knit organization of Cullyhanna and Crossmaglen families intent on maintaining pressure on the authorities to find Paul's killers. Jim and Stephen Quinn have known each other since the early 1960s, when they were both about sixteen or so. They met in a pub, something like that, Jim says.

As a young fellow, Jim had Republican feelings. He was elected to the Northern Ireland Assembly as a Sinn Féin candidate in 1982. But over the years he drifted away from the party, and he finally left it in 1996. He saw Sinn Féin becoming everything it had once despised—leaning away from its core beliefs to get votes.

A few years ago a schoolgirl asked him, When was Bobby Sands shot? Bobby Sands died in the hunger strikes, Jim explained. He wasn't shot. That's when he knew his day was past. He remembered his grandparents talking about the 1916 uprising like it was clear in their minds, but it was history to Jim, just as Jim and Bobby Sands were history to that girl. It's all relative. It depends what side of the years you're on, aye.

When Paul died, a friend rang him, Jim says. A young man been battered to death. He didn't know his name. Just that he was a

Quinn. The county is full of Quinns. A moment later another man called and told him who it was.

The next morning he drove to the Quinn house. About twenty people were already there, and more were coming. When somebody dies in these parts, families gather around from all over to pay their respects. That's how we deal with death here, he says. They all talked about what happened. Not a wee beating, they agreed.

Paul had a reputation, of course. He fought. As a Sinn Féin counselor, Jim had dealt with antisocial behavior: boyos breaking windows, stealing, making a ruckus. That kind of thing. Years back some young lads, sixteen, seventeen years old, were in a gang called Hard Core. They'd assemble, drink beer, get loud. People were afraid. Jim asked to speak with them. Five or six lads showed up at his office one night. He told them they were scaring people. Those five or six boyos never came to notice again.

Two other lads, however, didn't meet with Jim. They continued to cause problems, and when he caught up with them they were made to wear placards: I'M A THIEF, something like that. Made to stand in a public place where everyone saw them. They never did anything after that. They became good men, so they did. Better to wear a placard than to be taken to a shed and killed, aye.

If it was smugglers who killed Paul, why would they want to bring attention to themselves? Jim says. Smugglers don't kill. If they have a problem with someone, they either hit them in their wallet, ignore them, or set them up to be caught by the police. They don't fight. No one has named specific smugglers as suspects. No one's come forward to accuse smugglers except for Sinn Féin.

Why's that, you think? Jim asks.

Paul would get involved in pub brawls, his father tells me, but he never talked about it. Nothing to tell. As far as he was concerned, once the fight was over, it was finished.

One time, however, he had a fight with Tomas McCabe. Tomas was the son of Frank McCabe, who police allege is an IRA man. Young McCabe would often get into rows with the other fellows. He lived in a political home and felt entitled to rule the roost, so he did, Stephen said.

The fight happened in Newry, a forty-minute drive from Cullyhanna. A car driven by Tomas blocked Paul's car outside a disco.

They both got out, and Paul landed a punch. He wouldn't be bullied. A second boyo, one of Tomas's friends, told Paul he would see him shot.

Later that evening, Eileen McCabe, Tomas's mother, stopped outside a chippy where Paul was ordering food. Clad in only a nightgown, she threatened Paul with a hammer. You'll be found in a black bag, she told him.

About the same time, Paul had another fight: this one with Vincent Treanor, an alleged senior member of the IRA. Paul confronted Treanor after his sister Cathy accused Treanor of insulting her.

How long was this before he was killed? I ask.

Three weeks, maybe, Stephen tells me.

This man biting his nails to nubs sits across from me in a cluttered kitchen strewn with newspapers and dirty dishes.

He tells me to refer to him as an ex-IRA volunteer from Crossmaglen. He served in the organization from his midteens to his late forties. A farmer now, he fears the consequences of the IRA finding out he's spoken with a journalist.

Now ask your questions, he says.

If the man were younger, he would leave Northern Ireland. He loved it once because the people were all united, but he feels shame today. If it had been Loyalists or Brits who killed Paul, he could stomach it. But not one of your own. The IRA takes anyone now. Before, they would cherry-pick. Before, a man could fight with an IRA man, have a bit of a pub row, and it was forgotten. Not now. The boys about today have recruited hoods, psychos, moneygrabbers.

They're as bad now as the police were during the Troubles. Worse. In the old days, if the police stopped you, they'd shoot you. They didn't play by the Marquess of Queensberry rules, but they never battered you to bits.

The people in rural areas know what's going on. They watch who's moving what and where. Groups of men assembling would be noticed. Someone saw something when Paul was killed. They had to. But after thirty years of war, people know not to give the police information on IRA activities. The bodies of informers have been dumped in public places. Reason enough for the living to keep silent, aye.

Paul would have been just a wee thing during the 1994 cease-fire, the man says. Barely a teenager when the 1998 Good Friday Agreement was signed. A child of the peace process, so he was. Some peace, wha?

Had Paul survived, his beating would have been forgotten. It would have been considered housekeeping. An internal IRA thing. But he didn't survive, did he?

To know one of your own did this is soul-destroying.

A month after Paul's death, Ulster Unionist peer Lord John Laird asserted parliamentary privilege in the House of Lords to accuse Slab Murphy of approving Paul's killing. He said Murphy had ordered Nationalists in the area not to cooperate with the police. Laird named Vincent Treanor as the man who planned the killing.

Both Murphy and Treanor denied any involvement.

In 2008, Northern Ireland's Independent Monitoring Commission issued a report attributing the murder to local disputes. Some IRA members, or former IRA members, may have been involved, the report said, without naming the assailants. But the IMC insisted that there was no evidence that IRA leadership was linked to the incident.

Some of the killers, the commission's report concluded, were "accustomed over a substantial period of time to exercising considerable local influence, collectively and individually. This would have led such people to expect what they would consider as appropriate respect from others, [including] being able to undertake their activities—including criminal ones—without interference. They would find it very difficult to accept any waning in this influence and respect."

Stephen Quinn and I stand in the St. Patrick's Church cemetery, beside Paul's grave. He lies buried next to a friend who drowned while he and Paul were on holiday in Greece. Just eighteen, both of them. Paul brought his clothes home afterward. Another friend buried nearby died by suicide.

IN LOVING MEMORY OF OUR DEAR SON AND BROTHER PAUL
SAVAGELY BEATEN TO DEATH 20 OCTOBER 2007 AGE 21

Stephen folds his hands and closes his eyes and tells Paul about his day. How he took his seven head of cattle to the market in

Newry. It rained something awful. Gave them a good feed the
night before, aye. Last supper. He gives a short laugh. He tells Paul
to help him catch his killers and then pauses, his face a weather
of hurt.

A nurse leads the Quinn family into the surgery room on the evening of October 20, 2007. They see the ventilator tube protrud-
ing from Paul's mouth. They see the swollen left side of his head.
His right earlobe torn off. One of his front teeth cracked. Gray
face beneath the bright ceiling lights. Eyes with no color, not completely closed. The rest of him covered in a sheet. Beaten so badly
Breege is not allowed to put rosary beads in his hands. Still so
young-looking.

Paul's girlfriend, Emma Murphy, saw trouble coming three months
before he died. Paul lived in Silverbridge at the time, a village near
Newry. He told Emma the IRA didn't like him. Living on his own,
he worried they'd come and get him. He decided to move back
home.

   Stephen Quinn remembers the night Paul returned. He came
into the kitchen and Stephen asked him, as a joke, Are ye back
home, aye?

   I am, Paul said, and laughed a nervous laugh.

   Before he came in, Stephen saw him outside the house in a car
with three or four fellows. He didn't know if they were friends or
not. He didn't ask.

I try to contact Anthony and Connor, but they won't talk.

   I call Sinn Féin every day for three weeks, asking them to comment on the status of the Quinn investigation. I'm told someone
will call me back, but they never do. Finally a secretary says, We've
got all your messages. Stop calling. There's no point for you to call
anymore.

   I call back anyway, but this time I leave a message for Slab Murphy. I never hear from him.

   I call Vincent Treanor and leave a message with a woman I pre-
sume to be his wife. She's decidedly cool when I explain the purpose of my call. She takes my number, but I don't hear from him.

   I call Patrick John Quinn, owner of the shed where Paul was

killed and no relation to his family. A former IRA man, according
to the police. The man who answers refuses to identify himself and
tells me not to call the family again.

I call Frank McCabe, father of Tomas McCabe. His wife, Eileen,
answers, and I ask to speak to her husband. Just a minute, she says.
I hear her call for him in the next room. She gets back on and
asks, Who's calling? I tell her, and explain that I want to speak to
him about the Quinn murder. He's not here, she says, and hangs
up.

I call the press office of the Democratic Unionist Party. In 2007,
Sinn Féin and the pro-British DUP entered into a power-sharing
agreement to govern Northern Ireland. The DUP went into government with the Republicans on the strict understanding that the
IRA had ended all its militant activities. Proof of IRA involvement
in Paul's murder would endanger the very existence of the administration. The DUP refuses to comment.

Finally, I call Peter John Caraher, a senior South Armagh Republican listed by the Northern Ireland police as a veteran IRA
member. I met him on a reporting trip in 1993, when he spoke
to me about his son Fergal, who was shot dead in 1990 by a Royal
Marine.

I can still see Peter John's wife handing me a framed photo
of Fergal, her pale face lost in sorrow, her sunken eyes staring
through me. Not a word exchanged between us. Just the silent
offer of Fergal's photo. Surely, I thought, Peter John would understand the Quinns' need for answers.

Peter John remembers me and agrees to a meeting. On the day
of our appointment, however, he changes his mind. He explains
that he has the flu. He expects to be sick all day and the following
day. And the day after that and the day after that.

Good luck, he says.

It took Stephen Quinn twelve months to visit the hulking red shed
where Paul was beaten to death. He refused to look inside. He
thought about the beating and the bastards who did it and was
sickened looking at it.

I am quite convinced the IRA killed Paul, Pat McNamee tells me.

He cites the black military-style clothing the killers wore, the planning required to lure Paul to the shed, and the manner in which the shed was cleaned after the beating, leaving no weapons and little forensic evidence.

It's the modus operandi of the IRA, Pat says.

We are sitting at a long table in his Crossmaglen house, with pictures of his daughter and his grandchild looking out at us. Pat has a professorial air about him. Blue dress shirt, gray slacks, tie. Gray hair, trim goatee. An urban planner. But years before, he was a member of the IRA.

In 1978 he was jailed for kidnapping and possession of arms and ammunition. Four years later he was tried in a special criminal court in Dublin. He served six years in Portlaoise Prison. In 1996 he was elected to the Northern Ireland Forum for peace negotiations as a member of Sinn Féin.

As time went on, he began to disagree with the party's policies. Like Jim McAllister, he believed the real issues had been shoved aside to promote electoral success. He left Sinn Féin in 2005.

I knew Paul's family in the sense I'd know most families in the area, he tells me. In the IRA it was important for me to know who was who and where people lived. I would have seen him as a young fella knocking about. When I saw the pictures of him later, I remembered him. Quite a big lad. Bit of a terror. He did what young fellas do. He had a car. A bit of a racer.

He drove oil for people, Pat continues. He ran afoul of the IRA. When the Republicans stopped their military activity, they occupied themselves by making money. Some members worked in legitimate ways. Some got into smuggling.

Paul was a competitor, he says.

They would have been at the shed an hour before Paul arrived, Pat says. Some of them would have watched the road. At least twenty others would have been waiting nearby. For that many people, the operation had to have been authorized by the IRA leadership in South Armagh.

Do him, they would have decided.

Easy enough.

Get a line on his mates.

Easy enough.

Get his mates to lure him in.

Easy enough.

Why not just shoot him? I ask.

That would have involved firearms. A violation of the ceasefire and the decommissioning of weapons.

So they beat him to death instead?

Yes, Pat says.

I consider a billboard that stands above a closed Sinn Féin office in Crossmaglen.

MURDER!

Beneath the word is the smiling face of Paul Quinn, striped shirt open at the collar. Short hair combed forward. A relaxed smile. The shape of his nose, the blue of his eyes that will be passed on to another Quinn.

PAUL QUINN REFUSED TO BE BULLIED
AND FOR THAT HE WAS BEATEN TO DEATH

The billboard has faded from the rain and sun and the days that have turned into weeks, months, years. No one has been charged. Perhaps someone will decide to talk to the police. For their peace of mind, if nothing else.

YOUR COMMUNITY IN THE GRIP OF MURDERERS
IS THIS THE "PEACE" YOU SIGNED UP FOR?

On my last night in Crossmaglen, Stephen Quinn picks me up for dinner.

One last story before you leave, he says.

A year or so before he died, Paul was driving down a road with a farmer, a good Republican he worked for time and again.

Your man sees a picture of Bobby Sands and blows the car horn.

Why ye beep every time ye pass the wee picture of Bobby Sands? Paul asks the farmer.

To say hello to him, your man says.

Paul laughs. He doesn't have time for that.

The fighting's done.

The war is over.

PAUL THEROUX

The Wicked Coast

FROM *The Atlantic*

WHEREVER YOU LOOK on this coast, you see a Wyeth vignette. It was an icy diamond-bright day in late winter in midcoast Maine, under a cloudless sky, the tide ebbing from the ice chunks that encrusted the rocky shore like blocks of salt, the north wind whipping whitecaps across the bay. This stretch of water, the lower end of Penobscot Bay, known and charted and fished by Europeans for more than four hundred years, once teemed with cod as it now teems with lobsters. As for the particular details of seaside granite and tangled kelp and white clapboard houses and driftwood washed smooth by waves, it is clearly Wyeth country. The man known locally as Andy once lived and worked just down the peninsula, at Port Clyde. His painting *The Patriot* depicts the father of the man who still runs the nearby sawmill.

I was visiting a lobsterman friend to ask a favor. This man greeting me would himself suit a Wyeth portrait. He was warmly dressed, a heavy coat over a down vest, cord trousers, rubber knee-high boots, and a fisherman's thick rubber gloves. He was crouched in the sun on his own dock, surrounded by tall stacks of lobster traps.

"What are you doing here?" And he laughed, because he's used to seeing me in the summer. I laughed too, hearing "*doo*-in *hee*-yah."

I said I needed him to run me out in his boat to an offshore island where I had to transact a little business. Of course he said yes, no problem, did I want to go right now before the tide ebbed away?

We were soon on the water, the wind cutting my face, the islands glittering around us. The last ice age carved this coast, created the narrow south-trending peninsulas and lumpy granite islands, all of it now softened by tall spruce trees, "The Country of the Pointed Firs," as one of its literary chroniclers described it. In summer these trees perfume the coast and support osprey nests. My friend was telling me how this had been an awfully snowy winter. It was not a complaint—for months it had been perfect for snowmobiling up near Rangeley. Oh, yes, very cold, but he had warm gear and added that one day ("I am serious") a few years ago on that trail, the temperature was 37 below zero, Fahrenheit. And he laughed.

Most visitors to coastal Maine know it in the summer. In the nature of visitation, people show up in the season. The snow and ice are a bleak memory now on the long warm days of early summer, but it seems to me that to understand a place best, the visitor needs to see figures in a landscape in all seasons. Maine is a joy in the summer. But the soul of Maine is more apparent in the winter. You see that the population is actually quite small, the roads are empty, some of the restaurants are closed, the houses of the summer people are dark, their driveways unplowed. But Maine out of season is unmistakably a great destination: hospitable, good-humored, plenty of elbow room, short days, dark nights of crackling ice crystals.

Winter is a season of recovery and preparation. Boats are repaired, traps fixed, nets mended. "I need the winter to rest my body," my friend the lobsterman told me, speaking of how he suspended his lobstering in December and did not resume until April.

But his son, younger and stronger, was preparing, this week in early March, to set out his traps—eight hundred of them. His chosen area was 35 miles out to sea; with his stern man helping, he could bait and set one hundred traps a day. What I take to be heroic effort is an average day for men like him, and women too —it's not unusual to see a woman piloting a lobster boat and hauling traps.

I love talking to this man and his neighbors, because they are the enduring community of the Maine coast, making a living in the same fruitful and laborious way that people here always have. The coast was known to Europe from the earliest times. John Cabot claimed it for King Henry VII in 1497, Verrazano sailed "down east" in 1524, Captain Weymouth set foot here in 1605 and was rowed in a shallop up St. George's River, which he named. Charts made during these voyages were used by Europeans seeking fish. Indeed, as Bill Caldwell writes in *Islands of Maine: Where America Really Began,* fishermen from England, France, Spain, and Portugal were familiar with Maine's islands—so much so that by the early 1600s as many as three hundred foreign fishing vessels were working the waters off the Maine coast.

The Wawenock chief Samoset, who befriended the Pilgrims at Plymouth, was born a little way down the coast, at Pemaquid. (He knew English; some say he learned it from another Indian, who'd been kidnapped by English explorers.) Thoreau claimed that the wilderness of Maine was as wild as any on earth, and his *Maine Woods* (portions of which appeared in *The Atlantic*) is persuasive on that theme. I agree with Bill Caldwell that America began here, and it endures here in the same venerable way.

The landscape of the midcoast is summed up in the plangent lines that begin the poem "Renascence," by Edna St. Vincent Millay, who was born near here:

> All I could see from where I stood
> Was three long mountains and a wood;
> I turned and looked the other way,
> And saw three islands in a bay.

Many small towns I know in Maine are as tight-knit and interdependent as those I associate with rural communities in India or China; with deep roots and old loyalties, skeptical of authority, they are proud and inflexibly territorial. These traits, deplored by some people "from away," are the secret of their survival. I like these Mainers for their self-sufficiency; they are uncomplaining almost to a fault, indeed studied self-deprecation is the normal mode for such people, who superstitiously make a point of never boasting of a great catch. "Not bad" is passionate for a Maine lobsterman. They are renewed by a sustaining culture. My friend the lobsterman is also a volunteer fireman, as well as a trained (and unpaid) emergency medical responder. Onshore, whenever his pager summons him, he hops in his pickup truck and answers the call.

Late fall and winter is also a time when Mainers get creative. I know many painters, sculptors, and weavers who spend this time of year at their art. The expression *cottage industry* does not do justice to others' achievements in knitting, quilting, basket-weaving, bottling maple syrup. Many of these products are sold at the State of Maine Cheese Company on Route 1, halfway between Rockland and Camden. This modest but well-stocked cheese-maker sells cheese curd squeezed that same day, as well as seven-year-old sharp cheddar and a dozen other varieties.

Rockland, the commercial hub of midcoast Maine, was a blue-collar town originally based on shipbuilding and later on the fishing, granite, and lime industries. After Camden, just up the coast, became gentrified and prosperous, Rockland—with fishing in decline, and no longer an exporter of rocks—reinvented itself as a destination, with a world-class art museum, the Farnsworth (a showcase for three generations of Wyeths), and a renovated classic one-screen movie theater, the Strand, as well as good restaurants, bookshops, and a series of weekend summer festivals celebrating lobsters, blues, and boats.

Maine does not end at its coast. Its beauty is repeated in its islands, thousands of them if one also counts those rock ledges known locally as "knubbles"—small knobs—some of them supporting a tree or two. Traditionally many Maine islands were offshore depots for fishing and lobstering; some served as pastures for keeping cows, or for quarrying granite; lighthouses still stand on some of them. Some are privately owned, with summerhouses on them, and a look of defiant seclusion as though challenging John Donne's assertion that no man is an island. On the Maine coast, some men are islands.

Headed out with my friend that day to one of those granite islands topped by tall spruce trees, I asked him what he had been doing lately.

"Shrimpun," he said.

He and his son had spent the past few weeks trapping and netting shrimp. It was a hard business at sea on those windy, freezing winter days, hard too because the shrimp have a short shelf life unless they're quickly shipped, peeled, and frozen. They are medium-sized. The catch is not huge. The price that week was 75 cents a pound. Not much, but never mind.

"Tasty?"

"Wicked tasty."

MICHAEL GORRA

Letter from Paris

FROM *The Hudson Review*

DEAR H,

Victor Hugo put his readers on top of Notre Dame, asking them to imagine themselves as a bird sitting upon its towers in the late Middle Ages and looking down at the city spreading itself around them, the bridges and streets and palaces, spires and hovels and maybe the gallows too. But all I can do is put you up seven floors in our building on the Boulevard Edgar Quinet in Montparnasse, and with a view from our windows onto the functional Rue du Départ. Not a good view either, not really, or not entirely. In the morning, true, the metallic buildings of La Défense, way off to the west, do catch the pink of the sunrise. The Eiffel Tower is always there as well, more than a mile away but still close enough to look big, and on some nights it seems to go off like a sparkler, its lights popping red and gold as if it were shorting itself out. But there's another tower too, the fifty-odd stories of the Tour Montparnasse just across the street, and depending on where I stand it can entirely fill my window with its dull brown mass.

The view improves when I look down, turning my eyes to the esplanade that stretches between the Tour and the neighboring train station. There's a merry-go-round that rarely seems to attract a child, and a line stretching in front of the Parisian equivalent of the Times Square TKTS booth, buying discounted theater seats for that evening's shows. There's an ever-changing and yet never visibly used litter of construction materials—today it's huge wooden spools of black electric cables. Sometimes there's a group of break dancers, or balletic kick-boxers whose feet miss contact by one deliberate inch, and usually I can spot the three soldiers who perpetually patrol the square in berets and camouflage, two of them out front with automatic weapons and a third, usually older, walking ten yards behind them. In the dark of a winter morning they sometimes seem the only things moving out there, distinguishable not so much by their profile as by their pace, whose slow methodical steps don't appear to take them toward anything, not the bus stop or the taxi stand or the sliding doors of the Gare Montparnasse itself.

On Friday nights the roller-bladers gather on the esplanade toward ten, a cortege of maybe two thousand skaters marshaled by yellow-reflector-jacketed volunteers. Voices call, and as the sound echoes off the buildings it becomes a roar; then the swoosh of their wheels, and then something like silence. These moving packs aren't quite as big as they once were, but they're still exciting to watch, with the wild benign energy of a circus parade. I like being in the streets as they prepare to take off, and afterward make my own small loop through the *quartier*. There are dozens of restaurants here, few of them good—kebabs and crepes and cafés, chain steak joints and sushi shops, and now that it's warm out they all seem to have outdoor terraces, so loud and full and busy that you move down the sidewalk in a haze of secondhand smoke. It may now be banned inside restaurants and bars, but a lot of people here do still smoke, in a way that they don't anywhere in America, and sometimes I think that the sidewalks are made entirely of cigarettes and high heels, tap tap, puff puff. In passing another pedestrian you have to make sure you won't be accidentally jabbed by flame, and in fact other people's smoking has even made me lose sleep.

Not because I worry about their health—no, it's because the kids at the tough down-market club at the foot of the Tour Montparnasse come out for a drag at 4 A.M., and their voices can make the place seem as loud as day. The club empties for good around six, with a certain violence, and on most Sunday mornings I stand in the window with my first cup of coffee and watch the police cars come to pick up after a fistfight. The fights are short, brutal, and governed by a strict code. The club's bouncers won't let anything happen in the doorway, so the kids move a few yards down the street and begin; the police, in turn, are careful not to arrive until it's over. I suppose it could be worse—its American equivalent would probably feature knives and guns. But a boot can do a lot of damage, and most weekends there's an ambulance too.

In all this, I suppose, the area is only being true to its own past. I've been reading a lot about the history of Paris on this sabbatical year, and with special attention to Eric Hazan's account of the city's neighborhoods in *The Invention of Paris,* and one of the things I've learned is that in the later eighteenth century the barrier wall at which taxes were levied on goods coming into Paris ran along what's now the Boulevard Edgar Quinet. The tollgate was just a block away from our building, at the boulevard's intersection with the Rue de la Gaîté. Wine was heavily taxed as it crossed into what was then the city proper, but people could move back and forth for free. So the area just outside the wall became a nightspot, where one could drink on the cheap, and Hazan suggests that the ghost of the tax barrier endures today in the honky-tonk life of the Rue de la Gaité in particular, with its vaudeville theaters and porn shops, their windows painted dark and a curtain over the door.

Yet the area changes once I cross Quinet on the other side and enter the narrow Rue Delambre. It's one of those well-ordered little Parisian streets with separate shops for meat and cheese and fish, a florist and a greengrocer and two bakeries. I walk it half a dozen times a day, and it puts me out into one of the old fabled lands of American expatriation, the big bars and cafés of the Boulevard Montparnasse, places once fueled by Prohibition. You know the names—La Coupole and Le Select, Le Dôme and La Rotonde. I like the Select in the morning, when I sit inside at a battered wood table, spreading out whatever I'm working on and getting up occasionally to pet the house cat, Mickey. (*Mal élevé,* the *patronne* says as the beast walks across the bar.) And the café at the Dôme is a good place for a drink toward six, never too crowded and with most of its clientele a set of elderly regulars whom the waiters treat with exquisite courtesy. Though I'm not really interested in the Lost Generation, in the memories of Montparnasse or even the frenetic American city of the fifties, the *Paris Review* on the one hand and Elaine Dundy's 1958 novel *The Dud Avocado* on the other. I've made no visits to Hemingway sites, and have walked by Gertrude Stein's apartment on the Rue de Fleurus only on my way to dinner. But I have gone to the Closerie des Lilas and made a silent toast to that better Parisian A. J. Liebling, who found a welcome there, as he writes in *Normandy Revisited,* on the night of the liberation in August 1944.

My most regular pilgrimage, however, is to the Cimetière du Montparnasse, whose entrance lies a few hundred yards outside our door. Its tombs don't have quite the marquee value of the Père Lachaise, far away in the hilly twentieth arrondissement, where women leave a red lipstick imprint on the grave of Oscar Wilde, and the wandering youth of all nations gather to see Jim Morrison. But it's a better place for anyone interested in twentieth-century culture. Sartre once lived in our building, and he's stayed on in the neighborhood, under the same stone with Simone de Beauvoir. Ionesco, Brancusi, Brassaï, and Man Ray have their plots there as well. Eric Rohmer was buried here just last year, and Susan Sontag in 2004, though she didn't die in Paris. I found her grave by accident one morning last fall, a flat dark slab among other flat dark slabs, but the cemetery's office is perpetually out of maps and I haven't been able to trace it since. Beckett is easier, he lies on one of the main avenues, and my wife and I stood there on Easter morning, a German couple next to us snapping photos of the banana somebody had left there in honor of *Krapp's Last Tape,* where the fruit figures as a prop. And there was some other produce across the way, at the only grave here that seems to rival the various cults of the Père Lachaise. It belongs to the singer Serge Gainsbourg, dead now twenty years, and along with many flowers there was a litter of metro tickets and cigarette lighters, objects that had figured in his songs, and then a head of curly Savoy cabbage. I needed Google to explain that one, I'll confess—a 1976 album called *L'homme à tête de chou.*

My own most regular visit is to an older figure. Guy de Maupassant's presence here seems a bit incongruous, since like so many nineteenth-century writers he was a creature of the Right Bank above all. I might have expected to find him at the cemetery in Montmartre, where he set one of his best stories. "The Graveyard Sisterhood" is a bawdy little anecdote in which the speaker recalls the curious way in which he once acquired a mistress. While visiting the tomb of a former lover he noticed a pretty woman crying over a freshly filled grave. It was natural for him to console her; and when after many months they parted, he made her a suitable present. Sometime later he went back to the cemetery—and saw her weeping over a different but equally new grave. Another man was rushing to her side, and her eyes implored our narrator to keep silent. Which sets him to thinking. She had taken him in, he had never quite realized she was working, and now he wonders if the graveyards might not be full of the crocodile tears of women trawling for customers.

Well, nothing like that has happened on any of the half-dozen times I've gone to see Maupassant, though once another visitor did hand me a flier for a self-published book of essays. For I have never been alone with the author of "La Maison Tellier" and "Boule de Suif." There are always other people there, at this modest grave planted with roses, not a crowd but enough to make it easy to spot, and many of them leave notes. I read through them one day, a stack of small slips of paper that had been rained upon and then bleached by the sun, notes like the ex-votos at the shrine of a saint, thanking Maupassant for favors conferred—that is, for pleasure given—in French and Italian, Spanish and German and Japanese. English too, of course—though those, I'm sorry to say, are on the order of "Guy, you rock!" Which isn't exactly how I'd put it, and yet it's true enough. Certainly that sentiment fits his best novel, *Bel-Ami,* in which one always expects the hero to be found out, to be caught and exposed and punished, like Stendhal's Julien Sorel before him. But no: Maupassant's cheerful cad goes on cheating everyone until the last page, when he is rewarded with a millionaire's daughter and a wedding at the Madeleine, and the author's effrontery in pulling it all off is every bit as great as his character's.

Most of my reading this year has been in the French nineteenth century—more Maupassant, some Zola, a bit of Gautier. After making her way through the fat brick of *The Count of Monte Cristo,* my twelve-year-old demanded that I read it too, and for a week it made me feel as though I were twelve myself. So then I got busy. I followed the Musketeers out through two thousand pages of sequels to their deaths, and after finishing with Dumas moved on to Hugo; good enough, in *Notre-Dame de Paris,* to make me think about someday trying *Les Misérables.* I do it all in English, alas; I can handle Maigret in the original but not much more, and even that comes dreadfully slow. Still, Simenon is probably better when read slowly—speed ruins his sense of moody rumination.

Once past Simenon and Proust, however, the twentieth century becomes for me an unscratched territory, a land that contains the well-known names of so many unknown volumes that I don't know where to begin. Maybe that's why I took myself out one day to the newish tower blocks of the Bibliothèque nationale, along the river at the city's eastern edge. Not that I was looking for a book: all my needs have been filled by that superb expatriates' institution the American Library, which sits in the seventh in the very shadow of the Tour Eiffel. But the Bibliothèque also runs exhibits, and this spring's lead show is a celebration of the one-hundredth anniversary of Gallimard, the publisher of Gide and Malraux, Sartre and Sarraute, of the *Nouvelle Revue Française* and the tidy permanence of the Pléiade. There are many exhibits up in Paris at any one time, more than any amateur can possibly see, and the last year has brought an overcrowded Monet blockbuster at the Grand Palais and an entirely thrilling retrospective of Jean-Léon Gérôme at the Orsay. Manet is hanging now, and Caillebotte, and Odilon Redon, and yet for me it will be hard to match the fascination of the video clips, dust jackets, and documents that the Bibliothèque has put together.

The interest starts even before you enter, with the realization that the lettering on the library's permanent signage uses the same typeface as most of Gallimard's publicity material. An accident, a string pulled on some committee in the Mitterrand years? Who knows, but it does speak to the publisher's quasi-official stature. It makes the national library itself look like an accessory of the Pléiade. The show opens with a room of photographs, a Murderers' Row of the house's writers: Proust and Camus and Céline, Marguerite Yourcenar and Romain Gary and the firm's newest Nobel Prize winner, Mario Vargas Llosa. There's a vitrine with some famous manuscripts— *Le Deuxième Sexe, Les Faux-Monnayeurs*—and then in the next room a wall displays some of the firm's reader's reports. Many of these are on works first written in English, and some of them are signed by names as distinguished as those on the spines of the books themselves; that for Isak Dinesen's *Out of Africa* is by Raymond Queneau. Meanwhile Ramon Fernandez advises rejecting *Gone With the Wind*—only to be overruled by Gaston Gallimard himself, who winkled it away from another publisher when a dinner party conversation made him realize what a hit it would be. The editors tried out dozens of titles for it—*En plein vent? Aller au vent?*—before settling on *Autant en emporte le vent*, and when the film was released under that name in France the firm made the producers acknowledge its copyright.

Gallimard does many things, kids' books and detective novels and a series of heavily illustrated travel guides, marvels of book production that Knopf publishes in translation; one room shows the mock-up for a multipage foldout that depicts the belts of cultivation along the Nile. There are walls of advertising posters and dust jackets, and bookcases displaying the house's various lines, like the Folio series of paperbacks, their design as unmistakable as a Penguin but printed more crisply and on better paper too. For someone of my own obsessions the most interesting things here are the bits that define Gallimard's long history of publishing Faulkner. It began with a 1931 letter from the Princeton French professor Maurice-Edgar Coindreau, who was then busy translating *A Farewell to Arms*. He gave a brief progress report on the Hemingway and then followed it with two typed pages on his prolific new discovery. Gallimard released *Sanctuary* in 1933 and *As I Lay Dying* the next year, but Faulkner himself didn't get to Paris until 1951. A framed letter here records his thanks for the firm's hospitality in good though stiff French. *"Tout le monde doit bien aimer la France,"* he writes and then adds that in Mississippi there's now someone who loves it just a little bit more.

Tout le monde. The phrase reminds me of something Jefferson is alleged to have said—that everyone has two countries, his own and France. Would I go that far myself? I don't know, and yet there's one crucial aspect of our national life that I can experience more fully here than now seems possible in America itself. Videocassettes and DVDs have long ago killed off the revival movie houses in which I spent so many grad school hours—have killed them everywhere but in Paris, where on most days the cinemas around the Rue des Écoles give me a choice of half a dozen old American movies. The screens are on the small side, but you still watch in the dark with other people, as you were meant to. Schools in France let out early on Wednesdays, and so that's where my daughter and I are apt to spend the afternoon, sitting in front of *Notorious* or *Stagecoach* or *Top Hat*, sitting at home only and precisely because we are also abroad.

KENAN TREBINCEVIC

The Reckoning

FROM *The New York Times Magazine*

AFTER READING AN ARTICLE on Bosnia's tourism boom, my brother, Eldin, and I decided it was time to face down our past. We reasoned that we were really doing this for our seventy-two-year-old father, Senahid. If he didn't see the country of his birth or his childhood friends soon, he never would. Yet within days I became obsessed with creating a to-do list for our trip: 1) Take a picture of the concentration camp my brother and father survived; 2) visit the cemetery where the karate coach who betrayed us was buried; 3) confront Petra, the neighbor who stole from my mother.

The minute we stepped out of the car in front of our old apartment building, my hands began to sweat. We fled eighteen years ago, one year into the Bosnian war, and had not been back since. My father's friend Truly bought our apartment as a summer home in 2006, the year my mom died of cancer. (We were living in Connecticut by then.) Truly and my father both worked with the city's sports clubs and were close friends for thirty years. "You and your brother should know what your father did for this city and its people," Truly said when he greeted me. "That's why he stayed alive."

As we approached the building, I could see Truly's two pretty teenage daughters staring down at us from the third-floor balcony. I was reminded of what it was like to be twelve, shouting to my friends below as I rushed to get to karate practice. It still shocked me to recall that it was my coach who, put in charge of the city's special-police unit, arrived with the army van to cleanse the building of its Muslims. They marched to our door and told my father, "You have an hour to leave or you will be killed." We left and went to stay with my aunt. My father and brother were picked up a month later and put into a camp. My mother and I eventually made it back to the apartment, where we were all reunited three months later. We were the only Muslim family who didn't flee the building when the war began. But we lived in fear that someone would come back for us.

Inside, the building hadn't changed—the same impossibly high steps, the same brown mailboxes. Only the tenants' names were different. After the war, this side of town came to be populated by Serbs. Bosnians like us were now a minority.

As I walked into the apartment, I headed for my old bedroom. I used to lie on the floor peeping through the tiny holes in the shades that were drawn all day and night so soldiers couldn't see you and spray the windows with bullets.

Coming up to our apartment, I passed Petra, our old neighbor. She was in her late sixties now. When she caught sight of me, she put down her grocery bags and sat on the stairs to smoke a cigarette, hoping to avoid me.

I flashed back to the night she barged into our dining room and told my mother to give her the skirt she was wearing. The next day it was the dining room rug Petra wanted. A week later she invited my mother for coffee, and they sat with their feet resting on the stolen rug. Truly's wife promised my mother that she would never acknowledge Petra. "All summer long I walk by her as if I'm walking by a grave," she said.

Petra liked to tell the paramilitaries where Muslims were living so they could come and cart them away in meat trucks. Her husband, Obren, worked as a guard in the concentration camp. (It was the same one from which my brother and father were miraculously released, as prisoners were being transferred, hours before CNN arrived to show the world the atrocities.) While Petra requisitioned my mother's things, Obren brought me canned beans and plum jam. He remembered the time my father stood up for him during a tenants' meeting just before the fighting began. Years later, we learned he died of esophageal cancer. His wife has lasted almost as long as a Galápagos tortoise. The monsters always live.

As she approached our floor, her footsteps became halting, her breathing heavy. She fumbled for her key. Her eyes didn't meet mine. "No one has forgotten," I said. She put her head down. The door opened with a long sigh, then closed. There was silence.

I heard laughter coming from our old living room and joined my friends inside. Truly turned to his daughters and said, "If the two of you were only a few years older, you could marry one of the boys." They blushed, smiling. "Once they turn eighteen," I said, to make them less uncomfortable.

Later that night I reached into my pocket for my to-do list and crossed off item No. 3.

BRYAN CURTIS

The Tijuana Sports Hall of Fame

FROM *Grantland*

WHAT DO YOU WANT from Tijuana, my friends? You want to meet a girl? I can take you to the Hong Kong Gentlemen's Club. I can get you two-for-one drinks. (Actually, I know a guy: *three*-for-one drinks!) I'll show you a white donkey painted with black zebra stripes. The "Dr. House" Pharmacy and other places just out of reach of your copyrights. You want Che Guevara T-shirts, my friends? *I Ate the Worm* T-shirts? Wet T-shirts? Did I mention the Hong Kong Gentlemen's Club?

Me and my pal Eric, in lousy Spanish: "Do you know where we can find the museum of sports? The, um, place of the famous athletes?"

We do not want sex and drugs from Tijuana. We want to visit the Tijuana Sports Hall of Fame.

I hate to use an itchy word, but Tijuana is dead. Once, Avenida Revolución—the "Revo," in the gringo tongue—happily excreted pleasure. At age twenty, I walked its grime-covered sidewalks, dodged honors students from San Diego, and nosed into a bar where a stranger unfurled his hand and said, "Amphetamine?" (Nah, I'd stick with tequila.) But as Eric and I cruise the Revo at a nocturnal hour, we see boarded-up storefronts and hear the Proclaimers playing in empty bars. Even the calls of the touts ("Check this out, amigo") sound halfhearted, like the fight song when your team trails by three touchdowns. Tijuana, after its severed-head period, has entered a mind-bending phase. It's a gringo viceland without gringos.

Except, of course, these two gringos.

Now, about the Hall of Fame: Eric and I aren't sure it exists.
A motel owner, a shopkeeper, and a cabbie haven't heard of it.
They're not alone. I call Freddy Sandoval, a Tijuana native who
played third base for the Angels. "I didn't know we had a Hall of
Fame," he says. Freddy Sandoval's picture is *in the Tijuana Sports
Hall of Fame.*

One morning the cashier at Ricardo's restaurant gives us a tip.
We walk up Avenida Madero, past cheapo fast-food joints and auto
repair shops. We come upon a triangle of parkland bordered by
three noisy streets. A man and his two dogs are passed out in the
grass. Another sits on a park bench displaying his tricked-out bike.
We see two cops from a police force we have been eagerly trying to
avoid. And in the middle of this dingy urban still life, a bell tower
that looks like a giant white chess piece rises toward the sky. A
hand-painted sign reads, SALÓN DE LA FAMA DEL DEPORTE. The
Tijuana Sports Hall of Fame.

Balancing on four legs, the Hall of Fame proper begins about
three stories in the air. You can walk under the building and gaze
up at it. We climb the outer staircase, and the metal bows under
our feet. The final step feels like it could give way at any second.

Eric and I peek through the door. The Hall of Fame is as empty
as the Revo. We don't see any customers—or any employees. We
walk inside and sign the guestbook.

The Hall's first exhibit, on our right, is an odd photo collage
devoted to *lucha libre.* There are old wrestlers who look like Fidel
Castro, and new ones who look like Tijuana's answer to Doink the
Clown. On the left-hand wall, we come across an exhibit marked
"Golf." Only there aren't any photos of golfers. There are only
photos of the exterior of the Tijuana Sports Hall of Fame. "Maybe
the exhibit is on tour or something," Eric says.

Moving tentatively forward, I get interested in a team photo of
Equipo Vikingos, the 2000–2001 champions of Tijuana's amateur
baseball league. Los Vikingos, a swell-looking bunch of guys, are
celebrating with a well-endowed brunette in a leopard-print dress.
What's confusing is that I can't find photos of the team that won
the amateur title in 1999–2000 or 2001–2002 or any other year.
Los Vikingos and their valet, it seems, have been awarded a sin-
gular honor. The Hall of Fame is as idiosyncratic as your uncle's
mantel.

Another mystery photo: grim-faced Maria Hayde Gomez, described only as Tijuana's 1983 Youth Athlete of the Year. *¿Quién eras, Maria?* We see a glass case packed with strange memorabilia: a baseball glove with the name *Rudy Campos* written on it in marker; a leather jacket from Tijuana's hunting and fishing club; wrestling trunks; a photo of Esteban Loaiza.

The Hall bulges with sports history: *hundreds* of Tijuana men and women stare back at us from neat 11-by-14-inch black frames. There are chess players, archers, matadors. A geriatric woman bowling in brow-line glasses. A high school football team holding aloft its coach, a Mexican John Madden, after a big win.

The Tijuana Sports Hall of Fame has the soul of Canton, Ohio, and the inventory of a wall at Chili's. We have to know: What is this place?

Back downstairs in the park, I walk up to a man. I'd picked up a color brochure in the Hall of Fame and located a photo of the director.

How do I find this man? I ask.

The man in the park says, "He's dead."

Oh. I point at another man in another brochure. What about this man?

"He had a heart attack."

We'll try back tomorrow.

What do we *turistas* want from Tijuana? Well, first we want vice. Tijuana is our Larry Flynt. During Prohibition, vice was something as simple as getting a beer. Tijuana, *Liberty* magazine once proclaimed, was the city "Where There Aren't No Ten Commandments and Where a Man Can Raise a Thirst." Vice also meant sports.

In 1907 the mustachioed Mexican dictator Porfirio Díaz decreed that gambling was legal here. Tijuana Racetrack was opened less than a decade later by "Sunny Jim" Coffroth, the on-the-make son of a California state senator. (Americans and Mexican politicians were teammates in the creation of Tijuana's vice culture.) Americans crossed the border and walked a mere 150 yards to get to the track. Members of the clergy put up a sign at the border that read: THE ROAD TO HELL.

With sports, Tijuana was a clever demon. The horses ran in Tijuana on Sundays, when Santa Anita called such a thing unholy.

They ran during World War II, when Santa Anita was a Japanese internment camp. The city's Agua Caliente Racetrack popularized the "5–10" bet—later renamed the Pick 6—which drew thousands of suckers south in search of a payday.

The restaurants, hotels, and brothels that grew up around the racetracks and casinos became Tijuana's main street, later renamed Avenida Revolución, which became—under a few coats of irony—the official vicelandia of the gringos.

There were stadiums in Tijuana that felt like they were designed by Dr. Seuss. In 1947 an enormous jai alai palace was built on the grounds near our motel. A version still stands with JAI ALAI GAMES in giant letters on the outer wall and a statue of a player holding a *cesta* out front. A guard lets us inside and we can see that the betting windows have been perfectly preserved.

When American sports rejected you, Tijuana welcomed you. California's ban on bare-knuckle boxing led promoters to move a highly publicized 1886 bout just south of the border. Wyatt Earp served as ref. Dennis Rodman, when America tired of him, spent an end-of-the-trail season grabbing rebounds for the Tijuana Dragons.

If bullfighting is your vice, you can still find a $24 ticket to see bull-slayers like Humberto Flores and Lupita López. Ricardo "Cheto" Torres, who runs a boxing gym downtown, tells us he used to work the bullring in the 1970s. He sold seat cushions to *turistas* for five bucks. When the crowd threw roses to the matadors, sometimes drunk Americans stood up and threw their cushions.

In the bullring's parking lot, we notice a sign: MANAGEMENT IS NOT RESPONSIBLE IF YOUR CAR IS STOLEN, DAMAGED . . . OR CATCHES ON FIRE.

At the Tijuana Sports Hall of Fame the next day, Eric and I are surprised: there's another visitor. "What in the world are you doing here?" the man exclaims. This is Roberto Montaño, forty-two, who will guide us into the sports-obsessed mind of Tijuana.

"In Tijuana, baseball is the big thing," Roberto says. "I grew up as a Padres and Chargers fan." If you lived in Tijuana, you grooved on America's sporting vices just like America grooved on yours. Put up an aerial antenna and you could siphon off all the Padres and Chargers games.

"I grew up with Dan Fouts, Charlie Joiner, and John Jefferson,"

Roberto says, "and, on the Padres, Randy Jones and Dave Winfield. I remember when Ozzie Smith came up in 1978 as a rookie shortstop. I remember when the *Clippers* played in San Diego.

"I used to watch the Saturday Game of the Week. Joe Garagiola, Tony Kubek, Vin"—he pronounces it *Veen*—"Scully. My dad, who would be seventy-two now, was a Yankees fan. There weren't any Padres when he was growing up. Basketball wasn't big in Tijuana unless you were a sports fan like me. I remember Kareem, Magic, Worthy. And the white guy with glasses. What was his name?"

Tijuana has boxers like Érik "El Terrible" Morales, who keeps a gym in Zona Norte. But, interestingly, twenty years ago Tijuana was not a soccer town. Roberto and old-line *tijuanenses* will tell you soccer was brought by migrants from the Mexican interior who came to Tijuana hoping to get to the United States. Many got stopped short—it's a lot harder to cross near Tijuana than it used to be. They began the soccerization process, and satellites beaming in the Champions League did the rest. Tijuana's home club, the wonderfully named Xoloitzcuintles, just joined the first division of Mexican league.

We climb into Roberto's car. He's on his way to San Diego to go shopping, but he'll drop us in the red-light district. (My friends! I see you're back . . .) "Tijuana has grown so ugly," Roberto says as we cruise down the Revo. "Even in the seventies it was beautiful. Then a lot of outsiders came here to go to the States." While Americans fear an invasion of immigrants, Tijuana fears an invasion of soccer fans.

Roberto points down a side street and says, "Can you see the border fence?" We can just make it out, a string of silver tinsel glittering in distant hills. Even with an American passport, the lines to get back can take three hours.

At about that moment, a bile-raising smell wafts into the car. Roberto's wife and son cover their faces. "That incomparable Tijuana odor," Roberto says. "It smells like rotten dog." It smells a lot worse than that.

We accelerate down the lonely Revo. Roberto points out a woman walking away from us. "That girl in brown? She's a prostitute." Her? "I can tell. Her walk, her face . . .

"We miss the gringos, man," he says wistfully when he drops us off. "They all left, like the Mayas did."

*

Pink flamingos swim in the fountain outside the Agua Caliente Racetrack on the night of the dog races. See, Tijuana indulges America's upscale fantasies too. It is our Larry Flynt *and* our Robin Leach. Eighty years ago the Agua Caliente's casino was a great gringo mecca—"a dazzling, dream-like city," in the words of a pilgrim from *Vogue*. Its owners came to Old Mexico and built . . . Europe.

The casino was constructed in 1928, pre-Vegas. The chandeliers were imported from Italy. The columns were made of marble. Designer shops had a UN roll call of fashion. (You could take $100 worth of stuff back across the border legally. You smuggled the rest.) In his book *Satan's Playground*, Paul J. Vanderwood notes that the owners boasted that the Agua Caliente was built in the shadow of an ancient Spanish fort. This was horseshit, but there was a certain glamour in the image of a Spanish don leaning on the craps table. The casino's motto was "Agua Caliente, where all nations meet and speak the tongue of happiness."

A San Diego pensioner could feel like a rich man at Agua Caliente. Charlie Chaplin hung out there. Howard Hughes was photographed at the racetrack. Will Rogers played cards at the grandly named Monte Carlo across town, and Tijuana's top-ranked bordello was called the Moulin Rouge.

Lured by a fat purse, Seabiscuit outran an overmatched field at Agua Caliente's horse track. So did studs like Phar Lap and Round Table. By 1929, Tijuana's promoters—imagine Mark Cuban with fewer legal controls—were staging an annual $100,000 handicap, dwarfing the purse at the Kentucky Derby.

The grand old Agua Caliente was closed by Mexican president Lázaro Cárdenas in 1935 and later turned into a school. The new Agua Caliente, owned by Mexican oligarch Jorge Hank Rhon, is your basic, utilitarian casino. The drug war cleared the place of Americans: Naim Lajud Libien, director of the dog track, tells us that 5 percent of the clientele are from the north. I'd heard of one absurdly upscale touch, however. I'd heard Hank kept a private zoo on the premises.

Naim smiles. "Mammals, birds, what do you want?"

He boasts that Hank's menagerie rivals Noah's. "We have tigers. Lions. An ostrich. A giraffe."

". . . kangaroos, macaws . . ."

". . . peacocks, panthers . . ."

"... jaguars ..."

"... camels, buffaloes ..."

"... bears—black, grizzly ..."

"... *focas*. How do you say that? Seals ..."

"Come with me," Naim says. He leads us behind the first turn of the dog track, not 100 feet from where greyhounds will run. We see lions and white tigers—five, six, maybe seven of them—prowling listlessly in a chain-link cage. My notes end here. Naim hurries us away—this is just a "preview." You've got to be a high roller with a reservation to see camels, buffaloes, kangaroos, macaws ...

Tijuana, you might have heard, is frightening. Americans cross the border for this too. They don't want to be robbed or murdered, but they get a kick out of walking mean streets where such a thing happened to someone else. If you're scoring at home, Tijuana is our Larry Flynt *and* our Robin Leach *and* it's also our Freddy Krueger.

The Tijuana Racetrack opened in 1916, five years after the city was captured by rebels in the Mexican Revolution. Indeed, the Revolution led to a loud scream of panic in the United States, what historian Ricardo Romo called the "Brown Scare." For decades after, tales of murderers and pickpockets rippled through the Revo —some real, some the product of the hyper gringo imagination. You cross the border into Mexico and your sense of security melts away.

"There's a kind of mysteriousness about Mexico," says the historian Paul Vanderwood. "But even more than that, a kind of *unpredictability*. You never know quite where you're at, quite what's going to happen, you don't quite speak the language ...

"Entrepreneurs didn't really want to clean up Tijuana," he adds. "They may announce once in a while, 'We're going to do this and that.' But they want to leave that 'what's going to happen next?' kind of atmosphere."

The drug war sent Tijuana's danger from a semiromantic, *Touch of Evil* variety to a full-on, *Faces of Death* freak-out. The bodies piled up in 2008, when two lieutenants in the Tijuana Cartel vied for control of the city. They were El Teo (Teodoro García Simental) and the Engineer (Luis Fernando Sánchez Arellano). The Freddy-versus-Jason battle was a typical *narco* debate—the mutilated body as message. (A typical note, left atop eight headless, tongueless corpses: "Here you go Engineer.") This created a grimly ironic situation at Camp Pendleton: U.S. Marines, who were deploying to the most dangerous cities in Iraq, were discouraged by their commander from going to Tijuana.

The murder rate plummeted after El Teo's capture in 2010, and Tijuana is now a relatively safe city. But as with the revolution, a forensic residue remains. "I don't feel comfortable going sometimes," Freddy Sandoval tells me. "I'll just go and stay in my house." For this fear we can thank the American cable news networks, which have taken a complicated, regionalized problem and used it to make all of Mexico look like a bloody slaughterhouse. One night Eric and I see a lonely hot dog salesman on the Revo. We can't help but think the man's fortunes have been crippled, in an absurd way, by both El Teo and Bill O'Reilly.

But bloodstains are part of the reason Eric and I are here. We silently congratulate ourselves: we've made it to Tijuana. *Narco* Tijuana. Pull up a stool and hear a horror story. My friend, thank goodness you were not here two years ago, because a horrible thing happened at this very place. Have a drink and I'll tell you . . .

We return to the Tijuana Sports Hall of Fame and gaze up at the bell tower. As befits the city of the "Dr. House" pharmacy, it turns out to be a copy. A bell tower like this one guarded the old Agua Caliente Casino. The city thought it might be nice to rekindle the memories (glamour! vice!) and then turn the building over to sports.

Inside the Hall, we meet a man. He's sixtyish, tall, and strongly built, with dyed black hair. "I'm in charge," he says.

This is Felipe Domínguez Cobo, the acting president of Tijuana Sports Hall of Fame. There are two cool things about Felipe. One is that he's also *in* the Hall. We see pictures of him in tight basketball shorts. Point or shooting guard? I ask. "Shooting," Felipe says, looking slightly wounded that I have to ask. The second cool thing is his nickname: *El Caballo*—The Horse. Felipe graciously pretends he doesn't remember why his teammates started calling him El Caballo. "It was so long ago . . ."

We're high rollers here (actually, the only ones here), so El Caballo is going to take us to the *secret* parts of the Hall of Fame. He lifts a metal chain and we ascend a flight of stairs. Here, on the second floor, he points to an architectural model. "This is the future," he says—a ground-level Hall straight out of Cooperstown. The reason, Felipe says, is that the old men and women enshrined in the tower can hardly make the climb.

Next Felipe takes us up *another* flight of stairs. This is the really important room. The Tijuana Sports Hall of Fame. The stuff below is just memorabilia gathered after an announcement in the newspaper. (That would explain Equipo Vikingos—they answered the ad.) This room contains the finest sportsmen and sportswomen Tijuana has ever produced.

Look, it's Macario Rayle Preciado, the lefty slugger who, his Hall bio notes, is one of the most disciplined players in Baja California baseball. And isn't that grand old Jesús "Chucho" Peralta, the "father of bullfighting in Tijuana"? Miguel Ángel López, the professional wrestler known as Rey Misterio Sr., is here. His nephew Rey Jr. will be his tag-team partner someday—but you've got to be retired for five years to be considered for the Hall.

Eric and I find the jai alai legend Dr. Juan Valdés Martínez, who stopped his career to pursue a life of the mind just as Robert Smith left the Vikings. The bodybuilder Beatriz de Regíl González, who in her bio is compared to a beautiful flower in Tijuana's garden. There are expansive men like Benjamín Rendón Castrejón, a boxing judge, who says, "The sport of boxing is, to me, the philosophy of my life." There are haunted men like Carlos Pérez Acosta, a golfer, who says, "My life has been tragic, I lost my wife and my son."

The only thing more touching than the Tijuana Sports Hall of Fame's membership is its waiting list. Each candidate is asked to send a sports résumé to El Caballo and the executive committee. The local martial artist Roberto Proo Mendoza sent in a whole *book* crammed with photos, news clips, and certificates of achievement from the World Hapkido Federation. He tacked on sixty-four addenda. The Hall had no choice but to admit Master Roberto in 2008.

Now El Caballo takes us up a final flight of stairs. This is the fourth floor of the Tijuana Sports Hall of Fame, the top level of the bell tower. Only we see no bell here, just an old stereo system. The Tijuana Sports Hall of Fame plays a recording that sounds across Zona Centro.

To recap: Eighty years ago, Old Tijuana had a bell tower. It was built to convince Americans they were experiencing European luxury. Now we're standing in a copy of that tower—a Xerox of a dream of Europe. This tower is used to celebrate sports history. Sports attracted vice-hungry Americans to Tijuana, until they stopped coming because of violence. However, that violence may now be at a point where, like the vision of Europe, it's mostly a creation of the American mind. Finally, this bell tower plays a fake bell.

The Tijuana Sports Hall of Fame may be the most perfect encapsulation of Tijuana ever built.

After three days in Tijuana, Eric and I hail a cab on the Revo. We pop the trunk and see a well-worn wooden baseball bat lying inside.

You play ball? I ask the cabbie.

"That's for the bad guys!" he says.

We're not sure if he's kidding, but the three of us laugh together as we drive to the border.

My friends, why are you leaving? No girls? Just a bunch of athletes? Sure, it's okay. To each his own. You have seen a part of Tijuana. You have seen an even larger part, perhaps, of your gringo souls. Whatever else, my friends, you must promise me one thing. Okay? Promise me you'll come back.

KIMBERLY MEYER

Holy City of the Wichitas

FROM *Ecotone*

AN OMPHALOS IS an ancient religious stone, hollow and often beehive-shaped, its surface intricately carved. The most famous one was discovered at the Temple of the Oracle, at Delphi, but similar objects have been found in Rome, Iraq, Egypt. According to the Greeks, Zeus sent two eagles across the earth to meet at the center of the world, and there the Greeks erected a stone, perhaps the world's first omphalos, which they believed allowed them direct communication with the gods. The word means "navel."

In the Middle Ages, Jerusalem was considered an omphalos. To signify this designation, medieval cartographers frequently placed the Holy Land at the center of their maps of the world, where all the continents and rivers and seas met. These *mappae mundi,* while often adorned with precise geographic details, were attempts to represent an idea of God's orderly creation more than they were depictions of the world as it actually existed. At the center of their picture of the idealized world—and the center of spiritual existence—was the place of the birth and death and Resurrection of Jesus Christ.

The United States also has a navel. It's called Oklahoma, located, one might be tempted to say, at the buckle of the Bible Belt. But what I didn't know, until I lived in Oklahoma the first two years of my married life, is that America has a holy city as well. Ours is the Holy City of the Wichitas, a rusty red granite replica of ancient Jerusalem. It rises from the scrub-covered foothills of the Wichita Mountains, which are named, according to Native tradition, for the tribe whose ancestors were born from the rugged rocks.

In the Wichita story of the first creation, Kinnekasus, "Man Never Known on Earth," created all things. In the beginning, land hovered upon the water, and darkness was everywhere. Kinnekasus made a man and a woman, and afterward they dreamed of things, and when they woke, they had those things of which they had dreamed. The woman was given an ear of corn, and in her heart she knew that it was to be her food. But they were still in darkness. Then the man dreamed he should travel east and so he did, and in the east he found another man and together they made a bow and an arrow, which they used to shoot and wound a deer. A voice told them that they had done well, and now the darkness could move on, and time began. Later, the man and the woman themselves became the light. Woman, the moon. Man, the morning star. The man they had met in the east became Kinnihequidikidahis, "Star That Is Always Moving," and set off to follow the wounded deer and all the others of the herd, a chase that would last until the end of days.

When we married, my husband, Terry, was a lieutenant in the U.S. Army. We were stationed at Fort Sill, near the base of these same mountains in southwestern Oklahoma, just north of the Red River and Texas. From time to time his unit would practice artillery warfare out in the desolate hills. They'd be gone for a week, no showers, eating prepackaged MREs, sleeping in their cramped Humvees when they could. Terry would come back with red dust rubbed deep into the lines of his palms, into the creases of his neck.

One restless February, years after we had left Oklahoma and the army for Houston and civilian life, Terry and I returned to Fort Sill for the weekend with our daughters. We didn't have enough money to go anywhere more exotic or enough vacation time to travel anywhere farther away. So we packed up our station wagon and drove north out of the Piney Woods of east Texas across the flat bottoms of the Red River under gray skies, in bitter winter. Cows in the fields bore the brunt of the cold wind, unbroken by any tree. Barbed wire fences anchored by cedar posts stretched off into the endless distance. Telephone poles like barren crucifixes lined our way.

We stayed in Medicine Park in a small cobblestone cabin over-looking Medicine Creek, believed by the Wichitas as well as the other Plains Indians who came later—Kiowa, Comanche, Apache —to have healing powers. Not far from our cabin, Medicine Bluff loomed over the stream. This sheer precipice of rock is cleft from top to bottom by a jagged tear. In his 1875 account, *The Life and Adventures of a Quaker Among the Indians,* Thomas C. Bat-tey, a schoolteacher stationed at the Wichita Agency in present-day Anadarko, Oklahoma, recorded "the old Indian legend of Medicine Bluffs." Many years before, a group of Comanche trav-eling by horseback had arrived at the edge of the precipice and been forced to halt, unsure of how to proceed. But their medicine man, "uttering some words of Indian magic," rode his horse over the cliff and was borne across the creek to the opposite bank. He turned back toward his companions, but they were too frightened to follow, and too arrogant to go around. "To relieve them from their unpleasant position," Battey's chronicle notes, the medicine man "crossed the creek, and rode directly up to the perpendicular wall of rock, which rent at his approach, dividing the bluff into two parts by forming a chasm through the cliff several feet in width, through and up which he rode, rejoining his companions at the top, who then followed him down through the pass thus made, now known as Medicine-man's Pass."

According to Edward Charles Ellenbrook—lifelong resident of nearby Lawton, Oklahoma, adventurer, hiker, amateur historian, and author of *Outdoor and Trail Guide to the Wichita Mountains of Southwest Oklahoma*—native medicine men of various Plains tribes once climbed that escarpment for vigils. War parties came to the bluffs to fast and meditate before raids. Sometimes the sick or af-flicted were carried to the top and laid within a circle of stones to be healed. How the sacred becomes the profane: we used to picnic here.

Our cabin had a sleeping loft and at night the girls giggled and whispered up there after we turned off the lamps. I lay with Terry on the foldout couch downstairs and thought of the Wichi-tas' story of the first man and woman, dreaming things into being which they would need. The moonlight illuminated the painting on the wall above our bed—a landscape in gaudy oils with buffalo on the horizon and, against a setting sun, a quotation from Genesis: "And God saw every thing that he had made, and, behold, it was very good."

Jerusalem has long been two cities, one literal and one metaphorical. It was the City of David, conquered by that poet-king, who brought the Ark of the Covenant there, and whose son Solomon built a temple for it. When that temple was destroyed by the Babylonians under Nebuchadnezzar II, around 586 B.C., and the Israelites were exiled, Jerusalem became a symbol of all that had been lost. It was the homeland to which the Jews longed one day to return. "If I forget thee, O Jerusalem, let my right hand forget her cunning. If I do not remember thee, let my tongue cleave to the roof of my mouth; if I prefer not Jerusalem above my chief joy," laments Psalm 137, dating from the time of Babylonian captivity.

When the Jews finally did return to Jerusalem, seventy years later, they rebuilt their temple on the same site where it had formerly stood. The site of this temple, now known as the Temple Mount, encompasses some of the most contested real estate in the world today: the Western Wall, sole architectural remnant of the Second Jewish Temple; the Dome of the Rock, from which, according to Islamic tradition, Muhammad ascended to heaven, accompanied by the angel Gabriel; and the Church of the Holy Sepulchre—the tomb in the middle of the city in the middle of the world. That omphalos: the center of the center of the center.

The Church of the Holy Sepulchre had only recently been erected under the orders of Emperor Constantine when, in A.D. 333, an anonymous pilgrim made his way from Bordeaux to Jerusalem and wrote the earliest extant record of a Holy City pilgrimage. Like the sites he traveled so far to see, this brief *Itinerarium* itself became a precious relic worth preserving, a record of the beginnings of the great age of faith. Copied out by monks, three manuscripts remain, one each from the eighth, ninth, and tenth centuries. Much later the manuscript was translated into English by Aubrey Stewart, Esq., for the Palestine Pilgrims' Text Society in Victorian England. In his *Itinerarium,* the unknown author merely notes the towns and cities he passes through, and the distances in leagues between them, on his overland route across what was then the vast Roman Empire. Even in Jerusalem he does little more than list the sacred sites he visited: the house of the high priest Caiaphas with its scourging column "against which Christ was beaten with rods"; the Mount of Olives, where Jesus taught the disciples and where he prayed; a vault in which Lazarus, raised by the Lord, was supposed to have been laid. Over the centuries more sites and their associated relics would emerge, miraculously, it seems. By the Middle Ages, Christian pilgrims to Judea could visit countless places associated with Jesus's birth and life and death and Resurrection: the field where the shepherds kept watch over their flocks; the manger, encased in white marble; the house of Simon the leper and of Lazarus and his sisters, Mary and Martha; the muddy waters of the Jordan; the place near Mount Zion where Jesus broke bread during the Last Supper; the Rock of Calvary; the Stone of Unction; the empty Tomb. Pilgrims appear to have required "some visible and tangible evidence of our Lord's Passion to confirm their faith," writes Stewart, without irony. "For such persons the necessary aids to faith were provided in gradually increasing numbers."

Because this was February and because there was snow on the ground and because my daughters did not share my fascination for replicas of ancient sacred shrines in the middle of what most people might agree is nowhere, my husband stayed with them and built snowmen and drank hot cocoa while I headed to the nearby Holy City of the Wichitas. The Holy City sits on land in the 59,000-acre Wichita Mountains Wildlife Refuge, which was itself set aside from the Kiowa-Comanche-Apache Indian Reservation and declared a national forest on July 4, 1901. The refuge shelters American bison, Rocky Mountain elk, Texas longhorn cattle, white-tailed deer, and a remnant of native prairie that escaped the plows of pioneers only because the ground beneath was too full of stones. Fort Sill was originally a frontier fort, established to protect the settlements of those same pioneers from Native tribes in the border states of Kansas and Texas. It was here, in June of 1875, that Quanah Parker and his Quahadi Comanche tribe surrendered, ending the Indian Wars on the southern Plains. And in 1894, Geronimo and more than three hundred other Chiricahua Apache were brought here as prisoners of war, eight years after having surrendered in Skeleton Canyon, in the Peloncillo Mountains of northern Arizona. At Fort Sill the Apaches were held in scattered villages, where they raised crops and cattle, adapting, because they had no other choice, to this new, sedentary existence. Geronimo would spend the last fifteen years of his life at Fort Sill, dying of pneumonia in 1909, still a prisoner of the United States. Three years before his death, he dictated his autobiography to Steven Melvil Barrett, superintendent of education in Lawton. In the final chapter, he makes a plaintive appeal that he and his remnant Apaches be allowed to return to the mountains surrounding the headwaters of the Gila River, in Arizona. "It is my land, my home, my fathers' land, to which I now ask to be allowed to return," Geronimo entreats. "I want to spend my last days there, and be buried among those mountains. If this could be I might die in peace, feeling that my people, placed in their native homes, would increase in numbers, rather than diminish as at present, and that our name would not become extinct." His cairn, surmounted by an eagle, lies in the Apache cemetery at Fort Sill.

The thing about the Holy City of the Wichitas is that, replica though it may be, it's strangely beautiful, laid out along a low rise of scraggy terrain, where jagged rocks erupt from the soil and grasses and stunted oaks and cypress claw through the spaces in between. Beyond, farther hills and abraded mountains. Nothing —except a few telephone poles and the road that brings you here —man-made. The Holy City itself consists of a quarter-mile swath of crenellated structures made of the same native red granite that juts from the earth. It is anchored on one end by a sturdy chapel with two square towers, and at the other end by three wooden crosses. In between: a temple, an arched gateway, courts, a stable, the tomb. The Christ of the Wichitas, a white marble statue, stands 23 feet, palms open at his sides on the road approaching the Holy City, near the entrance. Encased in the red granite base of the statue is a white rock from the Mount of Olives.

Though the surrounding topography does resemble pictures I've seen of the Judean Hills, the Holy City itself strikes me as the vision of what someone who has never been to ancient Jerusalem, which I have not, might imagine it to look like. To be fair, this recreation was built not to replicate in exact detail the real Jerusalem but rather to stage an Easter pageant—"The Longest-Running Outdoor Passion Play Drama in America," as the cover of the program likes to remind its audience. Against a backdrop of cedar and stone, the Holy City of the Wichitas is a place where the devout come to see the story of their Savior reenacted before them, as the devout have been doing since the Middle Ages, when passion plays first began to be performed. Back then, through the visual representation of scripture, a largely illiterate faithful could feel the palpable presence of God. Similarly, the Holy City today and the pageant that takes place there represent an attempt to give body to a symbolic landscape the way Christ, as viewed by Christians, became the Word made flesh. The place is aligned with those Judean sites and relics that the translator Aubrey Stewart noted—a visible and tangible aid to faith.

When I drove up that winter morning, the cast was practicing for the upcoming performance. Teenagers leaned against what appeared to be the walls of the temple. Children in puffy, brightly colored coats chased each other around. Middle-aged men carried ladders from building to building. Women in earmuffs bustled about. During a break in rehearsals, I was lucky enough to get a tour from Richard Matthys, a retired printer from Lawton and that year's pageant director, and to meet some of the devoted cast and crew.

Matthys wore crisply pressed blue jeans and a flannel shirt under a hunter's camouflage jacket. His hands were those of a man who had worked them hard for the seventy or more years he'd been using them. When he spoke to me, he looked more at my chin than into my eyes. He explained that the narrative of the Holy City Easter pageant is composed of scenes plucked from the four Gospels and arranged to tell the story of Christ. "We have the whole life, from birth to Resurrection," he told me, clearly proud. "In South Dakota," he continued, referring to the Black Hills passion play, "they only focus on the last seven days. And Mel Gibson, he just shows only right there at the end." We walked across the grounds of the Holy City and arrived at a low-lying stone structure with a timbered roof, one long side open to us so that we could see in—more like the plastic crèches in suburban front yards at Christmastime than an actual stable. Matthys explained that this was the stable where the Christ Child was born because there was no room in the inn. Inside there was a manger filled with hay, and hovering over the roof, on a pole, was a blue neon star.

"We do use a donkey and a live baby Jesus," Matthys told me. "We've never had to use a doll." In past productions there have also been live cows and sheep. A riding club from the nearby community of Meers provides horses for the Roman soldiers. The Lions Club in Elgin loans camels, perhaps descendants of the U.S. Camel Corps, imported from Smyrna in the mid-nineteenth century to help the army during surveying missions in the West. And Jesus rides into Jerusalem on an honest-to-goodness ass. "We try to make it as back to the natural as we can," Matthys emphasized. Sweeping his arm out over a small field just below the stable on the hillside, he pointed out where the shepherds and the Wise Men come. "We used to have a cable with a star attached that would light up," he said. "Someone would be walking with the cord in the dark and all you could see was the Wise Men following the star to the stable. But we had to give that up. You would always hear it squeak." They also had to give up the possibility, during the Resurrection scene, of lifting Jesus up into the clouds on a cable. The Department of the Interior, which manages the refuge, said no way.

But this insistence on authenticity was something a number of the cast members would reiterate to me that February day. Bob Burgher, who at seventy-two was the oldest cast member and who had begun participating in the pageant in 1946, recalled that one year the temperature was one degree below zero. Someone bought the cast flesh-colored long johns to wear during the performance. "They said no," Burgher told me. "They wanted to be authentic. That's the kind of dedication you get here. It gets in your blood." Burgher himself seemed to be a model of that dedication. As a young man in the service, he had once taken a three-day pass just to participate in the pageant. "I flew out of Korea. Took a hop to Tinker [the nearby air force base]. Got into costume. As soon as the Hallelujah chorus was over, I headed back to Tinker." Another year he had three heart attacks while on set. "One guy had to hold me up. But I wouldn't leave to go to the hospital. I wasn't about to louse it up."

Before this city was built, the Easter service took place on a mountaintop, beginning in 1926, as Florence Guild Bruce records in her 1940 local history, *He Is Risen: A History of the Wichita Mountains Easter Pageant.* In the predawn hours of Easter morning that first year, Reverend Anthony Mark Wallock, an Austrian immigrant and minister of the First Congregational Church of Lawton, led his flock to a mountainside just outside Medicine Park, near the bluff sacred to the Native people, where the Comanche medicine man had rent the stones. At the summit, verses of scripture were read, interspersed with songs accompanied by violin—"In the Garden," "The Old Rugged Cross," "Christ Arose." As the sun began to ascend, five women enacted a tableau of the Resurrection: the three Marys (Mary the mother of Jesus, Mary the mother of James and Joses, and Mary Magdalene) and two angels stood by a whitewashed spot on the rocks—the door of the tomb.

Wallock was born on April 25, 1890, in Schildberg, Austria, a small village south of Vienna. In an article on the 1941 pageant, the *Daily Oklahoman* pointed out, with perhaps an outsize sense of Wallock's realm of influence, that Hitler too had been born in Austria, in a town not far away, and only a year earlier, and that "in each was to swell a singleness of purpose to dominate his life—but the purposes were direct opposites." The hagiography of Wallock's life, recounted in Bruce's *He Is Risen* and reprinted year after year in pageant programs, records that Wallock's parents immigrated to the United States when he was only two. He grew up in Chicago, was reared a Catholic, and would often spend his days cutting out stage settings and biblical figures from cardboard boxes, perhaps laying the early foundation for the religious drama that came to define his life.

In the years that followed that first simple tableau on the mountainside above Medicine Park, the production became more and more elaborate. Wallock wrote a script, based on the Gospels, that alternated hymns and chapters of scripture. It remains largely intact to this day. Over time he added more tableaux to the repertoire: Jesus healing the lepers, Jesus praying in the garden, the march to Calvary. One year an organ was carried up the hillside. He had electric lights strung along the pathway, and, at intervals, small stone shrines installed with glass-encased pictures showing the last days in the life of Christ. The Knights Templar, a Masonic group that takes its name from a medieval monastic military order whose mandate it was to protect Christian pilgrims en route to the Holy Land, began forming an enormous human cross at the beginning of each year's service. Though the pageant now takes place on the Saturday evening before Easter, in the early years it began in the wee hours of Easter morning, ending three or more hours later, at sunrise, with the Resurrection.

Every Easter the cast and congregation grew. According to Bruce and to various newspaper accounts, already by 1928 the audience was 1,000 people strong and the cast was 45. In 1932, 150 congregants took part in nine tableaux; 15,000 people attended. And by 1934, just eight years after the pageant's first performance, the cast of 500 actors performed for a crowd of 40,000 from all over the Southwest. Word seems to have spread first through the local *Lawton Constitution,* then the *Daily Oklahoman,* out of Oklahoma City. In 1932 the American News Reel Company shot footage of the pageant and released it to theaters throughout the country. The Columbia Broadcasting System began airing the entire pageant over the radio, beginning in 1939. The following year Ernie Pyle, a Scripps Howard roving reporter, attended the performance and wrote, "In Lawton is a master showman. He wouldn't call himself a showman, and probably wouldn't even like being called one. But he is . . . His creation is an Easter morning pageant. There are hundreds of them over the world. But Lawton's seems to have risen above the others."

Searching for a suitable site to which the growing pageant could be moved, Wallock stood in the Wichita Mountains gazing down upon what appeared to be a large natural amphitheater of granite. In the stones he saw the shape of a cross formed by the sunlight. In *He Is Risen,* he recalled of that moment, "This was God's garden first. When we discovered it, we were inspired by the majestic granite walls of Mt Sheridan in the background. The only inhabitants were the deer and the birds. A lone eagle flew over our heads. Like the Greeks, we believed it must have been a divine benediction." And as with the Greeks and the medieval keepers of Jerusalem, for Wallock these mountains seem to have been another omphalos, a place where God speaks directly to men who listen.

In 1934 the U.S. Department of Agriculture issued a permit for the use of approximately 160 acres of land, part of what was then still called the Wichita National Forest, but which just one year later would become the Wichita Mountains Wildlife Refuge. President Franklin D. Roosevelt eventually approved a grant of $94,000 (a little less than $4 million in today's dollars) from the Works Progress Administration for public improvements, which in this case meant building "the Holy City," as it was referred to in the WPA files. Among other, smaller structures, the WPA constructed watchtowers, the gateway to Jerusalem, the temple, Pilate's judgment hall, Herod's court, the Lord's Supper building, the garden of Gethsemane, the tomb, Calvary's mount, and the crenellated World Chapel, with murals and wood carvings inside by Irene Malcolm, who is remembered by Ellenbrook in his *Outdoor and Trail Guide* as "the Michaelangelo of the Wichitas." In the midst of the Great Depression, publicity for the 1936 pageant, the tenth anniversary, was nationwide: announcements were made over radio stations across the country; feature stories and maps appeared in the *Boston Globe,* the *Washington Post,* the *New York Times.* According to the April 13 *Daily Oklahoman* from that year, some of the congregation of a hundred thousand lit fires to stay warm and camped in tents all over the hills surrounding the Holy City. Three years later the same paper would report of these crowds that they resembled "the march of the refugee Spanish Loyalists lugging blankets, cots, mattresses, baskets of food, and portable cookstoves; they were dressed in warm old clothes, many of the women with their heads swathed against the chill of the night." On that tenth anniversary, as dawn broke over the mountains and the pageant came to an end, Wallock read a telegram from President Roosevelt over the public address system:

EASTER GREETING *by Western Union*
KMY103 104 GOVT NL=THE WHITE HOUSE WASHINGTON DC
REV ANTHONY MARK WALLOCK=
    DIRECTOR EASTER PAGEANT
TO ALL OF SINCERE FAITH THE DAWN OF THIS EASTER DAY IN
THE WICHITA MOUNTAINS WILL BRING THE SAME MESSAGE OF
HOPE THAT THE ANGEL OF THE RESURRECTION BROUGHT TO
THE HOLY WOMEN AT THE TOMB OF THE MASTER IN THE HILLS
OF JUDA STOP THE MESSAGE OF THAT FIRST EASTER DAY CO-
LON QUOTE HE IS RISEN UNQUOTE HAS EVER SINCE SYMBOL-
IZED FAITH AND HOPE AND NEWNESS OF LIFE AND STILL HAS
POWER TO STRENGTHEN AND SUSTAIN STOP IN GRATITUDE FOR
ALL THE RICH GIFTS WHICH EASTER BRINGS I JOIN MY HUMBLE
PRAYERS TO THOSE OF MY COUNTRYMEN WHEREVER THEY ARE
GATHERED THIS MORNING=
    FRANKLIN D ROOSEVELT

Colonel Arthur C. Goebel, famed airplane stuntman and speed flyer, wrote *He Is Risen* with smoke letters across the sky.

*

"This is the boat where Jesus starts calling his first disciples, Peter, James, John, and Andrew. They were fishing here and Jesus said to them, 'Put away your nets and come follow me,'" Matthys was explaining as we stood in the cold light beneath an inconceivably blue sky. Wallock had originally envisioned a Sea of Galilee as part of the Holy City. A dry creek ran through the grounds of the Holy City, and Wallock tried to expand this creek and then pump water from a well with a windmill, but what with the hard-packed earth and the scorching Oklahoma summers, they could never, as Matthys told me, "resurrect the river." As for the boat, weathered gray, it now lay amid the winter grasses. On its starboard side, in hand-painted block letters, were the words S.S. HOLY CITY.

Both the grandiosity of Wallock's vision for the Holy City Easter pageant and his desire for authenticity link this contemporary passion play not only with those of the Middle Ages, but also with those of the Renaissance, that time of the flowering of modern theater. Some productions employed music and scenery and hundreds of actors in elaborate costumes. Often they lasted too long to be performed in one sitting. In some, the scene of the Crucifixion took as long as it would have in reality. Georges Bertrin, an early twentieth-century professor at the Paris Catholic Institute, notes that in the 1437 production in Metz, the curé who was playing Christ nearly died on the cross. During that same performance, another priest, playing the part of Judas, was left on the cross so long that he collapsed and had to be lowered down and carried away. Prefigurations of the Holy City's Bob Burgher.

In 1927, only the second year of Wallock's Easter tableaux, the *Lawton Constitution* dubbed the presentation an "Oklahoma 'Oberammergau,'" after perhaps the world's most famous passion play. For much of its history, Oberammergau had been merely an obscure village in a small valley in the Bavarian Alps. But in 1632 the plague arrived in southern Germany, brought there, Vernon Heaton surmises in *The Oberammergau Passion Play*, by the Thirty Years' War. Great swaths of Germany had been ravaged by the contending armies. Waves of refugees washed over the countryside, fleeing marauding bands of mercenaries, abandoning the injured, the sick, and the dead as they went. In the forsaken villages, looted and pillaged, the dead lay rotting in their beds or in the streets. Rivers and wells filled with the filth of the slaughter and became contaminated. Garbage decayed in the alleys. Vermin flourished in the fly-infested heaps of dung. The plague was born, Heaton argues, "from this pestiferous charnel house."

When news of the arrival of the plague in Bavaria reached Oberammergau in late September 1632, the town fathers, otherwise known as the Council of Six and Twelve, closed off the city gates to anyone entering or leaving. This included Kaspar Schisler, a day laborer who had been working that summer beyond the walls of the village, at nearby Eschenlohe, and who found himself banned upon his return. He retreated to the mountains, surviving as best he could for a time, but one night he managed to evade the watchmen and sneak back inside, reuniting with his family. Three days later he died of the plague. Disease then swept through the entire village, killing more than eighty souls, half of the village's population at the time, as Heaton estimates.

Eventually, in a strange sort of wager with the Almighty, every living member, sick and well, met in the parish church and, again under the Council of Six and Twelve, made a solemn vow to God that they and their descendants would enact a passion play every tenth year, forever, in return for his intercession in eradicating the plague from their midst. Though the plague continued to decimate the countryside around them, not another citizen of Oberammergau died of the plague from that hour on.

Or so the legend goes. And the production continues to this day. In a vow ceremony every tenth September before the spring play, the villagers repeat this story to themselves and then formally renew their pledge to each other and to God. Origin stories too can be omphali, connecting what is made with what engendered it.

But this story derives from an old handwritten chronicle which was not set down until 1733, a century after the events it records, and there are problems with it. As the Shakespeare scholar and theater historian James Shapiro observes in *Oberammergau: The Troubling Story of the World's Most Famous Passion Play*, the death rate in Oberammergau rose steadily from October 1632 (when there was one recorded death) to March 1633 (twenty deaths), before declining steadily back to normal by July (one death again). However, as Shapiro acknowledges, if the parish priest, who enters the deaths into the ledgers himself, dies and is not immediately replaced, as was the case in Oberammergau, these records can be frustratingly incomplete. Still, the records show no abrupt end to the dying. Further, Kaspar Schisler's name doesn't appear in Oberammergau's death register from the time, though it does in a commemorative album bound together with it.

Regardless, the story the villagers have told themselves over the centuries is that the deaths stopped immediately after the vow. The townspeople's original devotional exercise has evolved into a massive production of more than two thousand volunteers and hundreds of thousands of spectators. Only residents of Oberammergau, and only those of impeccable character, have been eligible for parts. Here too authenticity is prized. In the past, Shapiro points out, young women delayed marriage for years on the off chance that they might be given the role of Mary or Magdalene. In 1990, with strictures loosening somewhat, a wife and mother of two played the Virgin Mary, but one angry theatergoer complained to the directors that "a woman who had sex at night had no business playing the mother of God by day." In addition to virginal authenticity, no wigs or false beards are permitted. Many of the men must begin growing their hair and their beards one year before the play. No makeup is used. Many of the participants spend their lifetimes on the village stage, starting as child actors and progressing over the decades to leading roles.

As Matthys and I were walking the grounds of the Holy City, we ran into Anita Brockwell, a wholesomely pretty middle-aged woman with a blond bob, who in her daily life raises pygmy goats and miniature donkeys and sells ceramic figurines, and is both director of wardrobe and the Virgin Mary for the pageant. She attaches a good-natured little laugh to the end of nearly every sentence, and she offered to show me the Angel House—which, on pageant night, doubles as the place of the temptation of Christ—where the angels' wings and gowns are sewn and stored. "This is the hierarchy of angels," she said by way of introducing the five or six mothers and daughters, all outfitted with gloves and earmuffs, who were inventorying the wings inside this unheated structure. "I call it typecasting, myself," joked one of the women. "Hells Angels," added another. Some of the old sets of wings are elaborately embellished with interleaved layers of white feathers. The newer ones have fence-wire frames covered with parachute fabric that has been cut into shreds. "To be an angel it's hard," said one woman of Comanche descent. The wings are heavy. The wind at the top of the hillside where the women must appear is stiff. "To be an angel, you have to be tough."

Matthys and I wandered over to Pilate's court and climbed onto a parapet between two towers. "Now this is where Jesus is brought before Pilate," he told me as we looked out over the rugged hills beyond, and to the grassy prairie and the buffalo. "The crowd is down below and some are saying 'Crucify him!' and one or two are saying 'Save him!'" We walked along the parapet as Matthys described how Pilate washes his hands and throws the cloth down to the crowd and says, "His blood shall be on you," freeing Barabbas instead of Jesus.

The implication is deicide: the Jews killed Jesus. A number of historians, however, including Marvin Perry and Frederick M. Schweitzer in *Anti-Semitism: Myth and Hate from Antiquity to the Present,* call into question the historicity of particular details of the Gospels' story of the passion of Christ. For one thing, they claim, in the Roman-ruled province of Judea, the notion of a frenzied Jewish mob holding sway over a prefect from Rome is improbable. For another, the act of Pilate's washing his hands of the blood of an innocent man is "a Jewish gesture and symbolic act," stemming from the Book of Deuteronomy, not a Roman one. And how would Pilate have rationalized the release of any prisoner to Emperor Tiberius? The story of the passion, they argue, is not history. It is kerygma—preaching.

As such, passion plays regularly sparked violence against Jews because of the accusation of murder inherent in this scene and others. Jewish characters often were costumed in outlandish hats with horns. They appeared bloodthirsty, allied with the devil, that other denier of God. In *The History of Anti-Semitism,* Léon Poliakov gives an example of one particularly gruesome scene from a late fifteenth-century passion play by Jehan Michel, bishop of Angers, where the Jews in Pilate's palace torture Christ:

> BRUYANT: Let us play at pulling out his beard
>   That is too long anyway.
> DENTART: He will be the bravest
>   Who gets the biggest handful.
> GRIFFON: I have torn at him so hard
>   That the flesh has come away too.

DILLART: I would take my turn at tearing
So as to have my share as well.
DRAGON: See what a clump this is
That I pull away as if it were lard.

"In a total identification," Poliakov writes of this scene and others like it, "the crowds lived Christ's agony intensely, transferring
all their rage to his tormentors, with a real massacre often following the depicted one." The carnage was acute enough to re-
quire the attention of the city governments. In 1338, for example,
Freiburg forbade the performance of anti-Jewish scenes. In 1469,
Frankfurt ordered special measures for the protection of the Jewish quarter during their passion play. And in 1539, Rome banned
its passion play altogether in an effort to prevent the sacking of the
Jewish ghetto there.

Hitler famously attended the passion play at Oberammergau
in 1934, during the jubilee season marking the three-hundred-
year anniversary of the original vow. After the performance, he
was given a gift from the villagers, a set of mounted photographs
of the play that was inscribed *To our Führer, the protector of the cultural treasures of Germany, from the Passion village of Oberammergau.*
Years after viewing the performance, at a dinner on July 5, 1942,
Hitler is recorded by Shapiro as having said, "It is vital that the
Passion Play be continued at Oberammergau; for never has the
menace of Jewry been so convincingly portrayed as in this presentation of what happened in the time of the Romans." In a perverse
and self-serving interpretation of scripture, he added: "There one
sees Pontius Pilate, a Roman racially and intellectually so superior
that he stands out like a firm, clean rock in the middle of the
whole muck and mire of Jewry." As Shapiro also notes, a significant number of the Oberammergau cast members had joined the
Nazi Party. Jesus was a Nazi, as were eight of the twelve disciples.
So was the Virgin Mary. Somewhat ironically, according to the Nazi
Party enrollment records only Judas was categorized as a "strong
anti-Nazi."

"In each was to swell a singleness of purpose to dominate his
life—but the purposes were direct opposites," the newspaper had
said of Anthony Mark Wallock and Adolf Hitler. From the beginning Wallock did insist that the Holy City Easter service be open to

all races and all creeds—especially remarkable given that this was Oklahoma in the era of Jim Crow. When the cast of the Oberammergau passion play was busy joining the Nazi Party and handing souvenir plaques to Hitler, Wallock was dedicating the theme of the 1936 service to the "Brotherhood of Men and Peace." His final tableau that year, the April 5 issue of the *Daily Oklahoman* reported, would be shrines of worship for the various races: a pagoda for the Chinese, a Japanese Shinto shrine, tepees for the American Indian. "Negroes and the brown race" would also have their place in the scene, though their shrines of worship were not specified. Behind these representative figures: lights which would represent the rising sun. At a signal, the groups representing the five races would move into formation, marching in a single column toward the light, followed by the rest of the cast, "while the glare of the artificial sun flashe[d] into the eyes of spectators."

Still, one wonders what to do with a passage from the exact same article proudly crediting Ron Stephens, district WPA director from Chickasha and a former army engineer, with "seeking out Ku Klux Klan members, who resurrected four hundred abandoned robes to be used by members of the cast in the Easter Service." While Brockwell reminded me that Indians have roles in the pageant—I had met the Comanche angel—and that the Lord's Prayer is performed in sign language at the opening of the play, she also felt it necessary to protest some accusation of prejudice against African-Americans of which, until then, I had not been aware. "We're not prejudiced," she told me. "We've had a colored baby Jesus. But you can't put them in a costume because they disappear in the dark. Philip Muse," she went on, mentioning one of the few participating black actors, "was put in as an angel. You could see this white suit with angel wings floating down the pathway, but no head. He's a disciple now."

Whether or not there is prejudice at work in the Holy City Easter pageant, the fact remains that while this place and this play once expressed a deeply sensed and widely shared worldview, each year it draws fewer and fewer participants and observers. All through World War II, attendance for the pageant still neared a hundred thousand. The Easter after the war ended, in 1946, the audience actually neared two hundred thousand, according to the *Daily Oklahoman* and the *Lawton Constitution*.

The Lawton Story, a movie version of the pageant, was even produced by Kroger Babb, the godfather of exploitation film, a genre which was, according to Felicia Feaster and Bret Wood in *Forbidden Fruit: The Golden Age of the Exploitation Film,* "a bizarre mixture of . . . saccharine morality tales interrupted by moments of raw, ugly truth." Babb's 1944 film, *Mom and Dad,* for example, follows the story of a young woman charmed into sex by a dashing pilot. After the pilot dies in a plane crash, she finds herself unexpectedly pregnant. *The Story of a Birth,* a movie within the movie of *Mom and Dad,* then presents detailed drawings of the female reproductive system followed by a graphic documentary of a woman giving birth, first vaginally, then by cesarean section. Given Babb's background with *Mom and Dad,* perhaps it's not so strange that he would produce *The Lawton Story,* which contains its own embedded nativity scene. The film premiered on Friday, April 1, 1949, in Lawton. President Harry Truman and his wife, Bess, were invited, though they did not attend. *The Lawton Story,* later recut and retitled *The Prince of Peace* after a dismal critical reception, is about a six-year-old girl, played by the relentlessly cheerful Ginger Prince, who persuades her great-uncle, a heartless banker, to see the performance of the Holy City passion play, after which, of course, he changes his greedy and iniquitous ways. Inside this frame story is lengthy footage from a daytime reenactment of the actual Holy City pageant.

The Lawton Story may have been the high point. In the 1950s the Holy City Easter pageant began to see a slow but steady decline. Now, in a good year, the audience might number a couple of thousand. The cast has also shrunk—to two hundred or so, "including animals," Anita Brockwell said. Brockwell, Burgher, Matthys—they have all mourned this falling-off, as well as the waning participation in the passion play. They blame television and other creature comforts, soccer games and T-ball practice and ballet, the laziness and greed of youth. As the older generation dies, the young people are not coming up to replace them. "It's the trend of the whole world—the change in times," Matthys told me. "I'd like to see that hillside covered again. But it'll never be."

In 1882 the Wichita Indians were removed from their village on the north fork of the Red River to a reservation 25 miles east of Fort Sill. From there the Wichita Mountains were just barely in sight. In 1900 reservation lands that had been held in common during the intervening eighteen years were divided into allot-

ments of 160 acres per person, with the remainder declared "sur-
plus lands" and opened up to non-Indian settlement. The Wichita
elders knew the end was approaching because their ancient stories
foretold the time of Dakawaitsakakide, "When Everything Begins
to Run Out." They knew that the things which they had needed
and which had been given to them in dreams would disappear.
That children of the same families would intermarry and cease
to have offspring, or that they would birth not human children
but animals. Then the animals, even the flowing water, would begin to speak to men. The morning star and the moon would be
human again, and the man who had been chasing the deer he'd
shot, an act that had set the universe in motion, would finally over-
take it and recover his arrow. "Furthering this belief [in the coming end]," writes George Dorsey, who recorded the stories of the
Wichita in 1904, "is the frequency with which the people in their
dreams converse with stars."

Medicine Bluff for the Plains Indians, the Holy City of the Wichitas for generations of Lawtonians, the Holy City of Jerusalem for
Christians and Muslims and Jews—why do we need these omphali,
visible and tangible manifestations of the longed-for and imagined? Is it because, as all the old mythologies say in one way or
another, we've been split umbilically from the divine? The cord's
been cut, we've been cast out from our native land, and we yearn
to reclaim that place where we can be connected again, however
briefly, to what we no longer possess. We're all exiles, longing for
home.

In Genesis, which begins the Bible, we have what scholars believe are some of the oldest references to the place that became
the actual Jerusalem; Revelation, and thus the Bible, ends with
John's inspired and imaginative vision of the otherworldly New
Jerusalem, to which those who believe will one day return. "And
I saw a new heaven and a new earth: for the first heaven and the
first earth were passed away; and there was no more sea," begins
chapter 21. "And I John saw the holy city, new Jerusalem, coming down from God out of heaven, prepared as a bride adorned
for her husband." Then, from "a great and high mountain," an
angel shows John this New Jerusalem of precious stones—jasper,
sapphire, emerald, topaz, amethyst. The streets are gold, the gates
are pearl, the river of the water of life clear as crystal. Growing in
the center, the tree of life, laden with fruit.

Saint Augustine saw human existence as a kind of exile from the divine, and the journey of the soul as a pilgrimage to God. In *On Christian Doctrine,* he describes a world permeated with signs which we must learn to read so that we can use them to reach God, who is our home. "Thus in this mortal life, wandering from God," he declares, "if we wish to return to our native country where we can be blessed, we should use this world and not enjoy it, so that the 'invisible things' of God 'being understood by the things that are made' may be seen, that is, so that by means of corporal and temporal things we may comprehend the eternal and spiritual." That last bit—*so that by means of corporal and temporal things we may comprehend the eternal and spiritual*—is what Jerusalem, both the real one, with its Calvary Mount and Stone of Unction and empty tomb, and the Holy City of the Wichitas, with its earnest facsimiles, tries to give those who come, seeking their spiritual homeland: a passing connection, through the things that are made, with the divine.

That April I convinced Terry to leave the girls with their grandparents and drive back up to Oklahoma so we could witness for ourselves the country's longest continuously run outdoor passion play. We arrived in Lawton late in the afternoon on Saturday and checked into the Best Western near the Comanche Nation Casino and Smoke Shop along the highway, then drove out to the Holy City. The sky was overcast and a cold, damp wind had begun to blow. In the refuge, low-lying wildflowers were starting to show though the russet winter grasses. Above us, hawks circled as if on pendulum strings.

When we arrived at the Holy City, the Christ of the Wichitas welcomed us with his open arms and the Gloryland Band was singing old-time gospel music out of a shiny blue trailer in the parking lot. Terry and I wandered into the gift shop—run by the nonprofit Wallock Foundation—to get presents for the girls in order to assuage our guilt over leaving them. Inside, we found Holy City spoons and thimbles and embroidered patches; Indian dream-catchers; snow globes with Native warriors on horseback; granite chips from the Holy City in small glass vials; bookmarks with cheerful, upbeat religious messages on them: *Prayer is a deposit in heaven,* read one. *Even on the darkest day, His light shines through to show the way,* read another.

Outside, the wind had picked up and there was a light mist. Silhouettes of cypress trees rose up against the gray sky. Behind the gift shop, concealed from view, were the riding club's trailers. Horses stood outside them, their red Roman blankets trimmed in gold and thrown casually over their backs like dressing gowns. The disciples of Jesus flirted with the girls of Jerusalem. Angels in white robes and wings walked among us along the stony ground.

I confess that we spent nearly the entire pageant inside our station wagon, drinking coffee and eating peanut M&Ms, trying to keep warm. The temperature had dropped into the low forties after the sun went down, and the wind across the open valley was piercing. We'd brought along a quilt, which we awkwardly wrapped around ourselves. Terry fell asleep. From time to time I would leave the car and nestle myself into the red stones, trying to find a spot protected from the wind where I could watch the pageant. From the loudspeaker across the hills, the disembodied voices of the narrators carried the story, and the actors gesticulated to the words while floodlights illuminated one scene after another and then went dark. It was all just as Richard Matthys had told me it would be—the blue neon star over the stable, the Magi leading the camels, Mary and Joseph and the real baby Jesus, who had come, as all infants do, to save the world. "Glory to God in the highest," the narrator with the voice of the Lord reminded the shepherds, and the choir sang "Angels We Have Heard on High" as the hills lit up the angels of the Wichitas, who had been lodging unseen in the rocks all along but now were visible to everyone, for there is nothing covered that shall not one day be revealed. There were the miracles too—the wedding at Cana, the cripple healed— which told us that if we asked, we would receive, and if we sought, we would find. There was the woman saved from stoning. Later, when Jesus made his triumphal entry into Jerusalem and upset the tables of the money changers, the high priest, perhaps sensing some new dispensation, proclaimed that this man from Nazareth had simply gone too far. Then Judas betrayed the Lord for thirty pieces of silver, and Pilate washed his hands of the whole affair. On the rooftop of the temple that would soon be destroyed, all except for the Western Wall, the risen Jesus appeared to poor doubting Thomas. "Blessed are those," the narrator intoned, "who haven't seen and who believe."

*

Just before the pageant had begun, while Terry was getting hot dogs for us at the concession stand, I'd gone into the Holy City's World Chapel. Here, beginning in 1940, Irene Malcolm, a local portrait artist and WPA muralist, spent nearly a decade of her life, unpaid, creating ceiling and wall murals and carving the wooden pews. In "The Impish Angel of the Wichitas," a 1952 article from the *Daily Oklahoman*, Malcolm is called a disciple of Reverend Wallock, and her work "an embodiment of the dreams he bared to her."

But this work seems utterly her own. In the vestibule, the walls are covered with tiles she shaped and fired from native clay, their green glaze the color of cedar needles. Sculpted into those tiles, which number nearly four thousand, is the Prayer of Saint Francis of Assisi. "Lord, make me an instrument of Thy Peace," it begins. "There is so much selfishness," Malcolm explained to the reporter. "I was searching for something to combat it and found this." Inside the chapel proper, a mural of Gabriel blowing a trumpet covers the entire ceiling. Behind the lectern, two other angels hold a painted scroll of the Lord's Prayer. Old iron sconces line the white plaster walls. Between them hang portraits of the disciples, also done by Malcolm. Even Judas Iscariot is here. "I painted Judas as a weak character, not as a wicked one," Malcolm told the *Daily Oklahoman*, a little subversively. "Judas was almost as bad as the rest of us."

I decided that my favorite works of Malcolm's were the two murals on either side of the pulpit: the Crucifixion scene and the Resurrection. The Wichita Mountains supply the background for both paintings. In the foreground of each, there is no Christ on the cross, no Savior dressed in white. Instead you see only the feet of Jesus: in the one, they are bloodied, the nail driven through; in the other, they are free of wounds, lifting into the air. Around his feet the faithful stare wide-eyed, unbelieving. Dashing past the Crucifixion is Malcolm's white dog, Emily, seemingly chasing some creature that has caught her attention, not at all aware of the man who happens to be nailed to the cross. She's completely missed the sign. In that newspaper article, Malcolm, seated for a photo on the top steps of a ladder near Gabriel, in the fleecy clouds, said, "Up here in Heaven, it's not as nice a place as they said it was."

Malcolm on the ladder, looking down upon her earthly homeland, recalls the Wichita myth of "the Woman Who Married a

Star," which George Dorsey recorded more than a century ago, as the Native people of the region began more and more in their dreams to converse with the stars, and the world of the Wichitas seemed to be coming to an end. A woman was watching the night sky, the story goes. She imagined that the stars might once have been people, dim stars the old ones, bright stars the young. There was an especially brilliant star that she was sure must have been a fine-looking young man and she wished to have him for her husband. That night she dreamed she was with the man who had been a star, and when she woke, she was sitting by a fire with an old man. She had been mistaken. He was the star she had seen from the earth and he claimed her for his wife. Time passed. There was a large rock which the man forbade her to move. But one day she disobeyed, and when she moved the rock, she could see the earth down below, through the chasm. Longing for her home, she made a rope of soapweed bunches braided together and climbed down to her native country, the land that had borne her.

When we'd come here with our daughters, in February, before the long drive back home to Houston we'd taken them out to the refuge to show them the buffalo and the place we used to hike when Terry was stationed at Fort Sill. Back then we would often head to an area called Charon Gardens, which the guidebook describes as "an untamed garden of Eden, a pristine, primeval wilderness." There, massive oval boulders of red granite balance precariously on ridges, and a sheer cliff drops down to a pool of deep water. But that wintry day we stood with our daughters at the edge of the precipice and looked out upon everything from a great and high mountain and beheld that it was very good. Above us was blue sky. Below, the cold dark water. Like angels, we hovered somewhere in between.

DIMITER KENAROV

Memento Mori

I

I WAS FIVE when my grandmother Parashkeva first took me to a funeral. She was the mayor of a small village in northern Bulgaria, and one of her responsibilities was to read eulogies for her dead constituents. Priests were no longer welcome back then, with their mumbling promises of a better world (what could be better than life in the People's Republic of Bulgaria?), so my grandmother became a secular priestess of sorts, a female Pericles. She married people and she buried them.

I remember my first body, laid out in a simple casket propped on two chairs in the garden of the dead man's house. Dressed in a black suit, he had a burning taper stuck in his lap, wax dripping onto his hands. It was a hot summer, the ripe tomatoes in the vegetable patch glowing bright as embers. A few black-veiled women wailed softly by the coffin, one of them swatting the gathering flies with the loose ends of her headscarf. I was standing at the head of the attending crowd, holding on to my grandmother, mesmerized, while she read out the eulogy she had written earlier that day on stationery paper. Her voice was clear in the heat, formal and martial, the voice of a schoolmarm tackling a patriotic poem. The wailing grew louder as she praised the dead man, his useful life as a mechanic, his good standing in the Communist Party.

An open trailer draped in black hitched to a red farm tractor pulled up next to the house. In one smooth motion the pallbearers shouldered the casket and loaded it onto the flatbed, then

helped the veiled women climb up. At an invisible signal, the
tractor revved its engine, shot up a plume of exhaust, and jerked
forward. Staggering, three gypsy brass players took up a drunken
version of Chopin's funeral march with the mourners following on
foot behind them. At every bump in the road, the tractor-trailer
jolted and shook out forgotten grains of wheat onto the cracked
blacktop.

II

My first dead man has been resting in the soft, fertile loam of
northern Bulgaria for almost twenty-five years now, but each time
I go back to my grandmother's village, his face is still there, on the
front door of his former house, on the fragrant lindens, on the
old telegraph poles, staring at me from the windows of the general
store and the shuttered bakery. He is clean-shaven and officious,
youthful-looking, his eyes ruefully fixed upon some invisible object in the distance.

This is not a gothic tale. There is nothing particularly ghostlike
about those sheets of A4-size paper with a passport-size photo of
the deceased—the fluttering, flimsy miniature tombstones are just
necrologues.

III

Necrologues are street obituaries that announce or commemo-
rate the passing of a member of the local community. MOURN-
FUL NEWS, the black header says, or FAREWELL, or SORROWFUL
REMEMBRANCE. The loose leaves quickly yellow in the sun and
molder in the rain—but their sheer numbers safeguard their existence. Among posters for the upcoming concerts of Madonna and
Elton John, among homemade ads offering English-language lessons and weight-loss recipes, peek out thousands of lusterless eyes.
Some municipalities have tried to contain the spread of necrologues by allotting special bulletin boards for that purpose, but
all efforts to sanitize and discipline urban spaces have come to
naught. The eternal border between the upper world and the underworld, the city and the cemetery, has disappeared in Bulgaria.

No one is truly dead without a necrologue, and yet necrologues are meant to keep the dead alive. As long as the photographic image of the deceased lasts, as long as passersby are willing to stop to look at that face and read the name, death has no dominion. "The life of the dead is placed in the memory of the living," Cicero once told the Roman senators, when trying to convince them to erect a bronze statue in honor of his late friend Servius Sulpicius Rufus. Memory has always been death's most dangerous adversary.

IV

Monastic institutions and churches recorded the names of their illustrious dead (kings, abbots, benefactors) in special registers called necrologies. On certain days of the year, these death rolls would be read out loud during service as both commemoration and prayer, for the road to salvation lay through the gates of memory. A soul could be easily lost if her name was forgotten.

Necrologues and obituaries trace their roots to that tradition. By the mid-nineteenth century many European and American newspapers had sections dedicated to the dead. Some were simple death notices, marking the date and circumstances of the passing, while others were elaborate biographical portraits of luminaries and celebrities, like the famous eulogy Emerson wrote for Thoreau in 1862: "His soul was made for the noblest society; he had in a short life exhausted the capabilities of this world; wherever there is knowledge, wherever there is virtue, wherever there is beauty, he will find a home."

It was around that time, with the ever-growing power and availability of printing technologies such as the steam-powered press (invented in 1814) and the rotary printing press (1843), that death burst through the bounds of newspapers and spilled out into the streets and squares. Few people today are aware that in the second half of the nineteenth century there were street obituaries in Paris and Vienna, London and Rome. Necrologues were hip; to die a modern death one had to have a necrologue. As late as 1957, the town of Santa Maria, California, was trying to deal with the proliferation of funeral notices in public places. Following the contemporary trend to censor morbid images, local officials finally outlawed the practice.

Today necrologues still survive in some Balkan countries, and Italy and Israel have their local versions as well, but only in Bulgaria
do the dead outnumber the living. Necrologues were, ironically, a
fashionable borrowing from Western Europe, a way for Bulgarians
—liberated in 1878 from the clutch of the dying Ottoman Empire
—to announce to the world their birth as a modern nation. There,
necrologues thrived.

V

In 1897, Hariton Ignatiev published *A Detailed Epistle,* in which he
prescribed a structure for necrologues. They should include, he
wrote,

> the names of all close relatives of the deceased, even the youngest
> ones;
> All distant blood relatives, as well as information pertaining to
> their children;
> Their names, nicknames, and the nature of their relation to the
> deceased;
> What kind of illness—prolonged or swift, severe or painless—
> was the cause of death;
> What was the age of the deceased;
> The day and hour of death;
> The day and hour the body will be taken out of the house;
> The church where the service will be held;
> If the deceased is not well-known, his/her house and street number.

The death notice, which Ignatiev also called "a funeral invita-
tion," was to be printed on a sheet of paper with black borders, a
Christian cross, or an allegory of death on top. He also advised the
use of cheaper paper when the deceased was an older person, and
glossier varieties for the youngest.

VI

When the Communists took over the Bulgarian government in
September 1944, they banned newspaper obituaries, deeming
them too morbid and backward for the brave new world they
planned to build. Unable to get rid of the sting of death entirely,

at least not at that socioeconomic stage of development, they did allow street necrologues to survive. For weren't they like the holy icons of the proletariat, every dead worker a pedestrian saint in disguise?

In 1949 the Bulgarian navy published a rather elaborate necrologue on the death of Georgi Dimitrov, the first Communist leader of Bulgaria, whose embalmed body lay for the next forty-one years in a glass coffin in a mausoleum in downtown Sofia.

> With a heavy heart, the officers of the Bulgarian Navy learned of the sad news affecting our whole nation and all progressive humanity: the death of our beloved teacher and leader GEORGI DIMITROV.
>
> In these decisive times, when our nation is straining every sinew to build Socialism in our country, we painfully feel the loss of the one, who led, inspired, and instructed us in the struggle for peace, democracy, and socialism.
>
> We don't despair in this cheerless moment, but like a granite rock we stand steadfast behind our favorite Central Committee of the Bulgarian Communist Party, the defender and heir to the work for which our eminent DIMITROV fought and toiled.
>
> We PLEDGE and stand under the OBLIGATION to do everything possible to strengthen the solidarity of our combat units, learning from the rich inheritance DIMITROV left to us—his living example and work.
>
> We promise to raise to the highest level our combat and moral-political readiness; we won't spare our strength and life to make DIMITROV's work a part of life.
>
> We will work relentlessly and tirelessly to learn from the rich experience of the MIGHTY SOVIET UNION—our defender and teacher, under the wise leadership of the mighty STALIN.
>
> We promise to preserve the eternal friendship between our people and the other democratic peoples, led by the mighty and majestic Soviet Union, the way comrade Dimitrov instructed us.
>
> We promise to guard like the pupils of our eyes our maritime border for the successful building of socialism in our beloved Motherland.
>
> DIMITROV DIED, BUT HIS WORK WILL LIVE FOREVER!

VII

By the end of the 1950s, with the growing availability of photography, the streets began filling with ever-greater numbers of

necrologues. Left with no other meaningful funeral rites, Bulgarians enthusiastically embraced them as the only available prayer
for the dead. The bereaved now added commemorative notices
to honor family and comrades who had passed away three and six
months ago, one and two and three and five and ten years ago. Often there were separate necrologues from family, coworkers, and
institutions.

Of course, the genre required a few political modifications. The
cross at the top of the page was replaced with the Communist star,
or, if the deceased happened not to be a member of the Communist Party, the space was left blank. Second, the textual template
needed to reflect the new atheistic values. Death became a manifesto, gushing about the merits of the laborer and the inconsolable pain resulting from the loss of productivity. "Today one workplace was left unoccupied," said one necrologue from that era.

History returned the joke in kind. After the Communist government passed away, on November 10, 1989, someone pasted the
following necrologue in downtown Sofia:

> A full three months have now passed since we parted with our be-
> loved Bulgarian Communist Party. We lost forever our dear mother,
> sister, and relative. We lost all purpose and the meaning of our lives,
> our bright future. Only the memory of the beautiful past remains:
> the red-colored memory of our dreams and hopes. Dear Party, our
> grief is great and inconsolable. Time is unable to heal this sorrow-
> ful separation. The memory of you, oh, dear Party, will rest in our
> hearts forever.

VIII

Without its photograph, a necrologue would be just an epitaph,
writing on the wall. It is the photograph of the face—there, but
not there—that captures the ghost of death in all of its peculiar
pathos. In a sense, all photographs are necrologues by default,
elegies to that which has already passed; the necrologue simply
exposes the essence of the photograph. "All photographs are me-
mento mori," writes Susan Sontag in her book *On Photography*. "To
take a photograph is to participate in another person's (or thing's)
mortality, vulnerability, mutability." And Roland Barthes, in his
very personal *Camera Lucida*, makes a similar observation. "Death,"

he says, "is the *eidos* of the photograph." He goes on to discuss the photo of a young man, Lewis Payne, who was condemned to die in 1865 for his attempt to assassinate the United States secretary of state William H. Seward and for the assassination conspiracy against Abraham Lincoln. Handsome and handcuffed, Payne is looking boldly into the camera, as if challenging time itself. "He is dead," Barthes writes in the caption, "and he is going to die."

IX

The textual framework of necrologues has always been a source of literary mystery for me. It is not uncommon to see two adjacent necrologues replicate the exact same content: just a few formulaic lines of verse or prose about love, sorrow, and memory.

> You left but didn't say "good-bye,"
> You started on the road alone,
> You left the pain alone to us
> And all the words you didn't say.

Or

> Where are you?
> Did you drown into the swell of the sea,
> Or did time engulf you in its folds
> Or did the wind sweep you away?
> But how should I believe you're there
> When you're in my heart?

Or

> Nobody really dies
> Until the living
> Love and remember.

But who writes these poems? Is there some great elegist, a Balkan Tennyson, churning out in-memoriam stanzas in his creaky attic? Funeral homes keep thick catalogs full of poetic kitsch for their clients' convenience, from which one could choose the rhyme that fits one's grief. I visited a couple of them by Sofia's Central Cemetery to look for answers, but nobody could tell me anything specific. "We just photocopied the catalog from our colleagues, and they photocopied it in turn from their colleagues" was the most frequent response I got. The original source, like that of a medieval manuscript, seemed to have been lost somewhere back in time immemorial.

X

In her article "The Fabric of Pain," the Bulgarian sociologist Emiliya Karaboeva came up with a set of statistics for the most commonly used words in necrologues:

Words expressing suffering occur in 39.56 percent: pain (12.82 percent), sorrow (9.34 percent), anguish (8.91 percent), grief (8.47 percent).

Words expressing loss are in 26.73 percent: want (10.21 percent), loss (5.21 percent), parting (2.39 percent), emptiness (1.73 percent), desolation (1.30 percent), deserted (0.21 percent), and expressions such as "She/He left us" (2.82 percent), "She/He is gone" (1.73 percent), "You are not here" (1.08 percent).

Words expressing love are in 35.43 percent.

Words expressing remembrance/respect are in 25.43 percent.

Karaboeva concludes: "The key words are love, pain, and sorrow, but the most important one is love."

XI

The English anthropologist Geoffrey Gorer published a seminal essay in 1955 called "The Pornography of Death," in which he claimed that twentieth-century Western societies have come to repress death in the exact manner that Victorians used to repress sexuality. It is a familiar argument today: the death taboo. An optimistic belief in progress and medical science has made us increasingly unwilling to face our mortality. Surrounded by technologies whose hourly upgrades seem to extend existence in perpetuity, we have forgotten that our own bodies cannot be loaded with 2.0 versions of life. The capitalist state, seeking to secure the obedience and productivity of its laborers and to guarantee the circulation of commodities, has sought to erase death from social memory.

Necrologues counteract these modern forces. There is something very primitive, almost masochistic, in such open displays of mortality, where private grief is shared by the whole community. Death is not only bared to the public eye; its image is continually reproduced, multiplied ad infinitum, like an Andy Warhol print. But this exhibition is not about celebrities anymore, not about Mao or Marilyn, but about the common folk, the masses. The dead do not disappear; on the contrary, they reappear simultaneously in all the places they used to frequent in life: the home, the local street, the marketplace, the workplace. The regular "Ivan," a government clerk who spent seventy-eight years in total obscurity, suddenly has his name and picture pasted all over town. He is omnipresent, like a god, a minor pop star wearing his Sunday best. Death in Bulgaria is the most powerful publicity machine.

But being famous is not the same as being important. Using textual and visual templates, necrologues publicize death on a grand scale, but they also erase individual auras. Unlike the biographical obituary, with its inherent belief in personal identity, all necrologues look essentially the same. The sad faces blend into each other like the tapestry of victims of some vicious dictatorship —the Bulgarian *desaparecidos*—or the casualties of a colossal, endless terrorist attack, a 24/7 9/11.

XII

Why must death be so memorable, so perfectly photogenic? What is the meaning of remembering so much pain? Freud was right: we need to decathect from the lost love object, or we run the risk of falling into melancholia, a state of "pathological grieving." The museum of modern memory needs some blank walls and empty spaces. Maybe the time has come for death to go paperless.

PICO IYER

Maximum India

FROM *Condé Nast Traveler*

THERE WERE FIRES, six, seven of them, rising through the winter fog. Groups of men, scarves wrapped around their heads, eyes blazing in the twilight, were gathered barefoot around the flames, edging closer. A near-naked man with dusty, matted dreadlocks down to his waist was poking at a charred head with a bamboo pole. There was chanting in the distance, a shaking of bells, a furious, possessed drumming, and in the infernal no-light of the winter dusk, I could make out almost nothing but orange blazes, far off, by the river.

How much of this was I dreaming? How much was I under a "foreign influence," if only of jet lag and displacement? Figures came toward me out of the mist, smeared in ash from head to toe, bearing the three-pronged trident of the city's patron, Shiva, the Ender of Time. In the little alleyways behind the flames was a warren of tiny streets; a shrunken candle burned in the dark of a bare earth cavern where men were whispering sacred syllables. Cows padded ceaselessly down the clogged, dung-splattered lanes, and every now and then another group of chanters surged past me, a dead body under a golden shroud on the bamboo stretcher that they carried toward the river, and I pressed myself against a wall as the whisper of mortality brushed past.

It was hard to believe that just three days before I had been in California, marking a quiet New Year's Day in the sun. Now there were goats with auspicious red marks on their foreheads trotting around, and embers burning, and oil lamps drifting out across the river in the fog. Along the walls beside the river were painted faces, laughing monkey gods, sacred looming phalluses. The shops on every side were selling sandalwood paste, and clarified butter oil for dead bodies, and tiny clay urns for their ashes.

Imagine finding yourself in a Hare Krishna celebration as populous as Philadelphia. All around you, people are shaking bells, whirling, singing joyfully, though their joy has to do with death, as if everything is upended in a holy universe. At the nearby Manikarnika Well, the god Shiva is said to have met the god Vishnu, usually an occupant of a parallel world. The result of this propitious encounter is that bodies are burned in public there — as many as a hundred a day — and the most sacred spot in the center of Hinduism is a smoking charnel-ground.

On paper, Varanasi is a holy crossroads, a place of transformation tucked between the Varana and Asi rivers, along the sacred Ganges. It is, many will tell you, the oldest continuously inhabited city on earth, as ancient as Babylon or Thebes. Because the city, now housing as many as 3 million (half a million of them squeezed into the square mile of the Old City), has never been a center of political power or historical conflict, it has been able to continue undisturbed, and fundamentally unchanged, as the most sacred citadel of Hinduism and a cultural hot spot. Bathe yourself in its filthy waters, devout Hindus believe, and you purify yourself for life. Die or be burned along its banks and you achieve *moksha,* or liberation, from the cycle of incarnation.

But if Varanasi means anything, it is the explosion of every theory and the turning of paper to ash. The heart of the city is a chaotic 3-mile stretch of waterfront along Mother Ganga on which there are more than seventy ghats, or steps, from which the faithful can walk down into the water. At the top of these steps stand huge, many-windowed palaces and temples that are all in a state of such advanced decay that they seem to speak for the impermanence of everything. At this very spot, the southeast-flowing Ganges turns, briefly, so it seems to be flowing back toward the Himalayas from which it came, and bathers on its western bank can face the rising sun. Varanasi's original name, Kashi, means City of Light, although millennia of dusty rites and blazing bodies and holy men showing no interest in normal human laws have also left it a city of shadows or, as the wonderfully obsessive Varanasiphile Richard Lannoy writes, a "city of darkness and dream."

The son of Indian-born parents, I am (in theory) a Hindu, and though I have never practiced the religion, I was finding Varanasi to be more a mad confusion than the sublime order that a good Hindu would see. Yet in the months before I made my first trip to the city, everywhere I turned seemed to lead there, as if by magnetic attraction. Writing on Buddhism, I was reminded that the Buddha delivered his first discourse at Sarnath, 6 miles from Varanasi. Meeting a professor of Sanskrit in California, I was told that Shankara, the great Hindu philosopher, had accepted his first disciple in Varanasi and was said to have met Shiva there, in the disguise of an untouchable, more than a thousand years ago. This was where Peter Matthiessen began his epic Himalayan quest, recorded in *The Snow Leopard;* this was where Allen Ginsberg was shadowed by local intelligence and confessed, of the city's residents, "They're all mad."

Varanasi seemed to mark the place where opposites were pushed together so intensely that all sense gave out. Its holy waters flow, for example, past thirty sewers, with the result that the brownish stuff the devout are drinking and bathing in contains three thousand times the maximum level of fecal coliform bacteria considered safe by the World Health Organization. Those old collapsing buildings along its banks, suggesting some immemorial pageant, are in fact not old at all, although they do confirm the sense that one has entered less a city than an allegory of some kind, a cosmogram legible only to a few. Everything is constantly shifting, flickering this way and that in the candlelit phantasmagoria, and yet the best description I found of twenty-first-century Varanasi—"There is movement, motion, human life everywhere, and brilliantly costumed"—was penned by Mark Twain in the nineteenth.

A city that is truly holy is as contrary and multidirectional as any charismatic human, and draws people almost regardless of their faith or origins. So perhaps I should not have been surprised that the minute I landed following the fifty-minute flight from Delhi and set foot in Varanasi, which was shrouded in a miasmal early-January mist, I ran into a Tibetan incarnate lama, an American Tibetan Buddhist monk I know from New York, and a ninety-one-year-old Parisienne I'd last seen attending teachings of the Dalai Lama's in Dharamsala.

"Oh," she said, unsurprised, "you are here too."

The Dalai Lama, I gathered, was giving his only official teachings of the winter and spring in Sarnath, right there, that very week.

The living capital of Hinduism is home too to fourteen hundred mosques and shrines, and every religious teacher from Jiddu Krishnamurti to Thich Nhat Hanh has spent time here; it was here that Mohandas Gandhi entered Indian political life in 1916 (when, at the inauguration of the local Banaras Hindu University, he spoke out against the filth of the city's holy places), and it was here that the French explorer Alexandra David-Néel received lessons in yoga from a naked swami before heading to Tibet.

I got into a car and entered the swirling river of life that in Varanasi reflects and flows into its central symbol. India specializes in intensity and chaos—part of the governing logic of Varanasi is that it is crowded with traffic and yet there are no traffic lights—and very soon I was careening through the crush (a riot in search of a provocation, so it seemed). Here and there an elderly policeman with a mask over his mouth held out an arm, and cars, cows, bicycles, and trucks crashed past him, willy-nilly. Dogs were sleeping in the middle of a busy road—Varanasi's Fifth Avenue, it might have been—and men were outstretched (sleeping, I hoped) along the side and on the pavement. I dropped my bags at my hotel, the Gateway, and in the course of the twenty-minute ride to the river, I saw two more jubilant corpse processions and two parades of children—in honor, I could only imagine, of the God of Mayhem.

"This is a very inauspicious time," my guide warned me from the front seat. "It is called Kharamas. Everyone stays hidden; no one talks about weddings, things like that. Everyone is silent. It is like a curse placed on the city."

I could find no mention of any such observance, but if this was Varanasi at its most silent, I thought, I couldn't imagine it on one of its frequent festival days. "The curse lifts on January 14," my new friend told me. "Then we celebrate." This was not cause for celebration to someone due to depart, as I was, on January 13.

At a Christian church, we got out and joined the crush of bodies pushing toward the Ganges. We walked along the path to the riverbank, dodging the refuse and excrement of centuries, and passed an almost naked man, staring right at us, sheltered by a small fire inside a hut.

"He's meditating?" I tried.

"Everything for him is ashes," came the reply. Philosophy is ceaseless along the Ganges, and usually causeless. Holy men sat on the ground under umbrellas, chanting and smearing paste and ash on their foreheads. "These sadhus, they like very much to live with cremation. They don't wear clothes as we do. They don't do anything like people who are living in the material world. They want to live in a world of ash." To come here was like entering one of the narrow, winding old cities of Europe—my birthplace of Oxford, in fact—in which you are back in a medieval mix of high scholasticism and faith.

A huge, bloated cow floated past us, and we climbed into a boat as five handsome young boys in elaborate gold pantaloons held up five-armed oil lamps in a glossy fire ceremony along the river. Fires were blazing to the north and south, and the air was thick with the smell of incense and burning. "Only in this city, sir, you see twenty-four-hour cremation," offered the boatman, as if speaking of a convenience store. In other cities cremation grounds are traditionally placed outside the city gates. Here they burn at the center of all life.

The next day, a little before daybreak, I walked out of the gates of my hotel to visit the river again. Only one man was standing there now, under a tree, with a bicycle-rickshaw—his eyes afire in his very dark face, and what looked to be a bullet hole in his cheek. We negotiated for a while and then took off into the penumbral gloom, the previously jam-packed streets under a kind of sorcerer's spell, quite empty.

To travel by bicycle in the dawn is to feel all the sounds, smells, and ancient ghosts of Varanasi; for more than a week the bicycle-rickshaw man would become my faithful friend, waiting outside the gates of the hotel, ready to guide me anywhere. The winter fog only compounded the half-dreamed air of the place, as figures loomed out of the clouds to stare at us and then vanished abruptly, as if nothing was quite substantial here, or even true. *"Unreal City,"* I thought, remembering a boyhood ingestion of T. S. Eliot. *"Under the brown fog of a winter dawn . . . I had not thought death had undone so many."*

On the Ganges, a Charon pulled me soundlessly across the water, past all the broken palaces, the huge flights of steps, the men and women walking down to the water, barely clothed, dipping their heads in and shaking themselves dry, as if awakening from a

long sleep. "In Varanasi," said the ferryman, "thirty-five, forty percent is holy men." In another boat, an Indian man with his young
wife and child had his laptop open in the phantasmal dark. Cows,
pariah dogs, and figures in blankets appeared in the mist, and red-
bottomed monkeys ran in and out of the temples. "Sir," said the
boatman, and I braced myself for an offer of young girls, young
boys, or drugs. "You would like *darshan?* I arrange meeting with
holy man for you?"

All this, of course, is the Varanasi of sightseers, the almost psychedelic riddle at the eye of the storm that entices many, horrifies
others, and leaves most feeling as if they are losing their mind.
But part of the power of the holy city is that it is shaped very con-
sciously—like a mandala, some say, a series of concentric sacred
zones—and as you move away from the river, you come out into
a world that is India's highest center of learning and refinement,
home to its greatest scholars for as long as anyone can remember.
  "It is such a beautiful city," said Pramod Chandra, an elegant
soul who comes from a long line of Varanasi thinkers and writers (and who is a professor emeritus of art at Harvard). We were
seated in his large, bare family home not far from the burning
ghats and the crumbling palaces. "If they did it up, it could be like
one of the great cities of Spain or Italy. The tall houses in the Old
City? If you go inside, you find abundant worlds there—courtyards
and inner spaces, everything. But the problem in India is always
bureaucracy. It's deadening." There was now, he said, a plan for
creating a futuristic overpass around the Old City, so as to turn the
maze of ill-lit alleyways into a kind of inner suburb.
  Because the buildings of Varanasi are only about 350 years old,
the city has always had to sustain its traditions in human ways,
through rites and ideas; it is not the stones or monuments that
give Varanasi its sense of continuity, as in Jerusalem or at Kailas,
but the unchanging customs passed down from father to son to
grandson. The professor recalled for me, over a long evening of
talk, the days when educated boys here learned Sanskrit from
pandits who came to their homes, committing to memory huge
swatches of holy text.
  So part of the deeper fascination of the City of Light, beyond
the visceral shock, is the way it brings together back-lane black
magic and high-flown speculation and, in so doing, serves as In-

dia's India, a concentrated distillate of the culture's special mix of cloudy philosophizing and unembarrassed reality. Spirituality in Varanasi lies precisely in the poverty and sickness and death that it weaves into its unending tapestry; a place of holiness, it says, is not set apart from the world, in a Shangri-la of calm, but a place where purity and filth, anarchy and ritual, unquenchable vitality and the constant imminence of death all flow together.

In Varanasi, as everywhere in India, the first rule of survival is that getting anywhere at all—from A to B via T, Q, and Z—is an ordeal; but settling into some quiet corner and joining in the rhythm of life around you can make for one of the most cozy and companionable stays imaginable. The center of life is Asi Ghat, at the southern end of the line of ghats, which has now turned into a foreigner-friendly neighborhood of eco-institutes and Salsa Dance Aerobics classes, pizza restaurants and compendious bookshops. And the epicenter of Asi Ghat, for the fortunate few, is the Hotel Ganges View, an unassuming-looking place whose thirteen rooms are usually filled with some of the most interesting Varanasi watchers you will ever meet.

Here you can find yourself sharing a table on a candlelit rooftop with a Danish psychiatrist working with trauma in Iraq, Rwanda, and Bosnia, and a German scholar of Hinduism. After dinner the low-ceilinged dining room was turned into a backdrop for an intimate concert, and as I sat there, being whipped up into the ether by two sarangi players and a tabla virtuoso, a gnomish man with tufts of white hair and a tweed jacket came in. He looked back at me and casually nodded, and I realized that it was a German singer of Sufi *ghazals* whom I had last seen in the Tiergarten in Berlin, talking of Ethiopia and Mali.

Varanasi has at times this feeling of being an insider's secret, marked on the invisible map that certain initiates carry around with them, and as the days went on, I came to see that the constant back-and-forth—the advance into the intensities of the river, the retreat to a place from which to contemplate them all—was part of the natural rhythm of the city. Every time I stepped out of my hotel to be greeted by my loyal friend with his rickshaw, I was pitched into the Boschian madness of a teeming, pell-mell cacophony in which, amid the constant plodding of beasts, I saw ads for an Institute of Call Centre Training, notices for "radio jockey certificate courses," signs for those dreaming to become "air stewardesses." The promise of the new India is that even the poorest kid in the slums, if he applies himself at a Brain Gym, can make it not to the NBA but to an MBA course, and to the once-unimaginable world marked out by the shining new malls and ubiquitous signs for McVeggie with Cheese. Such is the inclusiveness of Varanasi and the hundreds of gods it houses that the new is taken in as readily as the old.

We would clatter through the mob and arrive at the river, and I would be reminded how and why members of my own (Hindu, India-dwelling) family would often tell me, "Don't go to Benares [as Varanasi was long known]! It's just stench and crooks and dirt. Only tourists like it." In Aravind Adiga's Man Booker–winning first novel, *The White Tiger,* the narrator declares, "Every man must make his own Benares," a way of saying that for the upwardly mobile and up-to-the-minute creature of New India, the old city stands for all the ageless hierarchies and ancient rites that have to be pushed aside. Varanasi is the home of your grandmother's grandmother's dusty superstitions, and the new global Indian purports to have no time for it.

At the river itself, on the rare day when the fog lifted, men were blowing conch shells to greet the dawn, and women were pounding clothes upon the stone steps to wash them. Saried figures were stepping into the surging brown, and others were lifting their cupped hands to the rising sun. Varanasi, I thought, was a five-thousand-year-old man who may have put on an fcuk shirt and acquired a Nokia but still takes the shirt off each morning to bathe in polluted waters and uses his new cell phone to download Vedic chants.

There is another sight that helps to underline this ancient dialectic. Indeed, Sarnath, more or less a suburb of Varanasi these days, is to some extent the product of the same back-and-forth. Born into the higher reaches of Hinduism, the young prince who became the Buddha walked away from all the abstraction and ritualism of Brahmin priests in order to find his own truth, just by stilling his mind and seeing what lies behind our pinwheeling thoughts and projections. After he came to his understanding in the town of Bodh Gaya, he traveled to Sarnath's Deer Park and outlined his eightfold path for seeing through suffering.

To travel from Varanasi to Sarnath today is to undertake a similar journey, and one that retraces a central shift in the history of philosophy. As soon as you move out into the country fields and narrow roads on the way to the little village, the roar and tumult of the holy city begin to vanish, and you see Buddhist temples from all the traditions—and buildings with names like the Society for Human Perception—peeping from behind the trees. A beautiful museum houses Buddhas excavated in the area over centuries. One minute you're in the midst of the whirligig shock of crackling flames and darkened lanes, and thirty minutes later you are in a large, quiet park where monks in yellow and gray and claret robes are seated silently on the grass, meditating before the Dhamekh Stupa, originally set up here by the emperor Ashoka 249 years before the birth of Christ.

Because the Dalai Lama was about to offer teachings nearby, the pleasant park around the 143-foot stupa had been transformed into a busy, merry Tibetan settlement. As I looked out on the park, some Vietnamese nuns in triangular bamboo hats joined the Tibetans to pay their silent respects, while a Mongolian—striking in topknot and beard and rich silk robes—roared out his prayers. I went to listen to the Dalai Lama talk about the bodhisattva way of life, and when he was finished, the little lanes of the settlement filled with so many red-robed monks that it felt as if we had all ended up in Lhasa when it was a center of the Buddhist world.

On my arrival in Varanasi, it had seemed impossible to pull myself out of its hypnotic spell, its constant movement, its air of danger around the flames, where so many men (and it seemed to be all men) were waiting in such a state of restless energy that I could feel the sense of violence just below the surface of the Indian communion, in which a spark of misunderstanding can quickly turn into a blaze. On my third day in the city, my bicycle-rickshaw ran right into a procession for the Shia festival of Muharram, in which thousands of bare-chested Muslim boys were waving swords, shouting slogans of defiance, and carrying through the narrow, jam-packed streets 10-foot poles and silver-tinseled shrines that looked certain to collapse on us all at any moment. Two days later, the monthlong period of mourning was still blocking traffic.

But as the days went on, I realized that all I really had to do was sit and let life along the riverbank unfold around me. A crow was perched on a placid cow, now and then pecking bits of seed off the animal's cheek. A holy man fielded a cricket ball in the river and flung it back to the boys who had set up a high-speed game along the banks. Gypsies from the backpack trail drifted by, swathed in scarves and shawls.

I had been determined not to fall under the city's spell, nor to repeat the lines that so many millions of visitors have uttered, changelessly, for more centuries than I can count. I knew that Varanasi—India to the max—would stretch credulity in every direction, and I told myself to stay clear and alert, on the throne of pure reason. A part of me, lapsed Hindu, longed to stand apart. But as I kept returning to the ghats, I found myself thinking along lines I'd never explored before. Standing by the bonfires, suddenly noting how silent all the men around me were—the clamor was coming from elsewhere—I started to imagine what it would feel like to see a lover's body crumbling and crackling before my eyes, the shoulder I had grown used to holding every day for twenty years reduced to ash. I started to think about what one does with remains, and what exactly they mean (or don't). I felt the truth of the Buddhist exercises my friends sometimes spoke about, of seeing in every beautiful model the skeleton beneath the fancy covering.

I began to walk south along the river then, till I came to the other burning ghat—orange flames lighting up the surrounding buildings with their glow—and as I kept walking, the path grew deserted and dark till the only light came from far above, where a candle was flickering inside a rounded shrine. I walked on and on, deeper into the dark, knowing the steps and walkways of the city so well by now that I could dodge the areas where the water buffalo were wont to relieve themselves, and knew how not to get tangled in the kite strings of the little boys who raced along the riverbank in the uncertain light as if to tangle us all up in Varanasi itself. The decaying palaces up above, with their hollowed-out windows and interiors stuffed with refuse, or with huddled bodies, looked, when a light came on, like the homes of celebrants at some great festival who had long passed on—ghost houses.

That death could be a shrine before which everyone pays homage; that holy things, as a tour guide says in Shusaku Endo's haunting Varanasi novel, *Deep River*, do not have to be pretty things; that all of us are flowing on a river in which we will be picked up and

brought into a larger current; and that there can be flames marking the fires of heaven as much as of hell—all played havoc with
what I thought I knew.

A crossing ground, I began to think, is not just where the dead
move on to something else but where the living are carried off to
another plane, and where thought and sensation themselves are
turned around. "For Hindus," I had read in the work of the great
Varanasi scholar Diana L. Eck, "death is not the opposite of life; it
is, rather, the opposite of birth"—akin, perhaps, to leaving a cin-
ema by a different door than the one you came in by.

The following morning I ran into my guide from my first day,
always so eager to show visitors the beauties of his city.

"How are you, my friend?" I called.

"So good, sir. It is a beautiful day. More warm. No fog. Visibility
is good."

"So you think the curse is lifted?"

"Oh yes, sir. This all means it is the coming of spring."

The next morning, my last, I awoke to find the whole city covered in a pall of mist so thick that the ghostly towers and palaces
I could see from my room seemed to have unmade themselves
in the dark. Planes would not be able to take off or land. Trains
would be delayed twenty hours or more. Vehicles would crash into
one another, with fatal results. Down by the river, I could not see
30 feet in front of me, so that the smoke from all the fires—and
winter fog and pollution—made every figure I saw look like a visitor from another world. It could seem as if we were all trapped
now, spellbound in this sleeping world, and that the dense, fever-
ish, self-contained model of the universe was inside our bones and
had become our destiny, our home.

LYNN FREED

Keeping Watch .

FROM *Harper's Magazine*

Those who haven't lived . . . before the Revolution never
tasted the sweetness of life.

— Charles Maurice de Talleyrand-Périgord

SINCE THE END of apartheid, it has become commonplace
among South Africans, particularly middle-class whites, to mourn
not apartheid but the world that passed with it, a world that pre-
dated its demise by at least a hundred years. What they miss most
keenly is the safety they had enjoyed—at home, on the street, in
the car. In place of that world is now a sort of civil anarchy that has
caused many to leave the country and those who stay to take shelter behind high walls and electrified fences, alarm systems, panic
buttons, and security guards.

Not long ago, they point out, children were free to bicycle
around the streets and women to drive wherever they wished, day
or night. Cars could be parked without a guard to pay off. Restaurants didn't have to lock you in behind wrought-iron gates. Even
the vast numbers of poor were safer—just ask them how *they* cope
with this siege of violence.

And yet violence was always implicit in South African life, and
often explicit as well. If guns were scarce before the eighties, knives
certainly were not. Knife fights, flick knives, stabbings, stabbings,
stabbings—these were the daily fare of newspaper reporting during the fifties, sixties, seventies. And if they were largely confined

to ne'er-do-wells and Africans, well, we all knew it was only a matter of time before it was going to climb the hill to find us.

So when our garden boy came home half dead one day, stabbed just under the heart, I stared down at the wound as into an omen. There it was, a dark, moist, oozing thing, no distinction between dark skin and dark blood, and the gleaming white rib at the center of it. Even at the age of six or seven, I knew exactly what I was seeing: I was seeing the future. Except that for us, there would be no chance of a doctor stitching up the wound. For us, the knife was going to be drawn deep across the throat.

Much of my childhood anxiety was spent concocting ways to save myself when the Knife-at-the-Throat bloodbath actually came —where to hide, whom I could count on for help (the nanny, although at the top of the list, would, at least in theory, be part of the same knife-wielding rampage). We all knew how it would happen. One night, without warning, our servants would rise as one, snatch up knives from their various kitchens, and rush next door to slit some white throats. Turn around, and there, in the doorway, would be Josiah, the Sullivans' cook, eyes wild with *dagga* (marijuana) and their carving knife at the ready. Our own servants, we knew, would not be able to bring themselves to slit our throats. They'd go over to the Sullivans, or to old Mrs. Holmes on the other side. She was always complaining about the noise we made on the cricket lawn and wouldn't give back the balls we hit over the hedge. And so, in a sense, it would serve her right.

Meanwhile, I kept watch. On a Sunday afternoon, if Zulus were pouring down the hill on their way to their faction fighting, I would sit at the study window, keeping a firm eye on them. At that time faction fights were ritualistic affairs, and many Zulus were dressed in traditional warrior regalia—skins and rattles and headbands. They jumped and whistled and shouted and shook their clubs and sticks in the air, whipping themselves into a frenzy for the contest that was going to take place down on the soccer fields at the beach.

All it would take, I knew, was for one of them to leap our fence and come crashing through the bed of cannas for the bloodbath to start right there, at our house, never mind that that wasn't the way it was supposed to happen. It had happened already in Kenya with the Mau Mau, a phrase that could spark terror in the heart of anyone, let alone a frantic child checking behind the wardrobe before she could bring herself to leap onto the bed and under the covers.

And so when I woke up one night to the sight of a strange man at the foot of my eldest sister's bed, I was sure it had begun, and that no amount of cunning was going to save me now. We were at a holiday hotel in the mountains, my sisters and I in one room, my parents in the other, and the door firmly closed between us.

I lay as still as stone, moving only my eyes. My bed was lower than the others'—a sort of camp bed, brought in by the hotel and wedged into a corner. All I could see from down there was the man's hat, and the way his head bent over my sister's bed. Maybe he'd slashed her throat already, I thought, and was just checking to see if she was dead.

But what if he wasn't a native? What if he was a Coloured and didn't even have a knife? Coloureds, we knew, weren't going to rise up against us, because they were better off than the natives and wanted to keep it that way. Our Coloured housekeeper had a bedroom next to mine, and used the children's bathroom, and ate the same food as we did, but in the kitchen, and off different dishes.

I took another look, but it was impossible to tell. In the dark he could even have been an Indian. An Indian had once lured a girl in my class into an alley, and he'd made her pull down her pants, and a nurse, leaning out an upstairs window, had seen them down there and called the police. And after that the girl had seemed different, as if she had a birthmark down her face, or a limp, or a mother who had died.

But no one ever thought Indians would rise up and slit our throats either. They worked as waiters and gardeners and behind stalls at the Indian market. Some of them had shops down on Grey Street, and my mother knew them, and they knew her. Come the revolution, she said, the natives were as likely to slit their throats as ours. Everyone knew natives hated Indians. When the natives had rioted against them and burned down their shops, a native had thrown a brick at my uncle, who was dark and looked a bit like an Indian himself. And when Pillay, our gardener, had to use the toilet in the servants' quarters, they weren't at all pleased, the housegirl told me. Indians were dirty, she said, they stank of curry and hair oil, phew, and also they cheated you. Except that she called them "coolies," a word we were never allowed to use.

The man glided to the foot of my middle sister's bed. Now that he was closer, I tried to sniff for curry or hair oil. But there was only the smell of the room—coir matting and furniture polish. And outside the crickets were singing as if everything were normal. The window was wide open as usual, never mind that we were on the ground floor, because however much they threw the phrase around, my parents were far more concerned about fresh air than they were about the Knife at the Throat. At home, the French doors onto the verandas were fastened back day and night, upstairs and downstairs, the windows too. But when I worried about this, they just pointed out that the only invaders we'd ever had were monkeys, which would reach into the kitchen to snatch something from the table and then gibber up with it into the mango tree, the dogs in pursuit.

It was the dogs, really, that were meant to protect us. As long as they lay around our feet, cocking an ear for someone to chase —anyone, in fact, who didn't belong in the house—we were supposed to feel safe. Just let the garden boy emerge from the servants' quarters and they'd be after him in a pack, barking, snarling, snapping. The same held for Pillay, and for delivery boys, and for the Zulus pouring down the hill on a Sunday afternoon.

And yet what good were they now, here in a hotel in the mountains, with a man staring down at my middle sister? They were hundreds of miles away, at the kennels. And anyway, how many dogs would it take when all the servants rose up at once with their knives and sticks? Even Superman, our houseboy, had managed to slice Simba's ear with the stick he carried to protect himself walking between the kitchen and the garage, or back to his room in the servants' quarters. And when an enemy put a curse on him one day and he came to say he was leaving and wanted his wages, it was almost as if the dogs themselves were cursed too, because they just stood back and watched as he walked to the gate, carrying his cardboard suitcase.

The man turned toward my corner. And just as I was thinking that whatever he was I would leap up before he could get to me and scream at the top of my lungs—just then, he turned and walked over to the window. I pushed myself up a bit to see, and yes, there he was, climbing out, first one leg and then the other, and he was still wearing his hat.

As soon as he was gone, I jumped out of bed and burst through the door leading into my parents' room. But they were too fast asleep to take me seriously. Eventually, though, my mother did climb out of her bed and lead me back to my own, agreeing, for once, to close the window. And then, the next morning, as soon as I heard the early-morning tea trolley rattling down the passage, I was back at their bedside.

Something about my insistence must have caught their attention at last, because when he'd finished his tea, my father put on his dressing gown and slippers and came through to our room to question my sisters. They scoffed, of course—they'd seen nothing, heard nothing. But then, opening the window to let in some fresh air, he noticed some soil on the windowsill. And when he leaned out, there, in the flowerbed below, were four large footprints—two on their way in and two on their way out.

No one ever found out who or what the man was, and no one but me believed he could have had anything to do with the Knife at the Throat. And so on we went, doors and windows open, dogs in place, until the real terror began—coming not at all as we'd expected, but haphazardly, here or there, day or night, with guns as well as knives, because by then guns were almost as plentiful and cheap as hamburgers, and the dogs themselves were the first to be shot—until then we carried on with the paradise of our lives: luxurious but not rich, safe and yet threatened, carefree if one did not think too carefully about the future.

LUKE DITTRICH

Walking the Border

FROM *Esquire*

THE FENCE STARTS about 80 feet out into the Pacific. It's made of metal pylons and looks like a procession of old telephone poles, each jutting about 20 feet above the waves. The pylons are spaced tightly together, and there's a sign warning of additional barriers below the waterline. Once the fence hits dry land, it marches east across the beach, and then, on a little hill that begins where the beach ends, it changes. It becomes, in fact, two fences, a double barrier. Compared with the single-ply barrier on the beach and in the water, these two fences—sturdy square beams supporting tight rows of whitewashed steel spindles—look much more modern and formidable, like prison fences. One of the two fences picks up right where the beach fence leaves off and continues east along the actual borderline, while the other follows a parallel line a few dozen feet to the north of it.

The buffer zone between the two fences is reserved exclusively for the use of the U.S. Border Patrol, with one exception: at the top of the hill, there is a little door in the northern fence, and a sign informs that twice a week, Saturdays and Sundays from 10 A.M. until 2 P.M., U.S. citizens are allowed to enter. Then, if there happen to be Mexicans on the other side of the second, southern fence, the Americans are allowed to look at them and talk with them, though reaching through the fence or attempting "physical contact with individuals in Mexico" is prohibited. A portion of the American side of the visiting area has been paved with cement, in the shape of a semicircle, and there is an identical semicircle on the Mexican side of the fence.

The official name of this place is the "Friendship Circle."

A big marble obelisk stands in the center of the circle. There is a break in the southern fence to accommodate the obelisk, and some additional fencing around the break to keep anyone from trying to squeeze through.

In 1851 some men from something called the International Boundary Commission placed the obelisk here. Back then, the Mexican-American War had just ended, and Mexico had agreed to surrender more than half its territory to the United States, including the places now called California, Arizona, New Mexico, and Texas. The job of the International Boundary Commission was to come up with a map of the revised frontier between the two countries. They started here, on this beachfront hill, and installed the obelisk as their first survey marker.

Then they walked east, into the borderlands.

A geographer described accounts of the International Boundary Commission's expedition as the "stuff that dime novels are made of," complete with "deaths from starvation and yellow fever, struggles for survival in the desert, and the constant threat of violent attacks by Indians and filibusters."

Back then, of course, those surveyors had no choice when it came to transportation: in order to see the border, they had to travel either by foot or by horse.

Today there are lots of alternatives. You could fly from San Diego to the Gulf of Mexico in a few hours, or could drive the distance in a few days.

But there's still something to be said, when you want to really understand something, for slowing way down.

So this morning I'm taking my cue from the men who planted this obelisk.

I start on the beach.

I walk east.

The border's simple.

It heads due east from the beach straight across California until it hits the Colorado River, at which point it backtracks a bit, squiggling southwest along the river's edge before firming up again and slicing across the bottom of Arizona in two long straight lines. Shortly after reaching New Mexico, it suddenly jogs north for a few dozen miles, but then quickly resumes its straight, eastward course all the way to Texas, where it merges with the Rio Grande and rides out the final stretch to the Gulf.

The border's complicated.

From a distance it looks like an impossible tangle of Minutemen and La Migra, drugs and money, fence builders and fence hoppers. It's tempting to look away. But we shouldn't. The border is the place where we end and they begin, which makes it the definition of a defining place.

Planning a walk along the border, you quickly encounter certain problems.

One problem is political. The only feasible way to walk the actual borderline is to follow the dirt roads used by the Border Patrol, but a lot of those roads appear only on proprietary maps that the Border Patrol refuses to give out to members of the public. You can turn to online satellite imagery, but these days even that can't keep pace with how quickly new border roads are being plowed.

Another problem is geographical. The borderlands, whatever route you sketch through them, are a rough mix of deserts and mountains.

Sometimes problems meld the geographic and the political, because sometimes politics dictate geography. Example: I'm in an area known as Smuggler's Gulch, just east of the Friendship Circle. My maps show a deep ravine, one that drug and human traffickers used for decades to ferry their goods across the border. But a few years ago the Department of Homeland Security, armed with congressional permission to waive a number of environmental laws and regulations, sent in earthmovers to decapitate some nearby hills, filled the ravine with the resulting 1.7 million cubic yards of dirt, then topped it with a Border Patrol road and floodlights. Smuggler's Gulch, an ancient wrinkle in the earth, has been Botoxed. My maps are wrong.

My plan is to stick to the border roads where practical, where they exist, where I can find them. But I won't be too scrupulous about hewing to the line. Where there isn't a border road, or where the route looks more interesting a little inland, I'll let myself drift north. My first chunk is the 350 miles that now stand between me and Ajo, Arizona, including the 120 miles of open desert that immediately precede Ajo, a stretch called El Camino del Diablo.

And that leads to the final problem: water. El Camino del Diablo, like a lot of places along the border, is dry. One hundred twenty miles' worth of water weighs a lot more than I can carry on my back. If this were a century and a half ago, if I were one of those obelisk-planting surveyors, I'd probably have opted to bring along a mule.

Instead I've got a baby stroller.

"You need help?"

Feet digging, ankles stretched, calves tight, knees bent, back straight, shoulders up, head down, arms out, palms open, leaning forward, into the handlebar. The handlebar doubles as a rack to hang things on and dangles my quick-draw necessities: a Garmin GPS, a 32-ounce Nalgene water bottle, a Spot emergency locator beacon, and a can of Counter Assault Bear Deterrent pepper spray.

I look up, but I don't stop leaning. The stroller, if you add its own weight to the weight of all the gear and food and water inside it, weighs more than 120 pounds. The incline here, near the top of Otay Mountain, a dozen miles east of the beach, is steep, at least 45 degrees. If I stop leaning, the stroller will roll backward, over me, on down the slope.

The agent is standing on the top of the rise, looking down. He's holding a pair of binoculars.

"I saw you coming from a ways away," he says.

The border is approximately 1,900 miles long, and there are approximately 18,000 Border Patrol agents tasked with protecting it. That's nine agents per mile. Of course, these agents aren't posted at strict and regular intervals along the line. They move around, they cluster, and sometimes they pursue leads or man checkpoints up to a hundred miles from the frontier. But still. If you're walking the border, you're going to see a lot of Border Patrol.

I push the final few feet to the top of the rise and lock the stroller's wheels and stop to chat with the agent.

The eastern flank of Otay Mountain drops 2,000 feet into a deep valley that runs north to Highway 94 and south to Mexico. I can see the fence, about a mile away, and some cars passing by on the other side of it. That's where they cross, the agent tells me. It's best to spot them as soon as they hop the fence, when they're exposed, because once they enter the thick foliage of the valley, they become a lot harder to see.

I give him back his binoculars and keep walking. Otay Mountain is the highest peak for miles around, and this particular spot has a great view of the ocean. The chaparral that clots the slope —the redshanks, the monkey flower, the mission manzanita, the sugar bush—fuzzes into a blue-green pastel as the slope descends toward the Pacific, which coruscates mildly in the distance. Maybe it's just the pollution, the haze of the San Diego–Tijuana megalopolis, but everything has a soft focus up here.

I hope to average 20 miles a day, but the mountain is steep and the cart is heavy and I only make it 10 today before the sun drops away completely. I stop and make camp on a clearing beside the trail. I'm tired, and fall right asleep, then spend the rest of the night waking every couple of hours to the rumble and glare of patrols passing my tent.

At dawn I get up, get ready, and start again.

Coming down off the mountain is a lot easier than climbing up it, and I can relax a bit and let the rhythm of the walk begin to establish itself.

Every few miles I'll run into an agent, who'll ask what I'm doing out here. Sometimes he'll ask to see the soles of my shoes. Agents spend most of their time cutting sign, which is to say, they patrol dirt roads near the border, looking for fresh footprints or other sign of aliens. When they come across people who are not aliens, they often ask to see the soles of their shoes. That way they won't later confuse native sign for alien sign.

Sometimes I'll see agents even when they're not really there. I'll spot their bright white-and-green vehicles parked on almost every significant overlook, but it's not till I'm right up on them, peering through the tinted windows, that I can tell whether they're occupied or just expensive scarecrows. About a third are empty.

The trail from Otay Mountain feeds into State Route 94, and I follow the highway east for about 10 miles, then cut south toward the border again.

I spot a truck, and this one has an agent inside. I tap on the window and he rolls it down and gives me a nod. People call this town Tecatito on account of how it sits right across the border from the much bigger town of Tecate, Mexico. The agent's got the nose of his truck pointed straight south, where every so often someone walks out of the customs building and into America. A poster pasted to a wall in his line of sight features head shots of ten Hispanic men, along with details of the crimes they're wanted for, mostly smuggling, some kidnapping, some murders. I tell him I'm going across, that my hotel's a couple of miles away, that I'll have to walk through most of Tecate to get there. Does he think I'll have any problems, safetywise? Tecate's not too bad these days, he says. From what he hears, anyway. He's never crossed himself.

The passport-control booth is empty. Nobody's there to look at my ID or ask to see what's inside the stroller, so I just walk across the line.

Let me make my prejudices clear: I love Mexico. I lived in this country for a couple of years when I was a kid, and I used to go back all the time. I love the language, the food, the pace, the people, the temperature.

Let me make something else clear: Mexico scares me.

The last time I visited, I was driving around a small city with an off-duty police detective, and the car we were in was his own, and he wasn't wearing a uniform, and he was just cruising at first, relaxed, a big tough guy spinning stories about some of the scrapes he'd been in, but I'll always remember the jolt that went through his body when at a stoplight he suddenly realized he'd left his wallet with the badge in it lying open on the dash, and how fast he scrambled to snatch it and hide it away, and the look on his face as he shot glances at the other vehicles stopped at the light to see if anybody had noticed.

That kind of fear is contagious.

And I hate it, how this fear works its way into my experience, how it becomes as tangible a part of the background texture of Tecate as the uncatalyzed exhaust or the swollen-titted dogs or the snakeskin boots or the sweet little old lady who gives me directions to my hotel and then says, *"Dios te bendiga"* as I'm walking away.

Because if you scrape away the fear, if you dig through it, or just look past it, all the best parts of Mexico are still here.

Tonight I eat at a restaurant near my hotel and they bring me flank steak and grilled nopale cactus and homemade corn tortillas and flan and a couple bottles of the local brew and a shot of Tres Generaciones and it is, without a doubt, the best meal I've had in months.

*

"You weren't wearing those earlier."

He's got his flashlight aimed at my feet, at my three-dollar flip-flops. I tell him they're my camp shoes.

Agent Muñoz shines the light through a scrim of trees, toward the tent.

"Anyone else back there?"

No.

We're a few hundred feet north of the border, on a low rise beside a dry creek bed, 18 miles east of Tecate. It was a long walk today, pegged to the fence, lots of hills. The coastal flora had faded and hints of the high desert—tumbleweeds, the occasional cactus —had begun to show.

I'd already made camp and was just finishing my dinner when Agent Muñoz rolled up. He's edgy, keeps his gun holster, with its HK P2000 double-action pistol, angled away from me.

"Strange place to camp," he says.

I tell him I chose it for the location, because it's not right next to the fence, and because the trees are thick enough that I can't even see the fence, which means that nobody at the fence can see me. I tell him I chose it because that's one thing everyone told me was very important: to avoid camping right next to the fence, or even in places where I could be seen from the fence. Because I'm most vulnerable at night. Because bandits on the other side could spot me, scramble over, take whatever they wanted, then scramble back, untouchable.

Agent Muñoz listens, nods.

"You've never been here before?"

No, I haven't.

He shifts his hips, relaxes a bit.

"I wouldn't camp here," he says. "I don't even like to be here."

Everything I thought made this a good place, he explains, is exactly what makes it a bad place. This deep creek bed, shielded by its canopy of trees, is like Smuggler's Gulch before Smuggler's Gulch became Smuggler's Flat. The cartels love it, and drug mules come through all the time.

"We've got some pressure sensors buried farther up the creek," he says. "We send out a team anytime they get a hit. But that takes a while."

Should I pack up my tent? Would I be safer somewhere else?

He shakes his head.

"Nowhere's safe around here."

Before he gets back into his truck and drives away, he gives me the direct line to the nearest Border Patrol station, says I should call immediately if I see anyone.

"Tell them you're in the bottom of La Gloria. Everyone knows where that is."

The trees shimmer and wobble in the red glow of his receding taillights, and then it's dark again and I go and gather up everything I think I might be able to use as a weapon, including the pepper spray, a knife, and some hiking poles. I bring it all inside the tent, crawl into my bag, zip up, and lie there, waiting. Every so often I hear something moving outside, crunching seedpods or snapping twigs, and I turn on my headlamp and scoot up and try to look out through the tent's wall of mosquito netting, but the netting catches the light, and all I see is the wall itself. Then I turn off the light until I hear something else. Lying there in the dark, watching vague shadows on the polyester, it feels like a world of unknowns is outside pressing in.

Another gust lifts the dirt and sand off the road and spits it in my face, and I've had enough, so I take a break and lean sideways against the fence, my back to the wind. It's been blowing all day, fierce. The fence here, a few miles past La Gloria, is crude but strong, made from corrugated sheets of brown and yellow steel. The National Guard was deployed to build this stretch back in 2006, and every couple of miles a different engineering battalion marked the section it was responsible for by carving a piece of metal in the shape of its home state and welding it in place. The fence builders came from Hawaii, Wisconsin, South Carolina, and when they got here, they worked till they were done, even through the holidays, I'm guessing, judging by the spray-painted Christmas tree I'm leaning next to.

The fence is tall, 12 feet or so. It would be tough to climb over. And the steel of the fence would be almost impossible to tear through. But dirt is dirt, and from where I'm standing, I can see a spot where the dirt next to the fence has been dug up and there's a little hole underneath it, and I bet I could get down and crawl right through.

There's a sign on the other side of the road. It's bright yellow and busy with pictographs: a sun, some mountains, a rattlesnake, a cactus, and a little drowning man, one arm raised, sinking into a pool of water. CUIDADO! the sign reads. NO VALE LA PENA!

It's not worth the trouble!

But of course it is.

The returns are as stark and clear as those pictures on the sign. By the simple act of carrying his own body across the line, a man immediately boosts his earning potential sixfold. And if he chooses to carry something else along with his body, well, a pound of cocaine costs twice as much in Tecatito as it does in Tecate.

It's worth the trouble, and so every year roughly 2.5 million people in Mexico make the simple and consummately rational decision to make unauthorized entry into the United States of America.

It's worth the trouble, and so the fence, like the Border Patrol, has more than doubled in the last decade. But the incursions haven't stopped. Instead they've shifted. Back near San Diego, where the fence is particularly brawny and the density of the Border Patrol is particularly high, traffic has slowed. Here, where the fence is easier to conquer and patrols are less frequent, traffic has increased. The pressure on the other side remains the same, and as long as there is any gap, any weakness, it will push and probe until it finds a way.

It's worth the trouble, and so I wonder why I still haven't run into any crossers myself. The wind eases a bit and I lean back into the stroller and start moving again. I've been hearing things all day, seeing things too, little murmurs behind me or blurs of fabric in the chaparral or footfalls on the other side of the fence. I'll stop and look and listen, but then everything goes still and blank.

Eventually I come to a spot where the road and the fence split: the fence continues east over some particularly steep and rocky hills while the road jogs north. I follow the road until it crosses an abandoned train track, and then bump along over the slats for an hour or so until I reach Old Highway 80, which takes me back south. The highway brings me to a long concrete bridge, and there's a good view of the fence coming down out of the hills to the west, back onto the flats. At the end of the bridge there's a big weathered green-and-white painted sign that says, WELCOME TO JACUMBA. A smaller sign hangs beneath the big one. It features a little drawing of a woman dressed in a 1910-style bathing suit and the words JACUMBA HOT SPRINGS . . . ALL YOUR WANTS.

The manager's smoking a cigarette outside when I get there, and there are plenty of rooms available, and he gives me the key to one and I go and take a shower and change, and when I come back outside, the manager's still standing by the street, smoking another cigarette. He's a skinny guy, maybe forty, maybe fifty, with a tight-cinched belt and a sort of permanent smirk. There's a convenience store—Mountain Sage Market—across the street from the hotel, and it's open, and so's the Laundromat next to it, but most everything else here on the main drag—a car wash, a gas station, an antique shop—has gone out of business. In a vacant lot near the shuttered car wash, a clutch of Border Patrol agents are milling around, waiting for something.

I ask the manager about Jacume, which is the town directly south of Jacumba, right across the fence. I'd read about Jacume. The *Los Angeles Times* calls it a "black hole," says it's overrun by smugglers and that even the Mexican cops won't go near it. The manager tells me that Jacumba and Jacume used to be as close as their names imply, that before the fence went up, people from Jacume used to cross all the time to work day shifts and do their shopping here in Jacumba, and people in Jacumba used to cross all the time to eat or party in Jacume. Jacumba and Jacume, the way he tells it, used to be real border towns, meaning places where north and south sort of overlapped and mixed together. Now they're just towns on the border.

"I hear Jacume's real dangerous now," he says. "But I don't really have any idea what goes on down there."

A few minutes later, some sort of silent alarm must go off, because the agents in the vacant lot grab their M4s from the front seats of their vehicles and take off running toward the fence.

After Jacumba the fence road fades out again, and I have to stick to the asphalt. I stay on it for a week, averaging 25 miles per day.

Highways are their own sort of wilderness. They were never meant for walking on, and their unrelenting sameness, their day after day of minutely incremental progress, punches holes in your reservoir of memories, so that the narrative drains away and a whole week reduces to a dry heap of disconnected impressions.

The cherry-red semi that passes too close, too fast, and nearly pulls me into its wake.

The little leather pouch lying on the shoulder of I-8, the word *Columbia* stenciled on it, and the mix of pesos and pennies inside.

The flat I camp on off of Highway 98 in the Yuha Desert, and how long it takes me to find a clear spot for my tent, one without broken glass or bullet casings.

The days I take off in a hotel along the way, tending to my feet, hobbling back and forth to a Walmart pharmacy, trying Epsom salts, moleskin, Vaseline, duct tape, new socks, anything at all that might make the blisters hurt less.

The middle-aged guy in the hotel bar who proudly shows me his teeth, gleaming new crowns he bought across the border in Algodones for a third the price he would have paid in the States.

The bartender in the same hotel, who once spent a summer helping build the fence, telling a story about how the cartels cloned some of the vehicles and uniforms that belonged to one of the contracting companies, exact replicas, so they could drive their stuff freely back and forth, unsuspected, the whole time the fence was being built.

The Imperial Dunes, those odd chunks of Saharan desert on the eastern edge of California, buzzing all day and night with tricked-out hot-rod sand buggies.

The retired Border Patrol agent in Yuma who says he loved his job, then quotes Hemingway: "There is no hunting like the hunting of man."

The way the road rubs the same parts of my feet the same way, hour after hour, and how finally the blisters on my heels get bad enough that I start jogging instead of walking, just to change the point of impact.

The relief when I finally get off the highway in Wellton, Arizona, and the other emotion when I look south of Wellton, at the desert, the mountains, and the beginning of the Camino del Diablo.

In August of 1905, a wandering prospector named Pablo Valencia departed from Wellton and headed south into the desert in pursuit of a lost gold mine. He was about forty years old, 155 pounds, rode a good horse, and carried along with him two 2-gallon and two 1-gallon canteens, for a total of 6 gallons of water, along with plenty of bread and sugar and cheese and coffee and tobacco and a sort of wheat meal called pinole. The first day he rode 34 miles and reached the spot near the southern tip of the Gila Mountains where the trail from Wellton intersected with the Camino del Diablo. Just to the west, a steep slope led up to a place known as Tinajas Altas, or High Tanks, where eroded stone basins usually contain pools of rainwater runoff. Tinajas Altas is the only semireliable water source along the Camino, and Valencia refilled his canteens there. As it happened, a self-taught geologist named W J McGee had set up a camp nearby, working on a summer-long project to monitor the heat and humidity of the surrounding desert. The two men dined together on jerked mountain-sheep meat before Valencia saddled up again and rode east.

Eight days later, just as dawn broke, McGee heard an inhuman sound, like the roaring of a lion, near his camp, and followed it to its source. He later described what he found in a paper called "Desert Thirst as Disease," which ran in a 1906 issue of the *Interstate Medical Journal.*

Valencia, who just the week before had been "of remarkably fine and vigorous physique—indeed, one of the best built Mexicans known to me," was now

> stark naked; his formerly full-muscled legs and arms were shrunken and scrawny; his ribs ridged out like those of a starveling horse; his habitually plethoric abdomen was drawn in almost against his vertebral column; his lips had disappeared as if amputated, leaving low edges of blackened tissue; his teeth and gums projected like those of a skinned animal, but the flesh was black and dry as a hank of jerky; his nose was withered and shrunken to half its length; the nostril-lining showing black; his eyes were set in a winkless stare, with surrounding skin so contracted as to expose the conjunctiva, itself black as the gums; his face was dark as a negro . . . his lower legs and feet, with forearms and hands, were torn and scratched by contact with thorns and sharp rocks, yet even the freshest cuts were as so many scratches in dry leather, without trace of blood or serum; his joints and bones stood out like those of a wasted sickling, though the skin clung to them in a way suggesting shrunken rawhide used in repairing a broken wheel. From inspection and handling, I estimated his weight at 115 to 120 pounds . . . The mucus membrane lining mouth and throat was shriveled, cracked, and blackened, and his tongue shrunken to a mere bunch of black integument.

In the long history of people running out of water on the Camino del Diablo, there are two things that make the case of Pablo Valencia unusual.

First is the fact that W J McGee, such a meticulous observer, was there to chronicle it.

Second is the fact that Valencia survived and eventually recovered.

I walk south from Wellton for a day and a half before I reach Tinajas Altas, where I leave my stroller on the trail and scramble up the rocks to the lowest tank. It's half full of greenish, algae-topped rainwater. A quarter mile away lies the *mesita de los muertos,* a little mesa topped with anonymous wood and stone crosses under which lie the bones of sixty or so—no one knows the exact number—men, women, and children. Some of their bodies had been discovered within sight of these tanks, some right at the base of this rocky slope, poor souls too weak to pull their own desperate husks up to the water above.

I head east from Tinajas Altas, onto the Camino del Diablo, with 8 gallons in my stroller.

The geography, the remoteness, and the challenges of the Camino have remained more or less constant since Pablo Valencia's time, though there is one new hazard he would have found bewildering: a big chunk of it runs through the U.S. Air Force's Barry M. Goldwater Range. To gain entry, I signed a liability release that read, in part, that I accepted the "danger of property damage and permanent, painful, disabling, and disfiguring injury or death due to high explosive detonations from falling objects such as aircraft, aerial targets, live ammunition, missiles, bombs, etc."

The Tinajas Altas are less than fifteen minutes behind me when I hear a huge roaring sound. I look to the north and see, barreling toward me close above the desert floor, two F-16 fighter jets. Before they reach me, they pull up and shoot nearly vertical, chasing each other into the blue sky.

It's early afternoon, my third day on the Camino, and the sand on this part of the trail is too deep for my stroller, so I'm up on the thin crust of the surrounding desert instead, navigating around the cholla spikes and the ironwood stumps, my feet or tires or both occasionally dropping down into a rabbit hole, when I hear something behind me and I turn and there's a Border Patrol truck coming, kicking up dust. I stop and watch it approach.

Two agents. Both Hispanic, early thirties. Neither is wearing a uniform. The passenger gives a curt nod in my direction, but the driver offers a big smile, asks what I'm doing out here, and where I'm going.

I tell him.

"Ajo!" he says. "That's a long way away."

They drive off and I keep walking, and pretty soon I've fallen back into my stupor, not thinking anything at all, until about a half-hour later I notice that, way ahead in the distance, the same Border Patrol vehicle is stopped at a bend in the trail, just parked there, idling.

Your head does funny things.

You're all alone for hours at a stretch, except for the fighter jets and the occasional long-eared Sonoran rabbit, and you might think the solitude and the biblical terrain would lend itself to deep contemplation, but it doesn't, not really. You mostly find yourself falling into half-trances of no thought at all, just the constant plod, until some unexpected stimulus intrudes and seizes hold of your mind.

I start thinking about the guys in the truck. Why weren't they wearing uniforms? And why was the passenger so curt, so un-friendly? And why, for that matter, was the driver so friendly? Then I start thinking about the cartels and how good they are at cloning vehicles.

I move a little ways farther off the trail, though it seems a pretty futile gesture. People say things like "There's nowhere to run" all the time, but right now, besides me and these two guys there might not be another human being for 40 miles in any direction.

When I'm even with the truck but about a hundred feet off the trail, I look over and the driver is still sitting in the driver's seat, and he gives me another smile and a wave. I don't see the passenger for a moment, and then I notice that he's lying next to the truck, partly beneath it, looking at something on the undercar-riage, and there's a little toolbox next to him.

More hours, more miles. When the sun starts going down, I'm in a Martian landscape of jagged orange-black rocks, the Pinacate lava field. It's cold, below freezing, a lot colder than it's ever sup-posed to be in Arizona. By the time I've got the tent set up, my blood has slowed and the air is numbing my fingers. I eat quickly and then get into my bag wearing everything but my shoes, a wool hat pulled down over my ears.

I sleep for a while, until the wind wakes me.

The wind is amazing. This is a three-person tent, and I'm lying in the middle of it, and there would usually be plenty of floor space to my right, but now the wind has lifted up that whole side, ripping out all the stakes, and is blowing so hard that the floor has doubled over like a taco shell, coming down on top of me. It's a wonder the tent poles haven't snapped. I unzip my bag enough to get my hands out and push the floor up off of me and the wind whips the polyester around my hands, and if someone were outside watching the tent right now, I bet I would probably look a little like Han Solo stuck in the carbonite. Eventually the gusts die down and the floor settles and I zip all the way up again and try to sleep, but then I realize I need to piss.

It's 1 A.M. and the rocks don't look orange-black now. In the moonlight they just look gray, like everything else. I notice that a water bottle I left outside is iced up. The wind starts up again while I'm pissing, and I have to hold on to the tent with my other hand to keep it from tumbling off across the lava flow.

There's a red light throbbing in the distance. It's maybe a couple of miles to the north, just above the top of a mountain, and at first I think maybe it's a radio tower or something, but then I look at it longer and it doesn't look like a radio tower. It looks like it's floating. Like it's some sort of orb floating there above the mountain, stationary, throbbing, red. Another night I saw a different mysterious light, but that light was on the ground, and it looked like a flashlight beam, and I thought it was coming my way, and it scared me—because who would be out here and why would they approach my tent at night?—and so I had grabbed my satellite communicator and held it with my thumb poised over the SOS button and watched the beam until it disappeared behind some rocks in the distance. But this light tonight, this throbbing, floating, luminous orb, what the hell is it? It's not scary. Just intriguing. My camera's in the tent. I should get it, take a picture. But by the time I crawl back inside, I'm so cold that the idea of going back out into the wind, even to photograph a UFO, is just too much.

At dawn the light is gone.

*

The Camino del Diablo is older than America.

It extends from Tinajas Altas for a hundred miles, straight through the lava fields and sand dunes and cholla beds of the Sonoran Desert. Nobody knows who created the trail, but a thousand years ago it was already ancient, and young Papago Indians would make holy pilgrimages on it, testing their manhood. A regiment of conquistadores in pursuit of El Dorado may have ridden here in the 1500s, but the first Europeans who definitely set foot on the Camino were Jesuit missionaries in 1699, on the expedition that established the first overland route to the Spanish colonies on the West Coast.

It earned its name during the Gold Rush, in the 1850s. Hundreds of ill-prepared miners and their families dried up and died here, trying to reach the gold fields of California. The arrival of the transcontinental railroad in the late 1870s made the route obsolete, and hardly anyone else set foot in the wilderness around the Camino until recently, when other groups of strivers began to pass this way.

The Camino runs parallel and close to the border for most of its distance, and from the Camino north to I-8 there is an average of about 40 miles of open desert. As border security has increased around the more densely populated zones to the west, the Camino area, despite its challenges, has become a popular thoroughfare for migrants and smugglers. On a Saturday in May 2001, for example, fourteen men—a mix of former coffee farmers, citrus-plantation workers, Coca-Cola plant employees, and high school students—were dropped off near here, near where Mexico's Federal Highway 2 skirts the very edge of the border, and told that if they walked north, across the Camino del Diablo, across this desert, they would reach an American highway. And so they walked north. That evening they came up against the Growler Mountains, which they tried and failed to cross. They walked north along the edge of the range for most of the next day, and then for some reason they turned almost 180 degrees and walked southwest across the valley that divides the Growler Mountains from the Granite Mountains, walking all the way to the southern tip of the Granite range, back near the border, before turning again and heading northwest.

If you look at their route on a map, if you trace their increasingly lost and desperate wanderings, which lasted a total of five days, it looks like the stem of a weak seedling, the way a weak seedling rises up, doubles back down toward the earth, and then tries to rise again, reaching hungrily toward the sun.

Of course, they had more than enough sun.

And not enough water.

And when Border Patrol agents found them, there was little they could do but collect their remains and their belongings—the blue jeans, the belt buckles, the white shoes, the combs, the fake silver watches—and turn these things over to the Mexican consulate.

They had individual names—Julian, Arnulfo, Reyno, Claudio, Mario, Lauro, Enrique, Reymundo Sr., Reymundo Jr., Abraham, Edgar, Efrain, Lorenzo, Heriberto—but there were so many of them that it was much easier simply to refer to them as a collective. The Yuma Fourteen. None ever made it to Yuma, but Yuma is the nearest big city.

As in the case of Pablo Valencia a century before, there was nothing unique about how the Yuma Fourteen ran out of water or what happened to them afterward. More than a hundred people had already dried to death that year in this same desert.

But the sheer number of deaths, all at once, was impressive, and there was pressure to do something about it, to respond in some way.

Camp Grip, which was built in 2002, is one of those responses. The "Grip" stands for the forward operating base's mandate, which is to "get a grip" on this stretch of the border.

I see Camp Grip's radio tower come into view first, then the trailers and the trucks. The trailers are new and clean and there's a barbecue going outside one of them, and when I get close I can smell hamburgers cooking and it smells good. I ring the doorbell. I wait a minute and there's no response, so I ring the doorbell again and knock too. The air-conditioning unit on the side of the trailer is on, and it's loud.

An agent eventually comes to the door. He looks surprised to see me.

We chat a bit. Camp Grip has been a success, in the sense that traffic is way down from the worst times, he says. But there's still plenty of traffic. I tell him about the red light I saw last night above the lava field. He shrugs.

"There was a big group crossed last night near where you camped," he says. "We caught them earlier today, about twenty miles north. They could have had someone up in the mountains, scouting for them. That light might have been their go-ahead signal."

He walks to the barbecue and opens it up and grabs a spatula hanging from the side and flips the burgers.

"They've got scouts all over the place," he continues. "Camouflage. Radios. Binoculars. They're organized."

He squints up through the smoke from the grill, toward one of the mountains nearest Camp Grip, at the craggy, distant peak.

"They're probably watching us right now," he says.

The rising sun lights up the inside of the tent and makes everything glow orange, and I wait until the air warms a little and then I sit up and unzip my bag and look at my feet. Every morning, this is the first thing I do. The cold of the night keeps them pretty numb, so I can't tell until I see them whether they've gotten worse or stayed the same.

The worst blister is on the outer edge of the left half of my left heel. It looks sort of like someone cut a Ping-Pong ball in half and stuck it there, though not quite as round or symmetrical, and the fluid inside is not milky white like a Ping-Pong ball but is instead pinkish with streaks of brown. I pull out my medical kit and dig around for alcohol swabs and wipe off the blister and the tight red skin around it. I take some Handi-Wipes and lay them down on the floor of the tent and rest my foot on the wipes, then dig around in the bag again until I find the safety pin. Most of it spurts onto the Handi-Wipes as soon as I punch the holes, but I squeeze to make sure it's all out. I wipe it clean with alcohol again, wait a minute for it to dry, then smear on some Neosporin and cover it all up with a new bandage. Once I'm satisfied with my work on this one, I turn to the others.

Every day starts like this, and every day once I'm done, once I've pulled on my socks and squeezed back into my shoes, I try not to think about my feet at all until the next morning.

The trail arcs gently north from my campsite.

I get on it and start walking the final 16 miles to Ajo.

The New Cornelia Mine is an open pit a mile wide and a thousand feet deep, with an emerald pool of coppery rainwater at the bottom. I know that Ajo is just beyond the mine, but from the ground, approaching from the south, all I can see is a towering tailings dam, the junk rock left over from the ore-extraction process. It's the most massive dam of any sort in the country, 7.4 billion cubic feet of rubble, and it fills the entire horizon. For seventy years the people who lived in Ajo lived off the mine. They took from it what they could and piled the rest up high. Then copper prices crashed and in 1984 the mine shut down.

The trail has turned into a road, and I follow the road to the dam's leading edge, then around the dam to the northeast, until I reach the intersection with State Route 85.

I get on the shoulder and walk north. I'm looking forward to stopping for a while, to seeing my daughter, to letting my feet heal. I walk faster. Soon I'm on the outskirts of Ajo, passing by faux Spanish colonial buildings constructed during the boom years. They look a lot older than they are. When the men from the International Boundary Commission passed through this area a century and a half ago, mapping the new frontier, Ajo didn't even exist.

Behind me to the south it's a straight shot to the line, and there's not much between here and there except for the Ajo Border Patrol Station. The station opened on a patch of desert scrubland in 1987, when Ajo was just a backwoods old mining town with few prospects, and our biggest fears about Mexico concerned unfair trade agreements. The station looks a little run-down, a little overstuffed, too many cars crowded around too few buildings.

They've started construction on a new station, right next to the old one. Contractors from Tucson, soldiers from the Army Corps of Engineers, they're all down there now, clearing and grading the land, getting it ready. The existing station was designed for 25 agents. The new one will accommodate 360, with room for future expansion. When it's finished, next summer, it'll become Ajo's economic center, like the New Cornelia Mine once was. Soon one in four people living in Ajo will be either a Border Patrol agent, the spouse of a Border Patrol agent, or the child of a Border Patrol agent.

Twenty-seven miles farther south, the highway ends at the Lukeville crossing, and another new procession of steel and wire, built in 2008, marches east across the desert.

That's where I'll begin again, when I return.

MARK JENKINS

Amundsen Schlepped Here

FROM *Outside*

LOST IN A BLINDING WHITEOUT on a frigid day in 1896, encrusted in ice, the two Norwegian brothers finally stopped skiing. Disoriented and directionless, Roald and Leon Amundsen decided to bivouac. They dropped their immense backpacks, stepped out of their 7-foot-long skis, and began burrowing into a snowdrift.

After digging two cramped holes side by side, like shallow graves, they crawled into reindeer-hide sleeping bags. They were shivering terribly. It was January in the mountains of southwestern Norway, when snow and wind, darkness and biting cold—the wolves of winter—conspire to kill the unprepared. Having skied for three weeks to traverse the 100-mile-wide Hardangervidda Plateau, wandering in blizzards and bivouacking repeatedly, they were thin and weak. Their stove was inoperable, and they hadn't had food for two days.

During the night, blankets of snow piled up on them, at first muffling the sound of the roaring wind, eventually extinguishing it. The moisture from the brothers' slow breathing iced the interiors of their snow holes. The snow's weight nearly cemented their bodies in place. They were almost buried alive.

The next day, when twenty-three-year-old Roald woke up, he found himself encased in ice, unable to move. But Leon, twenty-five, having kicked off the snow through the night with berserk exertion, was able to escape. Only the tips of his brother's boots were still visible. Leon dug frantically for more than an hour, pulling Roald out just before he asphyxiated.

Later that day the brothers skied south off the Hardangervidda.

Frozen and hungry, they found their way to Mogen, a cluster of log cabins on the northern edge of a body of water called Vinjefjorden.

"They were saved by a farmer just over there," says Kjersti Wøllo, sliding homemade reindeer sausages onto my plate and pointing through a steamed window at the spot. Wøllo and her partner, Petter Martinsen, operate the cross-country ski hut at Mogen, which they've opened early, in March, just for us. My brother Steve and I have come to Norway to retrace the Amundsen brothers' journey across the Hardangervidda, partly as a tribute to our heritage (our mother's side of the family is Norwegian) and partly to better understand the courage and drive that made Amundsen unquestionably the greatest polar explorer of all time. Mogen is halfway along our ski route. For four days straight, we've been grinding into 60-mile-per-hour headwinds.

"Amundsen gave the farmer a compass for saving their lives," says Wøllo, a classic Norwegian beauty in her thirties, whose hair is pulled back in a thick ponytail. "His great-grandson still has it."

The attempt was Amundsen's second at crossing the largest mountain plateau in northern Europe; the first, in 1893, ended after a 40-below open bivouac in which he nearly froze to death. The Hardangervidda had turned out to be almost unconquerably cold and storm-whipped: the perfect polar prep school. Amundsen would later wryly recall that his ski traverse "was as strenuous and dangerous as any of my following trips . . . [T]he training proved severer than the experience for which it was preparation, and it well-nigh ended the career before it began."

It is often the close calls of a man's youth that set the course for his life. Ill-equipped and ignorant, flush with youthful hubris, Amundsen would never again make such mistakes.

"Adventure is just bad planning," he would famously say. And yet it was by getting slammed in his own back yard that Amundsen found the direction of his life.

One hundred years ago, in the fall of 1911, a team of five Norwegians led by the thirty-nine-year-old Amundsen began skiing south across Antarctica, the harshest continent on earth. They looked like Inuits, clothed entirely in furs, mushing fifty-two Greenland dogs pulling four sleds. Some 500 miles west, a team of fifteen, led by forty-three-year-old Robert Falcon Scott, a British naval captain, began setting out for precisely the same absurd location: the South Pole.

Scott's team consisted of four men driving two motorized sledges, ten plodding behind sled-pulling ponies, and two on skis. As British author Roland Huntford recounted in his extraordinary 1979 double biography, *Scott and Amundsen,* this was the start of one of history's last great adventure epics: a contest not simply between two men or two nations but between two philosophies.

Huntford was scathing in his critique of Scott, describing him variously as contradictory, confused, deluded, dramatic, irritable, and morose. Amundsen, on the other hand, drew his highest praise. "In the way an artist may be obsessed with his art," Huntford concluded, "Amundsen was obsessed with exploration to the exclusion of all else."

We all know how the contest ended. Amundsen got to the pole first and made it back safely with all his men. Scott also got to the pole—thirty-four days after Amundsen—but didn't make it back alive, dying of starvation with two other men in a forlorn tent 130 miles from base camp.

Having studied and experienced polar exploration throughout my adult life, I'm convinced that Huntford's tough, controversial take on Scott got it right, but that doesn't mean I don't have respect for the Brit. Scott and Amundsen were both courageous men, equally committed to their cause. Both had larger-than-life egos that could lead other men to sublime achievements or bring them unimaginable suffering.

But their styles couldn't have been more different. Amundsen was a brilliant tactician and an exhaustive strategist, Scott a rigid officer and obdurate romantic who failed to understand that the strategies of travel and survival developed by the Inuit were the keys to success.

Both men served long apprenticeships en route to their destinies. Amundsen was born into a wealthy family of ship captains, the youngest of four brothers. He spent half his wild childhood skiing in the rugged fjords and deep forests around Christiania (now Oslo), the other half in shipyards and on the ocean. His father, a ship captain, died at sea when Amundsen was only fourteen. Amundsen attended university to appease his mother, but he had an intensely pragmatic, rational mind that was well suited to a life outdoors and incompatible with the classroom.

Scott was born into a wealthy family of naval officers, with four sisters and a brother. He was a sickly child, gently teased by his sisters, and at thirteen he entered the Royal Navy as a cadet. An exceptional student, especially in mathematics, Scott went to sea for four years, returned to naval college, then went to sea again, sailing around Cape Horn.

Amundsen's heroes included a fellow Norwegian, Fridtjof Nansen, a fabled explorer and the first man to ski across Greenland. Nansen was an ethnologist before the word existed and learned how to survive on the ice from the Inuit, almost reaching the North Pole in 1895.

Scott cast himself in the mold of the tragic British hero Sir John Franklin, a dogmatic, siege-style explorer who perished in the Arctic in 1848 with all 128 of his men, starving after his two ships became hopelessly trapped in ice. When Scott was made an officer, the Royal Navy had ruled the world's seas for more than a century, but it had been gradually weakened by bureaucracy and nepotism. Scott wanted to be the man who restored that glory: he was known for his sly ambition, academic ability, and deep desire for promotion.

Amundsen decided as a teenager that he would become a polar explorer and never wavered, preparing himself in every way and signing on to a polar seal-hunting mission in 1894. He subsequently spent two years exploring the edges of Antarctica, then another three years, 1903–1906, in the Arctic on a quest to become the first to sail from the Atlantic to the Pacific through the ice-choked Northwest Passage. He not only completed this harrowing mission but became the second explorer to reach the magnetic North Pole.

It was during this expedition that Amundsen learned about dogsledding and igloo building from the Netsilik Inuits. What he saw impressed upon him the hard facts of polar travel: fresh meat could prevent scurvy (a disease caused by a lack of vitamin C), dogs and sleds were perfect for the poles, skis were fast and efficient over great distances.

In 1907, Amundsen published *The North-West Passage,* two unheralded volumes of straight, unadorned prose in which he underplays risk, takes struggle in stride, and heralds the primitive winter survival skills of the Inuit as supreme. Like Nansen before him, Amundsen was far ahead of his time, having the genius and openness to master the indigenous culture's ancient survival skills—an ability not simply ignored but often disdained by other explorers of the day.

Scott also spent three years, from 1901 to 1904, probing the edges of the Antarctic. Afterward he wrote an adventure classic, *The Voyage of the Discovery*, a man-against-nature tale that became a critical and financial success. And yet, regarding polar travel, Scott's national prejudices led him to conclude just the opposite of Amundsen: he insisted on the nobility of man-hauling sledges versus the efficiency of dogsledding, was convinced postholing on foot worked better than gliding on skis, and refused to believe that fresh meat prevented scurvy.

At the time the South Pole was the last great prize for explorers. English captain James Cook had been the first to sail across the Antarctic circle, in 1773; his countryman Edward Bransfield the first to set foot on the continent, in 1820; and another English captain, James Ross, the first to chart some of its coast. Ernest Shackleton, who had been with Scott in the Antarctic onboard the *Discovery* in 1901–1904, led his own ill-fated expedition to the South Pole, getting within 97 miles in January 1909 before turning back and almost dying of starvation during his retreat.

Later, in the summer of 1909, the American Frederick Cook, thought to be dead, suddenly emerged from the Arctic, claiming to have reached the North Pole in April 1908. Two weeks after that, American Robert Peary claimed to have done the same in April 1909. Newspapers were abuzz for months.

Today it's generally accepted that both Peary and Cook were lying, but at the time their claims changed the game completely. Scott and Amundsen, archrivals, immediately set their sights on the South Pole. The race was on.

At 845,595 acres, Hardangervidda National Park is the second largest wilderness area in Europe. When the Amundsens tried to traverse it, they winter camped, spending only one night in a hut called Sandhaug. Today, thanks to the Norwegian Trekking Association, there are two dozen huts on the treeless, wind-scoured plateau.

Using Amundsen's description of his ski trek and a topo of the Hardangervidda, Steve and I plotted a roughly 100-mile route from southeast to northwest, passing by eight huts. Two were staffed and served meals; the other six were self-service dwellings stocked with food, fuel, and blankets. Which meant that we could conceivably do a very light ski tour—no tent, no sleeping bags, no stove, no cookware, no food.

"But what if we get lost in a whiteout?" Steve asked. "Or get hurt, or move slow, or for whatever reason don't make it to the next hut? We'll freeze to death."

He wasn't exaggerating. Three weeks before we left, four Germans skiing hut to hut on another trail in Norway were found dead. Swallowed by a snowstorm, they froze within a mile of shelter. Four years earlier, two Scottish skiers attempting to cross the Hardangervidda hut to hut had been caught in a storm and died of exposure right on the marked ski track.

In the end, we each brought a foam pad and a paper-thin bivy sack, plus one shovel—just enough to dig in and survive a night out if necessary. Throughout the winter leading up to our trip, Steve, a headhunter in Denver and a former high school cross-country ski racer, hit the NordicTrack each morning at four; I skate-skied every day in Wyoming. Knowing that we had to be swift and smooth—or else—we toured together some weekends, through the worst conditions we could find, continuously testing and refining our gear choices.

Steve was expecting calamity and prepared for it. The Hardangervidda traverse didn't strike me as any more difficult or dangerous than some of my other trips—skiing across the heart of Greenland with a Norwegian and Swedish expedition, circumnavigating Yellowstone for a month on skis—so I arrogantly expected an easy eight-day tour.

The first five minutes on the Hardangervidda disabused me of this. The wind was so fierce, it had stripped much of the snow off the tundra. What snow remained was ice, and we were obliged to immediately stretch on our skins to avoid being blown straight backward.

"What'd I tell you!" Steve screamed, grinning ear to ear.

The first hut, Helberghytta, was empty and cold when we arrived. The cabin is named after Norway's most famous World War II resistance fighter, Claus Helberg, and its walls were lined with photographs from the secret mission he'd been part of to destroy a Nazi plant near Telemark that produced heavy water, an essential ingredient in the production of nuclear weapons. We fired up the woodstove, boiled canned reindeer meatballs we'd found in the pantry, burrowed under five layers of woolen blankets like kids in a fort, and felt deeply grateful not to be camping.

The next day the headwind was preposterous. We were repeatedly knocked off our feet, as if we were being slugged by an invisible boxer. At lunch we had to sit on our packs, backs hunched against the wind, lest they be blown away.

"Can't imagine having more fun," Steve shouted through his hood.

It took us more than eight hours to cover 14 miles to the Kalhovd hut. There we found sixteen Norwegians huddled around the woodstove, drinking tea and waiting out the storm. When our faces thawed enough for us to speak, they were shocked.

"Americans! Why woot you come here to Norvay?"

I mentioned my obsession with Amundsen, and Steve explained that our mother's maiden name was Smebakken—"smith on a hill." They nodded but still looked confused, clearly wondering why two people from the land of obesity would choose to ski through a storm in long, lean Norway.

The next day the wind remained ridiculous. The Norwegians altered their plans and ended their trip, going downhill with the wind. Steve and I did the opposite, skiing due west across Kalhovdfjorden, directly into the gale, not speaking and stopping only once to wolf sandwiches and energy bars while hiding behind a boulder.

It took us seven hours to go 14 miles. Without skins, despite the fact that the terrain was flat, it would have been hard to reach the next hut, Stordalsbu.

"Amundsen would be proud," Steve shouted as we arrived at the snug, clean, well-built Norwegian cottage. I made a fire while he cooked. My brother was lighthearted and talkative, unfazed by the unbelievable weather; I was both exhilarated and exhausted.

The next morning we crossed a pass in the first couple hours and began sliding downhill into a roaring opaqueness. When the terrain leveled out, we guessed we were somewhere near Lake Vråsjåen but needed bearings. As I was holding the orienteering compass over the topo and trying to triangulate, the wind ripped both map and compass from my hands. They disappeared in the maelstrom. Only partially unnerved, Steve pulled out an extra compass and spare maps and we huddled together.

"We're off course!" I yelled.

He looked worried. He knew that if we were really lost, we probably wouldn't survive a night out.

Following a hunch, we made a 90-degree turn to the south. We'd skied half a mile when the clouds cleared just long enough for us to get our bearings, locate the trail again, and identify our next pass. I laughed with relief, and Steve spanked his ski poles over his head.

We ascended the pass slowly, cowering behind rock outcrops where we could. Dropping down the other side was lovely at first. We telemarked over icy meadows and along a wiggling creek. But soon the topography tipped and we found ourselves in a steep defile. For hours we carefully downclimbed frozen waterfalls, zigzagged through birch trees, plowed into snow up to our waists, and cursed the Norse gods.

We reached the Mogen hut deeply grateful not to have broken a leg but well aware that the remaining trip would be both dangerous and challenging. Though there was a trail on the map, there wasn't one on the landscape: almost every day we were out, we had to navigate with map and compass through a howling white wilderness.

Amundsen and Scott arrived in the Antarctic in January of 1911, and each team knew that a historic contest was under way. Hundreds of miles apart, both teams built elaborate base camps on the Ross Ice Shelf and prepared to winter over. A single push to the South Pole—1,400-plus miles round-trip, with a dangerous haul over high passes through the Transantarctic Mountains—was impossible, so each team spent the Southern Hemisphere's autumn ferrying supplies to depots along their respective routes. When winter set in—June through August—darkness descended, and temperatures dropped to 50 below.

Amundsen's men, working in well-crafted snow caves, were urgently industrious through the dark season. They tested and altered their ski boots three times, each man cobbling his own boots to conform precisely to his feet to prevent frostbite and blisters. Their fur clothing was repeatedly evaluated on trial runs and then retailored by each member to fit perfectly, eliminating chafing. The men used a lightweight wind cloth to make tents that were nearly half the weight of canvas ones, then dyed them black with shoe polish and ink powder, for three reasons: to make it easier to find the tents in a whiteout; to provide rest for weary, snow-seared eyes; and to soak up warmth from solar radiation. In the snow-walled woodshop, the team's craftsman, Olav Bjaaland, redesigned their dog sleds, cutting the weight from 150 pounds each to 50. Bjaaland, a champion skier, fashioned custom skis for each team member.

Scott was satisfied with his wool-and-cotton clothing and confident in his ponies' ability to plow through snow pulling heavy sleds. The English expedition did not refine its systems. Scott believed courage trumped adversity and that character, not craft, would carry the day. In their base camp at McMurdo Sound, he and his men squandered the winter on esoteric academic lectures, amateur theater, soccer, and letter writing.

For Amundsen, nothing had been left to chance. Pemmican was weighed down to the gram, biscuits (more than 40,000) were counted individually, seal meat was laid in depot larders, sled compasses calibrated, dogs fattened. He had learned from the Inuit that deliberately courting danger was immature, if not immoral.

Scott was a big-picture man with visions of grandeur, and he left the details to others. Besides, for the first 400 miles he would literally be following in Shackleton's footsteps. To set his farthest-south record, Shackleton and three companions had plodded on foot, man-hauling massive sleds. Scott intended to do the same after using ponies and dogs for part of the route.

From the start, Amundsen moved quickly and smoothly. He could barely control the exuberance of his dogs, and the men could sometimes ride on the sleds rather than ski. His teams typically covered 12 miles in five or six hours, then set up camp, devoting the rest of the day to rest and recuperation. If the weather was nasty they built igloos. In the fall they had marked their depots with wide lines of flags in case they veered off course, so that even in storms they easily found their resupplies of food and fuel. For the Norwegians, all of whom were excellent cross-country skiers, it was a grand jaunt. A big ski tour.

Scott's two prototype snowmobiles (a third fell through the ice while unloading) had not been properly tested during the winter, and few spare parts had been cached, so they broke down and were abandoned after five days. The ponies, sweating all over their bodies, suffered grotesquely, Huntford wrote, their backs and flanks often plated in ice. Naturally, their sharp hooves punched holes in the snow. They were often wading up to their trembling knees, sometimes up to their freezing, huffing chests. Halfway to the pole, their fodder gone, the ponies were shot. From that point on, man-hauling began.

It was a given on both expeditions that some of the draft animals would be killed en route. Amundsen put down any of the sled dogs that came into heat, wouldn't pull, or became too belligerent, feeding them to the remaining dogs, his team, and himself. At one point, after slogging over the Transantarctic Mountains—a massive east-west chain with peaks of up to 15,000 feet—Amundsen slaughtered half his remaining dogs to supply both men and animals with enough meat to survive the final push to the pole and the return trip. The journey back, when men and beasts were mentally, physically, and spiritually fatigued, was even more crucial than the push out.

Having determined on previous polar journeys the precise daily nutritional needs of both man and dog, Amundsen had ten times the reserves of food at each depot as Scott. By skiing only half a day, Amundsen's team retained strength, vigor, and morale. Scott drove his team like he drove the ponies, his men pulling in harnesses twelve hours a day. They inevitably became weak, emaciated, and demoralized.

At Mogen, Wøllo and Martinsen fed us so well—and regaled us with so many remarkable stories about the pleasures of Norwegian life—that we might have given up our traverse right there. Thanks to a wealth of oil and natural gas, the government has accumulated the second largest rainy-day fund on earth, more than $500 billion. Every citizen has guaranteed government health care for life and a full pension. Unemployment is low, and there's essentially no poverty.

"I think I could live here," Steve said dreamily as we were falling asleep in our bunks. Alas, the next day we had to ski away.

The wind had at last abated, replaced by below-zero temperatures. We pushed back up onto the central plateau, stopping only for lunch and swigs of hot cloudberry tea. The snow was brittle and the landscape bewilderingly featureless—in all directions, there were snow-clad hills of identical height and shape. We set a map bearing and followed it precisely, deviating only to avoid steep ascents or descents.

When we reached the Lågaros hut, in midafternoon, it was so buried we had to dig it out to get in the door. We assumed we would have it to ourselves, but soon we heard shouting. Peeking out the frosted windows, we couldn't believe what we saw: three kite-skiers literally sailing in from nowhere. They dropped their packs beside the hut and then continued to kite-ski just for the fun of it, jumping and carving, sweeping in vast loops across the landscape.

When they finally came inside, they were jubilant. They were Norwegian, of course: two brothers and a woman. They'd skied 28 miles that day and still had energy enough to play. We'd come just 11 miles and were whipped. One was a soldier who had just returned from a year in Afghanistan; the other two were medical students. This was their third attempt to cross the Hardangervidda.

"The other times, the wind didn't cooperate and we had to trudge along on skis," one said with a knowing grin.

They'd spent three years testing different skis and kites and knew exactly what they were doing. They were also going with the prevailing winds rather than against them, as we were.

"Total traverse of the Hardangervidda will take us about three days," the woman offered, almost ashamed to admit the efficiency of their trip to a couple of cross-country masochists who would ski for eight days to cover the same distance.

They slept in the next morning, knowing they could fly another 20 to 25 miles in a matter of hours. Meanwhile, Steve and I slogged on.

The snow was rough and the landscape burning white. It was like skiing across a desert of sand dunes. With the wind down and navigation unnecessary, we knocked off the 16 miles to Sandhaug, the next hut, in a few hours.

One hundred and fifteen years ago, the Amundsen brothers had spent a night in this very hut. Arriving early in the afternoon, we had time to catch up on our journals, sketch out our route on the maps, hoover an extra meal or two, and toast our toes over the stove.

"I'm not sure life gets much better than this," Steve said before dozing off.

That night another storm blew in, and it began building drifts around the cabin. Just as we were turning in, five middle-aged, not particularly fit Norwegians burst through the door.

"Vat are you doing here?" one of them asked snootily. But they were more than happy to suck down all the snow we had melted and dry their soaked socks over the well-stoked stove.

The next day we were gone before they got up. It was snowing and blowing miserably. Within the first hour of skiing, visibility dropped until the sky and the earth fused into a single miasmic substance. At one point, looking down, I spotted two black dots far below me. Staring through depthlessness, I couldn't tell how far away they were. Five yards? Five hundred? I backed away from the gaping abyss only to realize that the distant dots were the tips of my skis.

Without depth perception, it became difficult to balance and impossible to move in a straight line. We were blindfolded by the whiteout 10 miles from our next hut. We had to stop.

"Have gone complately blind all day," Amundsen recorded in his journal on December 5, 1911. "Thick snowfall more like home." He and his team still skied 12.5 miles. The next day was no different, but Amundsen's team made their standard distance no matter what.

Scott, materially and mentally unprepared for such conditions, either didn't move on bad days or trudged moderate distances that required unconscionable suffering, his men straining to man-haul their monstrous sledges.

As Amundsen closed in on the pole, Scott was hundreds of miles behind. Neither knew of the other's position, which caused Scott enormous anxiety. He pushed himself and his men sadisti-cally. There were days when both Scott and Amundsen made the same mileage but Amundsen did it in half the time, economizing on effort and riding the sleds when possible. Scott all but killed himself and his men.

On December 14, 1911, Amundsen and his four teammates made it to the South Pole. "And so at last we reached our desti-nation and planted our flag on the geographical South Pole . . .

Thank God!" he wrote in his journal. His focus on his men, he stated that his teammates displayed the qualities he most admired: "courage and dauntlessness, without boasting or big words." He and his skiers had been in the Antarctic almost a year and had been skiing toward the pole for more than fifty days, covering some 700 miles. Aware of the need for proof, the Norwegians spent three days mapping twenty-four sextant readings to make absolutely certain they were precisely at the bottom of the earth. They left a sled, a tent, and a cheeky note of welcome to Scott, then headed home.

Scott and four men (all the others having been sent back along the way, fortuitously) arrived at the South Pole more than a month later, cadaverous, malnourished, tired, and weak. They found Amundsen's tent and his note. Wrote Scott: "Great God! This is an awful place and terrible enough for us to have laboured to it without the reward of priority."

"Do you have any idea where we are?" Steve yelled.

"No! But I know where we're going," I screamed back.

The evening before Steve and I got caught in this latest white-out, at Sandhaug, I'd been listening to the snow beating against the windowpanes like the wings of a frightened bird. Concerned about the next day's travel, I'd calculated four consecutive bearings in the warmth of the hut. There were three empty cabins between us and our next destination; the bearings shot like arrows from one to the next.

Abandoning any pretense of seeing where we were going, Steve and I set off in the direction of the first bearing. After skiing blind for five minutes, we stopped, held the compass directly over our skis, and found that we were ten degrees off course. The wind was too strong to ski without both poles, so we resorted to rechecking our bearing every fifty paces. It was tediously slow going, but we hit the first intermediary cabin dead-on. A drink, an energy bar, and onward.

We made the next hut by lunch. It was half buried, so we dug out a hole under the eaves, laid down our foam pads, ate deliberately, and ignored the swirling snow. On the map we were halfway to our goal, although we had been trapped in clouds all morning and had seen nothing but white on white.

We never found our third landmark cabin—it must have been entirely buried. At one point the clouds cleared and Steve pointed out a ridgeline.

"Maybe a click away?" he shouted. But the landscape was still playing tricks on us; it was three times that far.

At the end of the day we were traveling along a steep hillside, beginning to question ourselves, when our destination—the Hadlaskard hut—appeared out of nowhere to our left.

It was our last hut on the Hardangervidda. We feasted on reindeer stew, crackers heaped with Nutella and cheese, and thick squares of Norwegian chocolate. Since we were the only people in the hut, we dragged blankets from the cold bunk rooms, lay down on the couches next to the woodstove, and slept so well we snored.

As if the Norse gods were finally convinced that we were worthy of our little dream, the wind stopped blowing the next day—our last—the sun came out, and Steve and I slid effortlessly along. We glided atop the snow-covered Veig River, dropping into pockets of birch trees with summer cabins sprinkled among them. As we marched up over our last pass, it started snowing lightly. Warm, big flakes and no wind. We slid north off the Hardangervidda hardly poling, completing the traverse in Garen.

But now it didn't feel right to stop. After more than a week of abysmal weather, the conditions were suddenly straight out of a fairy tale, twinkling snow falling like goose down. We decided to do a big victory loop. Striding in rhythm, brothers in silent unison, we skied through the forest into the twilight.

As Roland Huntford clearly laid out in *Scott and Amundsen*, Scott was transformed into a hero by the English press when he should have been pilloried. On his expedition's ignoble struggle from the South Pole back to camp, petty officer Edgar Evans was the first to die, pulling to the last, collapsing in his harness. Cavalry captain Lawrence Oates was next, his feet so frostbitten they were gangrenous. On the morning of his thirty-second birthday, Oates crawled from the tent and limped into oblivion. Scott was still keeping his journal, writing for posterity, penning vainglorious letters of farewell. Marine lieutenant Henry Bowers, chief expedition scientist Edward Wilson, and captain Robert Falcon Scott, all skeletal and badly frostbitten, died in their tent in Antarctica sometime after March 21, 1911.

After reaching the South Pole, Amundsen and his team easily cruised back to base camp, covering 700 miles in just six weeks. In all, they had skied 1,400 miles in ninety-nine days. No one had died; hardly anyone had been sick. There was some frostbite, but no one lost fingers or toes. Amundsen had done everything possible to remove drama and danger from his expeditions, and for that he was, in a strange but tangible way, punished. Despite the fact that his South Pole expedition was the apotheosis of elegance and efficiency, arguably the finest expedition ever accomplished by man, he would be all but forgotten outside of Norway in the decades after his death, which came in 1928, when he perished in a plane crash, probably over the Barents Sea.

Huntford, who did as much as anyone to restore Amundsen to the adventure pantheon, thought his death was both a waste and a fitting end. Amundsen had been on his way to help rescue an Italian polar explorer, Umberto Nobile, who had disappeared during an airship flight to the North Pole. Nobile was rescued by someone else, so Amundsen could have stayed home. But for Huntford, it was a strangely appropriate exit.

"His end was worthy of the old Norse sea kings who sought immolation when they knew their time had come," he wrote. "It was the exit he would have chosen for himself."

MARK JENKINS

Conquering an Infinite Cave

FROM *National Geographic*

"PAST THE HAND OF DOG, watch out for dinosaurs," says a voice in the dark.

I recognize Jonathan Sims's clipped, British military accent but have no idea what he's talking about. My headlamp finds him, gray muttonchops curling out from beneath his battered helmet, sitting alone in the blackness along the wall of the cave.

"Carry on, mate," growls Sims. "Just resting a buggered ankle."

The two of us have roped across the thundering, subterranean Rao Thuong River and climbed up through 20-foot blades of limestone to a bank of sand. I continue alone, following the beam of my headlamp along year-old footprints.

In the spring of 2009, Sims was a member of the first expedition to enter Hang Son Doong, or "mountain river cave," in a remote part of central Vietnam. Hidden in rugged Phong Nha-Ke Bang National Park near the border with Laos, the cave is part of a network of 150 or so caves, many still not surveyed, in the Annamite Mountains. During the first expedition, the team explored two and a half miles of Hang Son Doong before a 200-foot wall of muddy calcite stopped them. They named it the Great Wall of Vietnam. Above it they could make out an open space and traces of light, but they had no idea what lay on the other side. A year later they have returned—seven hard-core British cavers, a few scientists, and a crew of porters—to climb the wall, if they can, measure the passage, and push on, if possible, all the way to the end of the cave.

The trail disappears before me into a difficult pile of breakdown—building-size blocks of stone that have fallen from the ceiling and crashed onto the cave floor. I crane my head back, but the immensity of the cave douses my headlamp's tiny light, as if I were staring up into a starless night sky. I've been told I'm inside a space large enough to park a 747, but I have no way to know; the darkness is like a sleeping bag pulled over my head.

I switch off my headlamp just to feel the depth of the darkness. At first there is nothing. But then, as my pupils adjust, I'm surprised to make out a faint, ghostly light ahead. I pick my way through the rubble, almost running from excitement, rocks scattering beneath my feet and echoing in the invisible chamber. Traversing up a steep slope, I turn a ridge as if on a mountainside and am stopped in my tracks.

An enormous shaft of sunlight plunges into the cave like a waterfall. The hole in the ceiling through which the light cascades is unbelievably large, at least 300 feet across. The light, penetrating deep into the cave, reveals for the first time the mind-blowing proportions of Hang Son Doong. The passage is perhaps 300 feet wide, the ceiling nearly 800 feet tall: room enough for an entire New York City block of forty-story buildings. There are actually wispy clouds up near the ceiling.

The light beaming from above reveals a tower of calcite on the cave floor that is more than 200 feet tall, smothered by ferns, palms, and other jungle plants. Stalactites hang around the edges of the massive skylight like petrified icicles. Vines dangle hundreds of feet from the surface; swifts are diving and cutting in the brilliant column of sunshine. The tableau could have been created by an artist imagining how the world looked millions of years ago.

Jonathan Sims catches up with me. Between us and the sunlit passage ahead stands a stalagmite that in profile resembles the paw of a dog.

"The Hand of God would be just too corny," he says, pointing at the formation. "But the Hand of Dog does nicely, don't you think?"

He clicks off his headlamp and unweights his gimpy ankle.

"When we first got to the collapsed doline, that skylight up there, I was with another caver and we both had four-year-old sons, so we were experts on dinosaurs, and the whole scene reminded us of something right out of Sir Arthur Conan Doyle's novel *The Lost World*," he says. "When my partner went exploring forward into the sunlight, I told him to 'watch out for dinosaurs,' and the name stuck."

Two decades ago the leaders of this expedition, Howard Limbert and his wife, Deb, became the first cavers to visit Vietnam since the 1970s. Back then the country's caves were legendary but unexplored. In 1941 Ho Chi Minh had planned his revolution against the Japanese and French in Pac Bo Cave north of Hanoi, and during the Vietnam War thousands of Vietnamese hid from American bombing raids inside caves. The Limberts, experienced cavers from the Yorkshire dales of northern England, made contact with the University of Science in Hanoi and, after obtaining sheaves of permits, mounted an expedition in 1990. They've made thirteen trips since, not only discovering one of the longest river caves in the world—12-mile Hang Khe Ry, not far from Son Doong—but also helping the Vietnamese create 330-square-mile Phong Nha-Ke Bang National Park, which now attracts a quarter million Vietnamese and foreign visitors a year. Tourists, who dramatically increase the income of local villagers, come to see the park's namesake show cave, Hang Phong Nha, which workers light up like a psychedelic rock concert.

Because of the dense jungle, the Limberts might never have found the caves without help from area residents. "Mr. Khanh has been with us from the beginning," Howard says, nodding toward a thin man smoking a cigarette beside the campfire. We're squatting around the fire just inside the entrance to Hang En, the mile-long portal that tunnels beneath a ring of mountains into the lost world. "Couldn't have done it without him," Howard says. Ho Khanh's family lived in a nearby village. His father was killed in the war, forcing Khanh at a young age to fend for himself in the jungle. For years he hunted all over this border country, taking refuge in caves when it rained, or rained bombs.

"It took three expeditions to find Hang Son Doong," Howard says. "Khanh had found the entrance as a boy but had forgotten where it was. He only found it again last year."

Stands of bamboo and other vegetation cover mounds of limestone here, making the place all but impenetrable. Below the surface, this part of Vietnam is one immense limestone block, says Darryl Granger, a geomorphologist from Purdue University. "The whole region was squeezed upward when the Indian subcontinent smashed into the Eurasian continent forty to fifty million years ago," he says. Hang Son Doong was formed 2 to 5 million years ago, when river water flowing across the limestone burrowed down along a fault, scouring out a giant tunnel beneath the mountains. In places where the limestone was weak, the ceiling collapsed into sinkholes, creating the gigantic skylights.

Anette Becher, a German caver and biologist, has found wood lice, fish, and millipedes inside the cave that are all white, which is common for creatures that live in the dark. And Dai Inh Vu, a botanist from the Vietnam Academy of Science and Technology, has identified the plants growing beneath the skylights, finding basically the same mix that grows in the forest above. But such science on the run is not the real focus of this expedition, whose central purpose is exploration. For cavers like the Limberts, discovering a cave as big as Hang Son Doong is like finding a previously unknown Mount Everest underground. "We've just scratched the surface here," Howard says of the national park, which was named a World Heritage site in 2003 for its forests and caves. "There is so much more to do."

When Howard and Deb first saw these enormous spaces, they felt certain they had discovered the largest cave in the world—and they might be right. There are longer caves than Hang Son Doong—the Mammoth Cave system in Kentucky, with 367 total miles, holds that record. There are deeper caves too—Krubera-Voronja, the "crow's cave," plunges 7,188 feet in the western Caucasus Mountains of Georgia. But for giant passages, there are few caves that can compare. At the time of the Limberts' discovery of Hang Son Doong, the largest passage was thought to be Deer Cave in Malaysian Borneo's Gunung Mulu National Park, which was recently surveyed at 1.2 miles long, 500 feet wide, and 400 feet tall. But as the explorers would eventually determine, using precise laser instruments, Hang Son Doong is more than 2.5 miles long with a continuous passage as wide as 300 feet and, in places, over 600 feet high.

"We weren't actually searching for the largest cave in the world," Deb says. But she's thrilled that the cave's newfound fame might improve the lives of local villagers.

After five days of hiking, hauling, and crawling, the expedition is still only halfway into the cave. Counting all the cavers, scientists, a film and photography crew, and porters, we are a team of more than two dozen, which seems to have slowed us down. Besides that, the going gets dangerous as we climb through the breakdown in Watch Out for Dinosaurs: one misstep on slick boulders could mean a fall of more than a hundred feet.

When we reach the next skylight, the Garden of Edam (another cheesy pun), it's even bigger than the first, almost as wide as the roof of the Superdome in New Orleans. Below the opening is another mountain of breakdown with a jungle of hundred-foot-tall trees, lianas, and burning nettles. As our time and supplies begin to run out, Howard decides the moment has come to send an advance team ahead to the Great Wall of Vietnam, to see if an assault is really possible.

The wall lies more than a mile away at the end of a corridor shaped like a V with a foot-deep trench of water at the bottom. Mud walls, sticky as peanut butter, rise 40 feet high on either side. It is not possible to walk in the trench, only to stumble. By the time you reach the wall, you're so covered in mud you appear to have gone swimming in chocolate pudding. The cavers named this passage Passchendaele, after the trench warfare battle of World War I in which the Allies lost 310,000 soldiers to gain only 5 miles of ground near the Belgian village of Ypres.

Climbing an overhanging 200-foot-tall wall of mud is technical, risky business, so you need just the right type of madmen. Luckily, Howard has handpicked Gareth "Sweeny" Sewell and Howard Clarke for the advance team. The two have been caving together for twenty years in the nastiest potholes in England. Clarky is a bull semen salesman, and Sweeny is a legal specialist who somehow convinced his wife that they should sell their one and only car so he could keep heading off on caving expeditions.

The first day at the base of the wall, as Clarky belays, Sweeny begins boldly working his way upward, drilling hole after hole. Almost all of the holes are too hollow to hold a screw from which to hang their ropes.

For twelve hours they jabber in their expletive-laden Yorkshire vernacular—"Ez bloody crap covered wit mood," Sweeny says at one point. Neither says a word about the true dangers of the task. Were any of the 6-inch screws to pop out, the rope Sweeny is hanging on would lose its anchor and he'd likely zipper the rest of the screws and plummet to his death.

On the second day of the climb, after bivouacking at the bottom of the wall for the night, Sweeny returns to his previous high point, with Clarky belaying again. Soon enough the whirring of his drill echoes through the domed blackness, Sweeny so high up we can see only the glimmer of his headlamp. At two in the afternoon —of course it doesn't matter a bit what time it is when it's dark 24/7—after twenty hours of drilling holes and climbing higher, Sweeny finally disappears over the wall, and some minutes later we hear *"AAΠOOOOO!!"*

Clarky ascends the rope next, then yells down for me, the words bouncing through the cave: "Well, ye comin' up or wat!"

At the top of the Great Wall of Vietnam we can literally see light at the end of the tunnel and start howling our heads off. The rest of the expedition will later tell us that they actually heard our hallos more than a mile away in the cave. Measurements made at the top of the wall will reveal that from the bottom of Passchendaele to the ceiling is 654 feet. It's just the three of us now, exploring. No human has ever been here before. We drop down off the backside of the Great Wall and begin ascending a staircase of rock toward the exit.

"Will ye look at deese!" roars Clarky, kneeling beside a dried-up pool. Sweeny and I gather around. Inside the pool, illuminated by our headlamps, are cave pearls.

Cave pearls are formed when a drop of water from the ceiling hits the limestone floor and throws up a speck of rock. This grain is jostled in its little cup of stone every time a drop hits it. Over thousands of years, a solid, almost perfectly round calcite pearl is formed.

Pearls are rare and in most caves are no larger than a marble. The cave pearls here are the size of baseballs, larger than any the cavers have ever seen. (Their preternatural size may be due to the enormous distance the ceiling waterdrops fall.)

"I 'ereby christen this passage Pearl 'arbor," Clarky announces.

Twenty more minutes and we're scrambling up and out of the cave. It is raining in the jungle. We hack our way far enough out into the forest to recognize a horizon and determine that this is not just another skylight, but that we have discovered the end of Hang Son Doong. Sweeny and Clarky are far too humble to openly express that we've just completed the first push through what is very likely the largest cave passage in the world.

AARON DACYTL

Railroad Semantics

FROM *Railroad Semantics*

3.30.11

EUGENE, OR — It's balmy out. That's what the waitress at Keystone said this afternoon as Sam and I gorged on buckwheat pancakes. It's windy too, and without a drop of rain (it was all spent yesterday), temperatures are at about 60 degrees with the sun occasionally breaking through the clouds—the type of Oregon day when you might spot a rainbow at any given moment. At dusk the sun retired slowly behind a heavy sky and I made my way down the Northwest Hwy, eyeing a northbound train sitting on the far tracks having its air hoses checked, and was meanwhile simultaneously being eyed by a worker on the rear of a line of trains backing into the industry tracks. I stayed motionlessly visible until dark enough, then crossed the industry tracks and disappeared into the yard where the northbound train sat hissing. There were several options to ride in case of sudden departure, but nothing preferred, especially in case of rain, and the very last car on the line, an old MP with Freddy, was the only open boxcar, but its doorway was exposed, facing west into the lights of the yard office. After walking the line on both sides I sat atop a car of huge rotund logs and drank all the beer I had, just listening to the sounds of the yard. When I later climbed into the MP boxcar I saw its floor was coming up at both ends like there had been an earthquake inside and the floor panels uplifted. I could actually see the ground and wheel axles through the floor on the front end so I lay in the back corner in the shadows. I did not bother putting my earplugs in, and instead focused on the constant multitude of hissing, snapping, popping pistons from idling engines echoing through the boxcar every split second. Occasionally a thunderous clanking of steel would reverberate on the track adjacent, jarring the entire boxcar like I was moving. Engines revved up and died down, backed up, picked up, and moved adjacent lines, and a train horn blared somewhere off in the distance. In all its chaos I felt relaxed—this is beauty to me: though a polluted, rusty, and industrial jungle so far the opposite of a place like Mt. Pisgah, it is beautiful to me in much the same way. Having spent so much time here I've come to cherish the solitude and privacy it affords me, and thinking on that I drifted off to sleep full and happy.

Later, the train pulled down to the departure tracks from a long slow crawl out of the yard, and it was a little hairy getting out of there. The very last car on the line screeched and rattled raucously back and forth as a white jeep followed the train, paralleling my boxcar the entire way. A worker switched the tracks and the train rolled slowly toward a pair of headlights shining brightly in through the boxcar door. As the train creaked along slower and slower I felt increasingly afraid that the last car would stop right in front of that jeep and they would look inside and pull me off. But oh-so-slowly my boxcar crept by. The train stopped briefly beside a large lumberyard just north of Eugene, then finally pulled onto the main line and began to highball. Bumping and bouncing along the dark land, through Junction City, across the Willamette River, along sowed fields spanning to the dark, milky horizon, the train felt like it was going to splinter and fall apart at any second —by far the bumpiest ride I have been on in a long time—and reminded me of my first ever train ride, on a Disko grainer to Kansas City some years ago. Balled up in the rear cubbyhole on the back end of a long junk train, I was thrust violently back and forth as the train clanked, shunted, and jerked endlessly along the miserable Missouri landscape. I remember thinking then that if I ever rode a train again I would surely have to wear a bike helmet the next time. Now, trying to lie down in that back corner was preposterous, thinking that I could get any sleep. On a surprisingly warm night I stood leaning out the doorway with the wind at my face, watching the valley roll by just like I used to. And as the train continued to rock violently, I had to be extra-careful to not end up another Michael Andrew Birkinshaw (the train had slacked and shunted with such a force that it already nearly jolted me out the boxcar door)!

Stopping at Shedd alongside a rancid-smelling cattle pasture and a cesspool pond of some sort with a road on the other side of that, a red light shone ahead . . . *With all Amtraks through for the night it could only be another freight this train is waiting on. (As long as I'm not at Marion I'm really not concerned.) It smells pretty fucking rancid as I stand pissing on the main line, watching Freddy's blink reflecting off the tracks toward two distant signal lights. It's warm out still, probably about sixty, and that and the wind doesn't help the stench any* . . . The signal looking south turned green and minutes later headlights shone distantly ahead as a southbound approached. It passed in a whirlwind of lights and roar and with two DPUs, and after it cattle stench filled the boxcar as frogs croaked wildly in the trackside watershed. The train stopped abruptly again before reaching Albany, on the main line behind a corrugated Oregon RV Appliance Repair shed, where again frogs croaked incessantly in the confusion, perhaps wondering if each other frog was okay. (I've heard this before in a train yard in Watsonville, California, where the main line borders acres of Driscoll strawberry fields, and where every time a train passed on the main line and I stepped out of the yard into the furrows I would hear frogs down in the watershed at the base of the ballast croaking wildly about all the confusion.) . . . *No doubt it must be putrid, as these amphibians are, cruelly, living in chemical runoff from the tracks. It's sad, but precious at the same time as they communicate to maintain some anuran solidarity* . . .

I awoke in the morning on a siding somewhere north of Salem . . . *Marion County probably* . . . where acres of grass (seed) sprawled out from the boxcar door and heavy clouds lingered west above distant I-5. Swollen fields held large puddles and a small single-engine plane flew back and forth over the land very low. It almost seemed like a remote control gig but was most likely spraying the fields. A very short train then blew by—the 0530 Cascades from Eugene making its morning run north. My train pulled forward a little bit, but only to stop again and I had no idea what was happening so I fell back asleep. Several hours later the train was on the move again, passing through Woodburn, where a small cemetery on the north side of town marks the spot from which southbound trains often stop on the main line to work. I realized then that I had been sided at Gervais—north of Salem indeed. Shortly thereafter, the train violently cut its air, stopping abruptly on the main line again. The smell of burned rubber snuffed my nose. I wondered if the train had possibly hit something or was just malfunctioning badly. It sat on the main line in a hilly area around a bend where a little road wrapped through the hills (a dirt access road or perhaps someone's driveway). A worker walked back and I heard him fooling around the back of the boxcar I was in, but he didn't look inside. The train then slowly pulled up to unblock a road crossing and I suspected the worker was riding the ladder on the back of the car so I remained still. But I don't know what happened to him . . . *It has been a manically unstable ride all the way from those rickety departure tracks in Eugene and I am quickly losing faith in my train. I feel like it's just going to splinter and fall apart or leave me here altogether . . .*

A malfunction of some sort definitely destabilized the train because after rolling again it again blew its air abruptly and smoke rose from the brake pads several car lengths ahead as the train stopped dead on the main line before reaching Coalca. I walked around the wooded riverbank for a while, then was just about to climb back into the boxcar when I checked back at the last second to make sure no one was looking but sure enough saw a worker in a bright green vest walking back my side of the train. I pretended to be taking pictures in case he saw me, then walked around the back of the train with a wide berth and, watching his feet from underneath the car, dodged him. He walked to the back end of the train and around it, and as he crossed over I cut through a coupler ahead of him and hopped back over to the other side. Then, as he continued up the other side of the train, I walked back to my boxcar and climbed safely inside.

3.31.11

Oregon City, OR—What a blower that train was. I rode the last car on the line, a dilapidated old MP boxcar with missing floorboards, and abandoned it twelve hours later at Coalca after a series of malfunctions. I put my thumb out on Hwy 99 but no one picked me up, and twenty minutes later the malfunctioning train clanked together and rattled off and I said Fuck it and walked the tracks north.

The section of tracks from Coalca to the recently shuttered Blue Heron Paper Mill in Oregon City follows the Willamette on a high riverbank of enormous, sometimes mossy boulders and a vertical cliffside that feeds the river waterfalls of runoff from the roller-coaster-like highway it holds. While several dilapidated marina buildings and other undetermined structural remains designate the area largely abandoned, it is rather superb if you take the time to observe its intrinsic qualities. A quaint little neighborhood sits a mile south of Oregon City with houses that face the tracks in an old-timey way and have little white picket fences with waist-high gates opening to pathways crossing the tracks to recreational river access. It looks like a small town on some discontinued shortline in the south, and is totally idyllic in that sense . . . *The thought of this being the very same view of the Willamette River the first settlers in Oregon saw two hundred years ago, and that the Kalapuya Indians had known long before that, is refreshing to my mind. However, behind me the highway cuts brutally through the rest of the landscape and everything is centered around easy access to that concrete trail. And of course Union Pacific renders the riverbank a constant threat, as is apparent from the tracks being strewn with deer carnage and the scattered remains of mammalian skeletons* . . .

I reached Oregon City with frustrated sweat upon my brow and wandered into a coffee shop to clean up and caffeinate myself for the day. From outside there I caught the #33 bus to Portland. A rather cramped ride to begin with, I had to sit in the front reserved-for-handicapped-persons seats across from a plump, sorry-looking goth girl clutching a library copy of a thick Stephen King novel and who sobbed into her cell phone to a no doubt equally pathetic white-bread boyfriend about her own personal problems as if it were a sorrowing, real-life soap opera. After hanging up she begged for stranger-comfort by making eyes at others and sobbing loudly for all to hear—her voluminous cleavage and cut-too-short denim skirt was an affront to all taste and decency. And then, if her life couldn't get any worse, the bus broke down at Silver Springs Road with Portland looming visibly on the horizon. The bus just quit, and all passengers—wheelchairs, travel packs (mine), and bikes alike—had to walk down the busy street to the next bus stop and wait to cram into an even more crowded next bus . . . *First it was the train that broke down repeatedly, huffing and puffing for hours before even nearing Portland, and now the bus. After getting this far it*

has taken me three hours just to get another five miles and I'm not even to
Portland yet. I should've went back to sleep and stayed with the train . . .

4.6.11

Portland, OR—It's not unlike Portland to suddenly revert to winter in the spring with freezing storms that make you run for shelter. While walking through the shadows of the already wet train
cars in Albina yard, a rogue sleet began and continued relentlessly,
thick and visible in the spectrum of the yard's lights. Skittle-sized
pellets of ice pummeled down on the Northeast Portland riverbank, careening loudly off the vertical steel walls of boxcars and
echoing oddly off empty tankers and hoppers. Wooden cross-ties
became white and slippery to the boot's touch, like from a fresh
frost. I took refuge under Going Street, but the bridge is not exactly conducive to human settlement—the concrete slanting up
to the road is too steep to climb and there is no room to lie at
the top, and the pillars below comprise one of Portland's hiviest
areas, to say the least. One headless line of trains sat on the departure tracks extending north past the bridge and after the sleet
had quelled to a drizzle I called several of the cars in to find them
destined for midwestern towns days and nights away. Because the
stock was mostly bound for BNSF yards (one of them interchang-
ing at a BNSF location in Washington and several others going
to Minnesota), my feeling was that the train was headed north,
mostly likely to Seattle to interchange there, then heading east.
On an ALY boxcar with no seal, I opened the door, put my stuff
inside, and with some beer I picked up at my favorite convenient
store (the Plaid Pantry at the top of the hill on Interstate) sat in
the boxcar door staring out into the wet night.

Around 2200 a northbound pulled down the main line and
stopped—a line of mostly empty well cars. It was Seattle-bound, I
presumed, and though wet, suicidal, and exposed to perhaps even
more wet, I climbed aboard and found somewhat of a ledge to lie
on at the front end of one of the cars so that if the rain did again
come, it would do so at an angle and spare me as much as possible.

I woke up somewhere in Washington getting dumped on—sound
asleep, just getting dumped on. The train was sided and I could

soon feel the wet beginning to seep through to my clothes as it collected in the grooves of my sleeping mat. I got my umbrella out and packed up my sopping sleeping bag and just sat there in the rain. (There's something about the alignment our solar body in the spring and the relative declination of the Pacific Northwest that just seems to suck the moisture from the sky at sunrise and sunset, the same way that the clouds then burn off around noon and reveal the day, only to reappear again around dusk.) With the sun rising bright in the overcast east and the landscape agriculturally nondescript—a barbed-wired-in distribution warehouse, I-5 moving along 200 yards to the west under lush, wet hills with fog cutting through the evergreens—I felt like I was still in the Wapato Valley. Looking ahead down the tracks it looked like my train was snaking out from the siding onto the main line, blocking it, but that was not the case. A series of long drawn-out horns eventually led to a southbound hotshot, and before it passed entirely, the empty train I was on clanked together and rolled off along the wet Washington landscape. Catching up to the rain that had previously woken and soaked me, I put my umbrella up and sat helplessly under it with my back to the front of the well car, hunched up with my knees in my sweatshirt trying to warm my painfully cold hands. Urbanity reigned on both sides of the tracks, confining me to remain down so that the only things I could see were the ground passing below and occasionally the tops of trains as I passed them . . . *I don't know where I am but my best guess is nearing Tacoma . . .*

On several occasions I tried to take notice of my surroundings, hoping to gauge some sort of claim on my trajectory, but nothing proved useful. (I saw Emerald Downs, a racetrack or something that I thought looked familiar, a sign designating the Black River and a small wooden trestle following it, and a multitude of BNSF freightage and rail equipment.) Suddenly the valley seemed to dissolve and immense hills grew around the train. Arms of the freeway overlapped in myriad spans, wrapping around each other and ultimately transporting the entire I-5 corridor to the east side of the tracks. Idle trains were passed and a Puget Sound Sounder snuck up from behind, no doubt seeing me plain as day sitting down in the well—that's when I knew I must be close. Busier and busier the landscape became as what looked like an airport took to the west side of the train and multiple tracks fed an increasing intermodel presence suggesting a nearby port: the Puget Sound. But I could not see water. The train then passed under a large scaffolding archway with the name Georgetown on it, telling, no doubt, but I didn't even have my maps to figure out where that was. As the train slowed I almost hopped off in case the Sounder had called me in, but it continued on so I stayed with it. But I could tell by looking at the ground below that it had switched tracks and veered off the main line, and again I had not done my research like I should have, and when I looked up and saw an intermodel yard with the name Argo, it only sounded vaguely familiar. Two workers stood on both sides of the train ahead operating a remote control engine and my train car stopped beside one of them. Vulnerable anyhow, I stood up, knowing the worker would see me but hoping he would not care, or at least that I could get safely out of the yard before anything could happen.

"Whooooa!" he exclaimed, obviously taken aback. He looked at his partner to confirm what he was seeing as I hopped off the train and walked up to him.

"You know that's illegal?" he asked in an obvious rhetorical question.

"Yessir!" I responded. "Can you tell me where is Argo?"

"You're in Seattle," he said, pointing to a distant dreary cityscape on the horizon that I then turned to see for myself.

"Yes! I made it."

"Where are you trying to go?"

"Seattle."

"Where did you get on?"

"Portland. Last night."

"Really?"

"Thank you, sir," I said, ending our brief conversation. "I'm getting out of the yard." And with that I walked briskly out of the yard and to a nearby street where I stood to catch the #106 bus downtown.

4.7.11

Seattle, WA—Seattle is wet and gray and cold and not unlike I imagined it would be: spitting rain. I am hanging out with Read, a graffiti artist wanted in several states, apparently (according to

The Stranger), and he is putting the final touches on his first gallery show as part of the Lawrimore Project, on display in a small storefront in a renovated old architectural office building in Pioneer Square, a skuzzier part of downtown. He has been up all night for the second night in a row hanging pieces, finishing an enormous black roller that looks like it could only have been accomplished with the aid of a projector, but wasn't, and organizing several hijacked newspaper boxes that he has repainted and claimed to display his own book *The Reader*—all inside this little bathroom-sized space with a high ceiling.

It was my first time in Seattle and Read and Herman Beans cordially showed me around. We spent the hours before the opening drinking at the Central, Seattle's oldest saloon (established in 1896), where a buffet of cheese ravioli and mini hot dogs adorned the corner. The dark, musty interior of the Central made me feel right at home as I drank Manny's, a local beer that everyone seems to prefer by the pitcher. By eveningtime hot dog vendors and shoe-shiners had set up on the sidewalk outside and patrons began to pour in from Friday's Art Walk. The night was a wild success (critics agree!), and one to remember on the streets of Seattle. Long after the gallery had closed, some envious coward threw a stereo speaker through the front window, breaking it and gouging the plaster on the back wall but otherwise doing no damage to anything. And no one really cared either. I think it enhanced the show, and if anything added to Read's credibility as a street artist. Last call later, five shots rang deafeningly into the musty night air, echoing across the Sound, and through the brick alleyways of Pioneer Square people scattered in all different directions. I passed out in the back of a big white moving van parked somewhere nearby.

[background noise]
ME: . . . buckin' shots.
READ: You guys all got fuckin' hella shook!
ME: That was the loudest thing I've heard in months, man!
[Read laughs]
READ: Was that shit pretty loud?
ME: It was so loud! It was echoing all across the bay . . . echoing all across the Sound.
[background noise]

*READ: Fuck. Isn't it crazy someone just . . . threw that fuckin' shit
    through the window?*

*ME: Ya. While you were buckin' shots, right? Coincidence? Who
    knows . . .*

DRUNKEN BROAD: Definitely obnoxious coincidence.

[Read looking for his phone charger]

READ: Is this my charger?

ME: You're not gonna find that thing in this mess.

READ: All right. Fuck it . . . find that shit tomorrow.

[door shuts]

*DRUNKEN BROAD: What are you doing? Don't you know what you're
    doing?*

[inaudible talking]

DRUNKEN BROAD to ME: You get it, right?

READ: Let's go! Call Jamie. See if Jamie still wants to hang out.

ME to DRUNKEN BROAD: Halfway . . .

*DRUNKEN BROAD: What the fuck are you doing with a gun you
    have to shoot into a bush at the same time this weird random
    coincidence at the same time happens that you don't know
    anything about?*

ME: What hath Fortuna spun my way?

READ: I didn't shoot that shit in the bush. I shot it in the air . . .

4.9.11

Tacoma, WA—I preyed on trains from the Amtrak station, which
conveniently borders a small BNSF yard just down the street from
the Greyhound station on Puyallup Ave., where there are also two
gas stations to acquire food and beer while waiting. The tracks are
fairly busy considering both UP and BNSF share trackage rights, as
well as Amtrak, which runs at least six trains a day. Just south of the
Amtrak station was a loading dock with several boxcars backed up
to it, across from which the yard sat fairly full. However, no trains
were on the outer five main lines, which meant that everything
was either being received or classified which was about the way
it looked to me, as there were no units in sight. Since it's Saturday and the business with the loading dock was closed, I sat there
writing and watching. Directly across from me sat an old green
BN caboose made into the middle of a string of miscellaneous

cars that I had my eye on from minute one. After several patient moments of looking out, I crossed the tracks to find the caboose wide open and accepting of me. Actually, it was the perfect place to wait. It had a bed, desk, table and chairs, two second-level seats that looked out over the top the trains, and several compartments to hide stuff in. I could've stayed there for days!

The main line quickly proved to be extremely active, as I thought, with three northbounds (two BNSF and one UP) moving through, one of which stopped for about an hour to work. I made a beer run across the street and found an obscure beer called Schmidt, with one of the most atrocious labels I have ever seen—a sepia-toned buck standing in the woods as if it were being viewed through the scope of a gun. That's what I got a six-pack of and drank while sitting in the upper level of the caboose looking out across the yard. It soon became apparent that, at least on this day, southbounds are not as frequent as northbounds. Trains destined for Seattle, Everett-and-beyond, and British Columbia–bound coal cars almost never stopped coming through, and most of them I could have caught on the fly (I think), if I needed to. I actually contemplated catching out north and reestablishing myself back up in Seattle for a clean catch south, out of Argo. But then again, I really didn't have any idea how these southbounds behaved, and I didn't want to give up on Tacoma so soon. Besides, I was pretty comfortable in the caboose.

It was a nice day in Tacoma, which doesn't necessarily mean warm or sunny—just not raining. Derived from the native *Tahoma,* a name given to the great mountain looming over the city, Tacoma sits south of the yard on a jut of land in the Commencement Bay part of Puget Sound. A railroad town founded in 187? by Northern Pacific, Tacoma very much has the feeling of a port city with an array of bridges linking to nearby islands. There are docks galore, seafood restaurants, a waterfront conducive to people traffic that stretches the length of the city's shoreline, and boats—in harbors, at ports, docking and undocking—surround the city at bay. Tacoma is not a sprawling expanse, but rather a town stacked on steep hills that provide an upper-handed view across the Sound of Vashon Island (the second longest [behind Long] island in the continental U.S., which stretches all the way to Seattle), and of monumental, glaciated, fine-beer-inspiring Mt. Rainier dominating the eastern horizon. Unfortunately, I did not get to spend much time in Tacoma, but perhaps another day . . .

By evening's onset seven northbound trains had come through, four of which were catchable on the fly. The seventh northbound was a damn fast line of BNSF maroon hoppers and after that the first southbound of the day pulled into the yard, a short line of doublestacks that did not seem too promising, so I made another six-pack-of-Schmidt run.

The eighth northbound of the day, a loaded BNSF coal train doing a good 35–40 mph, was no doubt headed to Vancouver, B.C., to be exported. There were very, very few markings on the line of silver bullets, and it had two DPUs pushing. The ninth northbound was another line of BNSF maroons . . . *Whistle Blower, 7/09 —Low Expectations; Joins; DCH Bend Over, Oregon; Texican Gothic; and several Ewoks* . . . A DPU pushed this line as well, which suggests it too is going a longer distance than just Seattle.

I finally lost track of how many northbounds came through— ten or eleven or twelve—but another southbound did finally pull into the yard after sunset and it was not a stock of cars that I had seen occupying the yard thus far, which made me think it was not going to stay. After cutting its air, the units broke off, carrying with them the first half of the train. In the cover of darkness I left the caboose and walked the line back. It consisted of a lot of Canadian grainers, old BN hoppers, and some obscure boxcars that I quickly determined were loaded. After walking both sides of the line I found only a big-belly Canadian hopper with a filthy porch facing into the wind. But since it's spring in the rainy Northwe(s)t, I needed to find something more suitable to ride. Most of the boxcars had seals on their doors so I didn't try to open them, but I came upon a NOKL boxcar without a seal and managed to open its door, and it was indeed empty (however, there was still a seal on the other side's door). I placed my bags inside the boxcar and rested my feet by dangling my legs out the door. A unit passed behind me on the main line and I climbed over and saw it to be a southbound, but I didn't get to see if the units were UP or BNSF. The train was short too, anyhow, and though it stopped briefly, I let it go and went back to the boxcar.

Trains clanked on the shove, my boxcar lurched, and the train

eventually departed south on a steady curve about the dark shim-
mering bay, passing under cathedral-like bridges, through multiple industries, grain mills, sidings stocked with a plethora of BNSF
maroon hoppers stretching for miles, cut through a short tunnel
beneath an overpass, and then delved into a longer tunnel that
stretched for about a mile—the Nelson-Bennet Tunnel. Curving
eastward underneath Point Defiance and submerging me in as
great a pitch black as I have known, the tunnel then spit the train
out along the eastern shore of the Puget Sound . . . *The tunnel was
a good mile long and I could not see my hand passing over my face . . .
just pitch black for a good two or three minutes and the train came out
right along the Sound . . . now just barreling along its shore . . . it's wide
open and there's an arch bridge ahead—a big Golden Gate–like bridge
arching over the Sound . . . there's an island in the middle and the Sound
looks like the Willamette up in Oregon City if the Willamette were three or
four times as wide, wider than the Columbia . . . it's beautiful and wide
and dark and milky and also reminds me of the Gorge as the train rounds
along banks of huge boulders, occasionally passing slender sand beaches
. . . I can see why the early explorers once mistook this for the mouth of
the Northwest Passage . . . barreling along . . . a train approaches in the
distance with bright headlights . . . now diverging readily from the Sound
and going over a sort of dried-up area where the water has receded like at
low tide . . . crossing I-5 into a woodsy area . . . still barreling along at
45–50 miles per hour, toward Olympia, I suppose . . . the only problem
with this boxcar is the door keeps—every time the train shunts the boxcar's
door closes a little bit more and I have to push it back open . . . I know that
it's a pressure-release door that can't just lock me inside . . . (I don't think
I'm going to get stuck in here, but I don't want to take any chances . . .) I
wedged my water bottle, which fit pretty generously, into the crease, and also
a beer can, but I don't think that's really going to do any good. (Hopefully I
won't be locked in this boxcar by morning. If I am, it will be a slow painful
death in which dehydration will be the key factor . . .) I have only one bottle
of water, so if I die, I'll die doing what I love—a noble cause . . .*

*I'm somewhere in Washington—not sure where. I slept all night in that
boxcar on a siding somewhere, and it rained the whole night, but I was
comfortable . . . now in a yard somewhere in Washington and the train just
started moving again . . . wet and gray . . . old BN cars and lumber . . .
headed south without any signs telling me where I am (I'll have to figure*

that out by deduction) . . . moving steady . . . a small lake of some sort to the west of the train car . . . hills across that with fog clinging to the tops of them . . . very low cloud cover . . . lots of empty and abandoned docks, and posts sticking out of the water . . . moving steadily at 30–35–40 miles per hour through a kind of marshland . . . everything is wet and gray yet still pretty—milepost 1048—and there's lots of lumber and industry around . . . the lake widens and shows its true character as a bay or marina with boats out—not as wide as the Sound, but still a wide bay (this could be Longview, or around there) . . . a whole line of trains that was in Tacoma last night is now down here in Washington—Ridgefield—they must've passed me in the night, and now I'm passing them . . . Fidel siding . . . now pulling into Fruit Valley, wherever the fuck that is (a lot of familiar cars hanging out in this yard, though, that I can already tell). There's a light, spitting rain and I'm on a jeep path in between two lines. The line I just got off, it's probably going to stay here for a while. However, a line across from it is getting air-hose-checked by a guy on an ATV, and taking that to be the line that's going to move first, I climb over to it . . . rain picking up, almost becoming sleet . . . a train horn in the distance sounds like a crossing horn, not a start-up horn . . . I hear this train ticking air and even sense it nudge a little bit . . . workers on ATVs always unnerve me and one looks to be coming down on each side of the train . . . (I've got to get off this porch when the worker comes because I don't know if the cubbyhole's going to cut it . . .) shit! [sound of ATV revving] Dude's right across from me on an ATV . . . he just rolled straight past as I hid behind a wheel axle . . . a light rain in Vancouver—I'm just going to go ahead and say this is Vancouver. I've been here for about an hour and no trains have left. That same line of boxcars from last night in Tacoma that passed me and that I then passed at Ridgefield this morning just pulled into the yard and is now sitting on the line next to me. I'm waiting for a move, anything to get me closer to downtown Vancouver so I can just take a bus to Portland . . . (there's something coming in between these two trains . . .) BNSF coal cars, loaded, just went north, and there's definitely a guy on an ATV down there working on this line . . . (sounds like an Amtrak coming through . . .) [Amtrak approaches] . . . it's the Cascades . . . [Amtrak roars by] . . . (kind of seems like strange timing . . .) a guy is coming down my line on an ATV doing something or another—I have to keep an eye on him . . . just left the north end of that Vancouver yard, or Fruit Valley, or whatever it's called, by jumping on a line when it started to move, then getting off when that line stalled and another line started to move and catching on to that other line on the fly . . . it's spitting rain and I'm on the move again, trying to just get back across the river to Portland. Time will tell where this train will take me, but hopefully it's not headed east. (I didn't really think about that. Hopefully I'll be able to get off before then if it is) . . . lots of whistles . . .

Contributors' Notes

Notable Travel Writing of 2011

Contributors' Notes

Bryan Curtis is a staff writer at *Grantland* and a contributor to the *New York Times Magazine* and *Texas Monthly*. He travels frequently with the photographer Eric Roberts.

Aaron Dacytl is a photographer, writer, adventurer, and train enthusiast. A 2010 graduate of Portland State University, he prefers to travel by freight train as well as to work seasonally. In his spare time he makes *Railroad Semantics*, a zine devoted to independent travel, railroad culture, and history. He lives in Eugene, Oregon.

Luke Dittrich is a contributing editor at *Esquire*, where he writes on subjects ranging from lost atomic bombs to teenage hit men. His forthcoming book, *The Brain That Changed Everything*, is about Henry Molaison, who in 1958 underwent an experimental operation at the hands of Dittrich's grandfather. The operation obliterated Molaison's ability to create new memories, and Molaison went on to become the most important human test subject in the history of science, revolutionizing our understanding of how memory works. An *Esquire* article Dittrich wrote about Molaison is featured in the 2011 edition of *The Best American Science and Nature Writing*.

Lynn Freed's work has appeared in *The New Yorker*, *Harper's Magazine*, *The Atlantic*, *Southwest Review*, *Georgia Review*, the *New York Times*, the *Washington Post*, the *Wall Street Journal*, *National Geographic*, and *Narrative Magazine*, among others. She is the recipient of the inaugural Katherine Anne Porter Award from the American Academy of Arts and Letters, a PEN/O. Henry Award, fellowships, grants, and support from the National Endowment for the Arts and the Guggenheim Foundation, among others. Born in South Africa, she now lives in northern California.

J. Malcolm Garcia is the author of *Khaarijee: A Chronicle of Friendship and War in Kabul* (2009) and *Riding through Katrina with the Red Baron's Ghost* (2012). His articles have been featured in *The Best American Travel Writing* and *The Best American Nonrequired Reading*.

Michael Gorra is the author of *Portrait of a Novel: Henry James and the Making of an American Masterpiece* (2012). Winner of a National Book Critics Circle Award for his work as a reviewer, he has taught English at Smith College since 1985. Earlier books include *The Bells in Their Silence: Travels through Germany, After Empire: Scott, Naipaul, Rushdie,* and, as editor, *The Portable Conrad.* An earlier essay appeared in *The Best American Travel Writing 2004.* Gorra lives in Northampton, Massachusetts, with his wife and daughter.

Peter Gwin is a staff writer at *National Geographic.* His assignments have led him to the Sahara's largest Stone Age graveyard, the oldest known tyrannosaur, and Nazi U-boats sunk in the Gulf of Mexico. A native of Fayette County, Georgia, he is based in Washington, D.C.

Pico Iyer is the author of two novels and eight works of nonfiction, including many found on the travel literature shelves — *Video Night in Kathmandu, The Lady and the Monk, Falling Off the Map,* and *The Global Soul.* His most recent book, *The Man Within My Head,* which came out in early 2012, is about Graham Greene, hauntedness, and the moral and emotional conundrums that travel quite wonderfully throws up.

Mark Jenkins is a seasoned climber, contributing writer for *National Geographic,* and former monthly columnist for *Outside* magazine. His books include *A Man's Life: Dispatches from Dangerous Places; The Hard Way: Stories of Danger, Survival, and the Soul of Adventure; To Timbuktu: A Journey Down the Niger;* and *Off the Map: Bicycling Across Siberia.* He has written for *Men's Health, Backpacker, Time, The Atlantic,* and other media.

Dimiter Kenarov is a freelance journalist and contributing editor at the *Virginia Quarterly Review.* His work has appeared in *Esquire, Outside, The Nation,* the *International Herald Tribune,* the Pulitzer Center on Crisis Reporting, and *Boston Review,* among others. He currently lives in Istanbul, Turkey.

Robin Kirk is the author of three books, including *More Terrible Than Death: Massacres, Drugs, and America's War on Colombia* (2004) and *The Monkey's Paw: New Chronicles from Peru* (1997). She is the coeditor of *The Peru Reader: History, Culture, Politics* (2005) and coedits Duke University Press's World Readers series. Kirk's essay "Best Ever Dog" was featured in the summer

2010 *Oxford American*'s "Best of the South" issue. An award-winning poet, Kirk also won the 2005 *Glamour* magazine nonfiction contest with her essay on the death penalty. For twelve years she was a researcher with Human Rights Watch and covered Colombia and Peru. She teaches at Duke University.

Kimberly Meyer has written for *Ploughshares, Kenyon Review, Ecotone, Oxford American, Georgia Review, Agni, Southern Review, Brain, Child, Crab Orchard Review, Natural Bridge,* and *Third Coast.* Currently she teaches in a great books program in the Honors College at the University of Houston and is at work on a book about the recent journey in which she and her daughter retraced the medieval pilgrimage route of Felix Fabri, a Dominican friar from Germany who traveled to the Holy Land and St. Catherine's Monastery in the Sinai Desert in 1483.

Monte Reel is the author of *Between Man and Beast: A Tale of Exploration and Evolution,* which will be published in 2013. His first book, *The Last of the Tribe,* came out in 2010. Previously he was the South America correspondent for the *Washington Post.* He and his family currently split their time between Chicago and Buenos Aires.

Henry Shukman is a prizewinning poet and novelist. His most recent novel, *The Lost City* (2009), was a *New York Times* Editor's Choice. He lives in Santa Fe, New Mexico, with his wife and two sons.

Thomas Swick is the author of two books: a travel memoir, *Unquiet Days: At Home in Poland,* and a collection of travel stories, *A Way to See the World: From Texas to Transylvania with a Maverick Traveler.* He has written for a number of publications, including *Missouri Review, American Scholar, North American Review, Oxford American, Wilson Quarterly, Ploughshares, Boulevard, Smithsonian,* and *Afar.* This is his fifth appearance in *The Best American Travel Writing.*

Paul Theroux is the author of many highly acclaimed books. His novels include *A Dead Hand, The Mosquito Coast,* and most recently *The Lower River,* and his renowned travel books include *Ghost Train to the Eastern Star* and *Dark Star Safari.* He lives in Hawaii and on Cape Cod.

Kenan Trebincevic was born in a town called Brcko in 1980 to a Bosnian Muslim family that was exiled in the Balkan war. He came to the United States in 1993, went to college in Connecticut, and became an American citizen in 2001. He works as a physical therapist in Greenwich Village and lives in Astoria, Queens, amid 10,000 other former Yugoslavians. His work has appeared in the *New York Times Magazine* and the *International Herald Tribune*, on the *New York Times* op-ed page and *Salon.com*, and on an American Public Media radio show called *Bosnia Unforgiven*. He is currently co-authoring a memoir about his exile called *The Bosnia List*.

Iraq veteran turned journalist **Elliott D. Woods** is a contributing editor at the *Virginia Quarterly Review*. His *VQR*-sponsored website, Assignment Afghanistan, won the 2011 National Magazine Award for multimedia, and his essay "Digging Out," about the economic potential of Afghanistan's mineral reserves, was a finalist for a National Magazine Award in reporting. Woods's work has also been honored by the Overseas Press Club of America. His writing and photography have appeared or are forthcoming in *Granta, BusinessWeek, Mother Jones, GQ, Outside, Time, Slate,* and the *New York Times*. He lives in Charlottesville, Virginia.

Notable Travel Writing of 2011

SELECTED BY JASON WILSON

CAROLINE ALEXANDER
   The Man Who Took the Prize. *National Geographic,* September.

ELIF BAUTMAN
   The View from the Stands. *The New Yorker,* March 7.
J. S. BROWN
   The Codeine of Jordan. *Bellevue Literary Review,* Fall.

DAVE DENISON
   Your Total Strike Feeling. *The Atlantic,* November.
GEOFF DYER
   Poles Apart. *The New Yorker,* April 18.

HALEY SWEETLAND EDWARDS
   Our Own Apocalypse Now. *WorldHum,* March 7.

DAVID FARLEY
   Bad "Carma." *WorldHum,* August 11.
   A Chip Off the Old Bloc. *Afar,* May/June.
MICHAEL FINKEL
   Here Be Monsters. *GQ,* May.
JONATHAN FRANZEN
   Farther Away. *The New Yorker,* April 18.

KEITH GESSEN
   Nowheresville. *The New Yorker,* April 18.

CLARE MORGANA GILLIS
    What I Lost in Libya. *The Atlantic,* December.
ELENA GOROKHOVA
    From Russia with Lies. *New York Times Magazine,* October 23.
S. C. GWYNNE
    The Lost River of Divine Reincarnation. *Outside,* August.

ERIC HANSEN
    The Killing Fields. *Outside,* August.
LEIGH ANN HENION
    In the Glow of Night. *Washington Post Magazine,* September 18.

PICO IYER
    From Eden to Eton. *Harper's Magazine,* November.

SAKI KNAFO
    Operation Iraqi Vacation. *GQ,* April.

ANDREW MCCARTHY
    The Art of the Deal. *National Geographic Traveler,* January/February.
DAISANN MCLANE
    Can Japan Recover? *Slate,* August 30.

LAWRENCE OSBORNE
    A Pilgrimage of Sin. *Harper's Magazine,* March.
EVAN OSNOS
    The Grand Tour. *The New Yorker,* April 18.

TONY PERROTTET
    The Secret City. *Slate,* December 5.

DAN SALTZSTEIN
    Greek Paradise, Lost. *WorldHum,* September 21.
AMY LEE SCOTT
    BabyLand. *Southern Review,* Spring.
NEIL SHEA
    Under Paris. *National Geographic,* February.
GARY SHTEYNGART
    The New Russia. *Travel + Leisure,* October.
JESSE SMITH
    Let's Put On an Air Disaster Drill! *Smart Set,* June 21.
SETH STEVENSON
    Why Would Anyone Go to Burning Man? *Slate,* September 18.

JOHN JEREMIAH SULLIVAN
   The Last Wailer. *GQ,* January.
PATRICK SYMMES
   Sand Storm. *Outside,* May.

DAMON TABOR
   Like Butterflies in the Jungle. *Harper's Magazine,* February.
GUY TREBAY
   The Global Nomad. *Travel + Leisure,* October.

SIMON WINCHESTER
   How Fast Can China Go? *Vanity Fair,* October.